The Pleasures of Virtue

The Pleasures of Virtue

Political Thought in the Novels of Jane Austen

Anne Crippen Ruderman

ROWMAN & LITTLEFIELD PUBLISHERS, INC.

ROWMAN & LITTLEFIELD PUBLISHERS, INC.

Published in the United States of America
by Rowman & Littlefield Publishers, Inc.
4720 Boston Way, Lanham, Maryland 20706

3 Henrietta Street
London WC2E 8LU, England

British Cataloging in Publication Information Available

Library of Congress Cataloging-in-Publication Data

Ruderman, Anne Crippen,
The pleasures of virtue : political thought in the novels of
Jane Austen / by Anne Crippen Ruderman.
1. Austen, Jane, 1775-1817—Political and social views.
2. Politics and literature—England—History—19th century.
3. Women and literature—England—History—19th century.
4. Political fiction, English—History and criticism. 5. Virtue in
literature. I. Title.
PR4038.P6R83 1995 823'.7—dc20 95-11163 CIP

ISBN 0–8476–8100-9 (cloth : alk. paper)
ISBN 0–8476– 8101-7 (pbk. : alk. paper)

Printed in the United States of America

♽™ The paper used in this publication meets the minimum requirements of
American National Standard for Information Sciences—Permanence of
Paper for Printed Library Materials, ANSI Z39.48–1984.

Cover photograph © 1994 The Art Institute of Chicago

To my father and mother

Contents

Acknowledgments

My work on Jane Austen began when I was a graduate student, and I am pleased to acknowledge my gratitude to my teachers. I owe much to Saul Bellow and the late Allan Bloom, who encouraged me to pursue my interest in Jane Austen and supervised my doctoral dissertation. They showed me by their example how lively and humane the study of literature could be. David Grene also served on my dissertation committee and offered valuable advice. This book benefited especially from the encouragement and criticism of David Bolotin and Werner Dannhauser, who read an earlier version of the manuscript. Among the friends who discussed Jane Austen with me over the years are Peter Ahrensdorf, Alice Behnegar, Janis Bellow, and Steven Kautz. I would like to thank them. I have profited from agreements and disagreements with the work of many Austen scholars, as I indicate in the endnotes. My husband Richard has been my main support at every stage of this work, in more ways than can be mentioned here. The dedication acknowledges my greatest debt.

Introduction: Virtue and Happiness

The titles of Jane Austen's novels are one obvious sign of the moral context of her writing. Although some of the problems they raise (say, the relation between ''sense'' and ''sensibility'') have been much-analyzed, not enough attention has been paid to the way in which the novels generally display her thought (such a word seems justified) about the most fundamental moral issues, especially the connection between virtue and happiness. Austen's critics have tended to focus on either her moralism or her concern for individual happiness, and, for the most part, have not confronted the fact that she defends both and says that they can and must be intertwined. Jane Austen is an unusual novelist and an unusual moralist in her seriousness about the possibility of human virtue (as something distinct from rights and duties) and of happiness. To fully appreciate her work, we must take note of this context, and—taking a cue from her own admonitions[1]—not assume that because she is only a novelist she cannot be a great moralist.

The fact that there has been no agreement among critics of Austen about the moral and political bearing of her novels suggests to me a problem with the many historicist methods of analysis that have been applied to them. The current controversy about Jane Austen's politics has been shaped by critics who stress either her defense of moral virtue or her defense of happiness to the exclusion of the other. Claudia Johnson, beginning from Austen's clear support for individual happiness, has tried to situate her in the context of modern philosophers of individual rights and politically radical literature of her time.[2] Marilyn Butler, arguing for a quite different historical context, has concluded that Austen is a conservative in a sense that Butler thinks is not applicable to our

1

own day.[3] Although the idea of a political concern in Austen's books is relatively new, the underlying dichotomy in this debate is not. Critics have long disputed whether the novels favor "self" or "society"; whether she writes to defend English bourgeois society[4] or is socially subversive.[5] The novels often have been interpreted historically or ideologically.[6]

Given this, it makes sense that Austen's suggestion that virtue leads to happiness has not been more acknowledged, for such a view is rejected by the modern philosophers who set the terms of all the various historical contexts usually suggested for her. Some of Austen's most thoughtful critics have made explicit the way in which the "self versus society" dichotomy that they defend is the product of modern philosophy. Avrom Fleishman, in his provocative book on *Mansfield Park*, explicitly argues for a link between Austen and Hobbes:

> If this war of ego is carried on by each against all, society is indeed as Hobbes described it, *bellum omnia in omnes.* Yet for Jane Austen the amazing fact about this struggle is its constancy and continuity: society is permanent organized hostility, and for better or worse it is the only permanence we can attain.[7]

This argument for the natural asociality of humans is implicit in the interpretations of many critics who see the novels in terms of such things as empowerment, autonomy, and competing wills. It is not uncommon to see *Pride and Prejudice,* for example, called a "fantasy of female autonomy . . . of female power"[8] in which Darcy is Elizabeth's "oppressor,"[9] or to hear Fanny Price referred to as a "representative of an oppressed sex."[10] When a critic such as Harold Bloom says that Jane Austen writes about the triumph of the will—the "crucial need of her heroines to sustain their individual integrities"[11]—he similarly sees Jane Austen's world as one of competing wills searching for power and autonomy.

In this fundamental assumption, there would seem to be little disagreement between feminist and traditionalist critics. Alistair Duckworth, arguing for Jane Austen's conservatism, says:

> The best solution, clearly, is neither society alone, nor self alone, but self-in-society, the vitalized reconstruction of a social totality . . . the simultaneous reception of what is valuable in an inheritance and the liberation of the originality, energy and spontaneity in the living moment.[12]

Duckworth arrives at a compromise between the view that Jane Austen supports the claims of the individual and the one that she defends the claims of society, by suggesting that humans can and must construct their own identity. Such picking and choosing amongst tradition and originality may not, however, be as exhilarating as Duckworth implies. Lionel Trilling argues that Jane Austen writes about the ''difficult and exhausting'' life in which moral choice is dictated by the '' 'kind of selfhood' one wishes to assume.''[13] What all these views share is the belief, which underlies all of modern philosophy, that humans are not directed by their nature toward any particular end.

I would suggest that Austen's presentation of love and marriage raises some questions about the assumption that human beings are essentially alienated and malleable, not naturally directed toward virtue or society, and that society is ''both the horizon of our possibilities and the arena where we destroy each other.''[14] Austen shows society to be neither so good nor so bad. Her heroes and heroines have a horizon beyond the societies in which they find themselves, and yet they can see what about the conventions of their time is worthy of respect. Not even the most proper of Jane Austen's heroines take their moral bearings exclusively from the wisdom of their society: Elinor Dashwood, for example, has never recommended that her sister ''subjec[t] her understanding'' or ''conform to their [acquaintances'] judgment in serious matters'' (SS 94). Austen rather suggests that even conventional propriety makes a distinction between noble and base conduct that the best characters wish to respect.

Virtue is not something each individual constructs for herself, nor something imposed by society. Austen's ironic use of the word ''duty'' in the following passage illustrates this:

> Being now in her twenty-first year, Maria Bertram was beginning to think matrimony a duty; and as a marriage with Mr. Rushworth would give her the enjoyment of a larger income than her father's, as well as ensure her the house in town, which was now a prime object, it became, by the same rule of moral obligation, her evident duty to marry Mr. Rushworth if she could (MP 38–39).

As the duty to marry at 21 turns into a duty to seek a large income and house in town, it is clear enough that there is no real ''moral obligation'' to marry Mr. Rushworth. It seems impossible to conclude, as one critic does, that this scene is an example of Jane Austen's belief that ''duty is what you make it, what you want it to be.''[15] Duty is precisely *not* what Maria Bertram wants it to be here. It is important to see, too, that the problem is not that Maria has not deferred to society: her choice of a husband and her wedding are "very proper," and might "stand the strictest investigation" (203, cf. 39). Yet the author leaves no doubt that she has, objectively, violated duty:

> In all the important preparations of the mind she was complete; being prepared for matrimony by a hatred of home, restraint and tranquillity; by the misery of disappointed affection, and contempt of the man she was to marry. The rest might wait (203).

In a similar way, Mary Crawford's philosophy—that "it is everybody's duty to do as well for themselves as they can" (MP 289)—is implicitly criticized when we see her use it to defend the ambitious but extremely unhappy marriages of her London friends (MP 361). When it is said of Mr. Elliot in *Persuasion*, " 'To do the best for himself,' passed as a duty," (P 202), it is clear that rational self-interest cannot prescribe duty. Jane Austen is not at all convinced of the modern belief that pursuing one's own desires will serve the good of others, that it is virtuous to care for oneself.

Austen's suggestion that there is a natural content to virtue shows an outlook that is more classical than modern. It is important that Jane Austen never speaks of choosing a "kind of selfhood" or of the "integrity of the *self*" (to my knowledge she never uses the word at all in this sense), but often speaks of *mind* in a sense that describes not only intellect but also the seat of human virtues—"rectitude and integrity of mind" (SS 127), "delicacy of mind," "elegance of mind" (e.g., P 5), "modern minds and manners" (P 40), to name a few cases.[16] Such language suggests something substantial that belongs to human beings as such—a human nature—and it is consistent with this that she does not show her people creating their unique "self" from their own desires (duty as "what you want it to be").

Austen, in other words, rejects the radical individuality that is a premise of modernity. To be sure, her characters have feelings and desires that are personal, and *one* purpose of propriety is to protect these sentiments from the notice of others.[17] But Austen shows to a surprising degree that it is not one's feelings and desires but rather one's character and actions that most define who one is. Furthermore, virtue has a permanent, objective content that defines what the *best* sort of character and actions are. This is evident even in her portrayal of love matters, which we might think would be most individualistic of all. The manner in which two people fall in love, as Austen shows it, is not fated or incomprehensible. Truly good qualities will always earn the respect of those who can discern (PP 231–2, P 5), and, while this respect is not love—it is crucial to Austen's point that love is not simply admiration—the concern that two good people take in each other can lead to the most lasting kind of love. Even Anne Elliot and Frederick Wentworth's romance begins from "the encounter of such lavish recommendations": they each have qualities that would be admired by any person "of real understanding" (P 5). Of course, she is not implying that all virtuous people are the same, but only that its cultivation, instead of drawing out individuality, aims at one standard of excellence. Austen insists that Captain Wentworth is not the *only* man who could have suited Anne as a husband (28) and that only her circumstances make this seem to be so. The author's belief, in all the novels, of the possibility of "the cure of unconquerable passions" (MP 470) is a sign of her suggestion that what is most fundamental about a person is not his or her feelings and desires, but rather the character that determines what the nature of those feelings will be.

Another sign of Jane Austen's unmodern doubt that humans can be anything they want to be, and her belief that human nature is perfected by virtue, is her clear suggestion that the reward of virtue is happiness. The narrator of *Pride and Prejudice* is sympathetic to Elizabeth's fear for her sister: "how little of permanent happiness could belong to a couple who were brought together only because their passions were stronger than their virtue" (PP 312). Even the mistaken separation of Anne Elliot and Captain Wentworth that causes them to lose eight years of happiness is not blamed on their failure to put passion first so much as on their failure to be sufficiently convinced, early on, of each other's true merit. Austen is well aware that virtue is not always rewarded, nor vice punished, in a worldly way. The conniving Lucy Steele of *Sense and Sensibility* ends up with more money and status than the long-suffering Elinor, and is thus content, in her own way:

> The whole of Lucy's behavior in the affair, and the prosperity which crowned it, therefore, may be held forth as a most encouraging instance of what an earnest, an unceasing attention to self-interest . . . will do in securing every advantage of fortune, with no other sacrifice than that of time and conscience (376).

Moral condemnation is light and humorous here, and the narrator is content to give an idea of the quality of the happiness of Lucy and her relatives:

. . . setting aside the jealousies and ill-will continually subsisting between Fanny and Lucy, in which their husbands of course took a part, as well as the frequent domestic disagreements between Robert and Lucy themselves, nothing could exceed the harmony in which they all lived together (377).

Elinor and Edward's happiness, in which "the ready discharge of duties" seems to contribute to their increasing attachment to each other, is presented as more substantial (377).

Austen, then, stresses the pleasures of virtue. Her heroes and heroines are distinguished from those around them by the cultivation that lets them find noble things pleasant. This association between virtue and happiness is in accord with Aristotle rather than with Kant, the foremost modern philosopher of virtue.[18] Alisdair MacIntyre has pointed out that "when Jane Austen speaks of 'happiness' she does so as an Aristotelian."[19] Critics of the novels, however, have tended generally to follow Kant in looking for moral virtue to be pure, free of a concern for one's own happiness. David Kaufmann (making explicit what is implied by many others) argues that behavior in the novels that seems "deeply masochistic" to us—he cites Elinor Dashwood's refusal to reveal her secret about Lucy—shows that "one could compare Austen to Kant without doing vicious damage to either."[20] I would argue that real virtue is never masochistic in the novels, and that Austen, unlike Kant, goes out of her way to show how virtue benefits the doer (of course, she does not say this is its motive). In the case at hand, for example, Kaufmann omits the fact that for Elinor to keep her secret is "no aggravation" to her, but is in fact a "relief to her"—partly because she is "stronger alone" (her sister and mother would not help her self-command) and also because "their tenderness and sorrow must add to her distress" (141). Austen insists that Elinor is *not* inflicting pain upon herself, and yet this does not mean she is selfish. Contributing to *their* sorrow would truly give pain to *her*. Austen's acknowledgment of the fact that virtue is not pure and selfless seems to reflect, paradoxically, a greater belief in the possibility of *genuine* attachment to others. Elinor keeps her secret simply because she must—because it is good and noble to do so—and her happiness consists in this nobility. As Austen puts it of Elizabeth Bennet, "self, though it would intrude, could not engross her" (PP 278).[21]

The dichotomy between virtue and happiness defended by Kant lies, for example, behind Claudia Johnson's argument that the novels are not conservative:

> Works of fiction on the conservative model tirelessly exhort us to accept infelicity as the condition of life . . . but Austen's novels are pervasively concerned . . . with achieving a more expansive, and personally fulfilling happiness.
>
> In none of the novels can conservative ideology be entirely overcome, but in all . . . its basic imperatives—benevolence, gratitude, family attachment, female modesty, paternal authority—are wrested from their privileged claims.[22]

Johnson suggests that Jane Austen sees such things as gratitude, family attachment, and modesty as "conservative ideology"—that is, in the service of a political agenda—and not virtues good either for their own sake or for the sake of happiness. The whole debate over whether Austen staunchly defends the *status quo* or is a social subversive implies that she defends either society or individual happiness, but not both: virtue, however much it serves others, does not bring "personally fulfilling happiness." Virtue is sometimes even associated with death by Austen's critics: Fleishman says Fanny Price's role is "to deny the pleasures of life in favor of the pleasures of principle, which feel like death,"[23] and Trilling implies much the same when he associates "the sanctions of principle" and "the wholeness of the self which is peace" with Lady Bertram's "vegetable" existence.[24] (It is hard to imagine how Lady Bertram—wholly guided by her own comfort and the opinions of others—could be seen as a representative of principle.)

As for Fanny, the pleasures of principle are not death-like but the opposite—of *attachment* to others. In general, Austen suggests that the capacity for real attachment and love is the highest pleasure of virtue. Fanny's ability to feel not just deeply but *rightly* (the novels always make this distinction) gives her the true "sensibility which beautified her complexion and illumined her countenance" (235). Her deep affection for her brother is a credit to her in "all who had hearts to value anything good" (235). In *Persuasion*, Austen points out that there is no comparison between the happiness of "generous attachment" and the happiness of selfish pleasure (P 185); such a contrast is always implied in the novels. We can consider a negative example that proves the same point. One influential book argues for Jane Austen's secret admiration for the novels' villains, especially the unpleasant Mrs. Norris of *Mansfield Park*, whom these critics see as "a parodic surrogate for the author," and praise for being "quite openly dedicated to the pursuit of 'pleasure and activity.'"[25] Perhaps the most startling aspect of this argument is that Mrs. Norris is *happy*. The ultimate result of Mrs. Norris's *seemingly* self-serving nastiness is that she "had never been able to attach even those she loved best" (MP 466). Such attachments to others do not seem to be possible without virtue and the feeling that comes from it, and the reader is less led to moral outrage than to pity for the sadness of Mrs. Norris's life. In fact, the punishment for vice in the novels is loss of love; the result of the habits of idleness and lack of self-control for Henry and Mary Crawford, Willoughby, and Lydia Bennet is the inability to make truly happy matches (see MP 458 and 467, SS 331, PP 231).

Austen's novels show that attention to self-interest is not the way to happiness—many of them point out that virtue requires a capacity for self-denial (e.g., SS 350, P 12)—but at the same time they do not ask the impossible, that self-concern be obliterated. Here again, we see a sort of classical moderation. Austen, like Aristotle, implies that the pleasures of self-control are the truest pleasures.[26] Wrongdoers in the novels are not punished but rather left to the natural consequences of their actions. Willoughby's "misconduct . . . brought its own punishment" in the loss of the woman who could have made him happy, but Austen goes on to point out that "he lived to exert, and frequently to enjoy himself. His wife was not always out of humour, nor his home always uncomfortable" (SS 379). Henry Crawford has more "wretchedness" for his actions because, with more sense and feeling than Willoughby, he knows more what he has lost (MP 469). In these cases and others Austen blames the habit of pursuing "immediate pleasure" for the loss of these greater pleasures (MP 467). Only a writer who believes that morality is connected to happiness could feel so little need to dole out punishments.

By arguing that Austen's outlook is essentially classical, I do not mean to suggest that she is part of the self-consciously neo-classicist, or Augustan, eighteenth-century tradition. Elinor Dashwood in *Sense and Sensibility* speaks of "admiring Pope no more than is proper" (SS 47), a phrase that seems an apt summary of how the novels relate to these attacks on the Enlightenment. Austen's comedies do not presume an ideal, earlier age and, as Marilyn Butler has pointed out, "she is far less critical of contemporary society in its essence than Ben Jonson, Dryden, Swift, Pope or Fielding had been."[27] What I am suggesting instead is an agreement with the classical defense of moderation as fundamental to virtue and to happiness. It would be possible to use her novels to illustrate the view of human nature put forth in Aristotle's *Ethics*, which is not at all to say that she meant them to do this.[28] She may never have read Aristotle.[29] Like him, however, she does not give an account of the source of virtue (she does not discuss *why* a particular character is virtuous, except to attribute it, in part, to habit and education), but rather looks at the world and describes what virtue and happiness seem to be. (And her conclusions rescue Aristotle from the charge of representing only "Greek" thought.) Surely the fact that she has remained so popular a novelist might make us hesitate to assign her to one particular historical context, or to one "partisan meaning."[30] My argument is that the novels themselves defend the enduring possibility of human virtue and happiness, and because of this she can be somewhat complacent about the deficiencies of society that she gives us signs of seeing.

I say *somewhat* complacent, for Austen does not dogmatically disdain any connection between politics and morality. She strongly defends England over France, for example, which I will discuss later. Certain political orders better contribute to virtue than do others. Especially in *Emma*, but to a significant degree in all the novels, Austen suggests that the most true and open attachment between two people requires a certain kind of upbringing, one that fosters taste and measure. In *Persuasion*, for example, the Elliot family's inability to lead a measured life is the reason they must abandon their estate, and Anne and Wentworth's union is founded on the possession of real taste and moderation.[31] The virtues Austen emphasizes (e.g., moderation, prudence and modesty) are not especially egalitarian ones, being not easily cultivated in all circumstances. But the fact that morality has a social basis cannot allow us to conclude that social and economic conditions, for Austen, "guarantee the morality."[32] Austen's most scathing attacks are against those snobbish characters—the John Dashwoods, the Bertram sisters, Mrs. Elton, Sir Walter Elliot, and others—who have a sense of superiority due to their social status or money.

While frank about the importance of money, Austen always ultimately denies its preeminence. Similarly she acknowledges the need for bodily satisfactions, while not deriving morality or happiness from them. Austen suggests that some people, at least, are able to free themselves from being dominated by these things. She is elitist, to be sure, but it is an elitism not in defense of wealth and class but in defense of the enduring possibility of a human life that both benefits others and perfects oneself. The old view of, for example, Winston Churchill—who said, on reading *Pride and Prejudice*, "What calm lives they had, those people! No worries about the French Revolution, or the crashing struggle of the Napoleonic Wars"[33]—may have more weight than is typically granted today. Her heroes and heroines are able to live lives of real virtue and form lasting attachments because they are to some extent free of political or domestic urgencies.

By suggesting that Austen's thought is not formed by the modern philosophy that underlies her (and our) time, I do not mean that she was not aware of it and in a certain way responding to it. Recent scholarship on Austen has greatly furthered our understanding of the political debates she undoubtedly knew. I would argue simply that her response is not entirely partisan, but comes to a great extent from a perspective that would be foreign to both Jacobins and anti-Jacobins, or to both feminists and reactionaries. In short, Austen's defense of happiness as a natural human end rebuts those things that others would put in its place—be it power and rights or respect for tradition.

To begin with the latter, it is apparent that Austen's seriousness about happiness as the end of virtue makes her differ from other eighteenth-century moralists. Duckworth, arguing that Austen is a Burkean conservative, says she has faith in "an inherited structure of morality."[34] Yet, Austen's novels do not ever appeal as much to tradition as to nature.[35] When the novels criticize radical changes or "improvements," it is because such changes are in bad taste, and not simply because they oppose a worthy tradition. Duckworth suggests that Jane Austen's fondness for preserving trees, which he sees as a symbol of organic continuity, is a sign of her opposition to "a radical attitude to a cultural heritage."[36] But there is, in fact, implicit criticism of this sort of tradition when the narrator of *Sense and Sensibility* says that the Norland estate has been secured in such a way as to give its owner "no power of providing for those who were most dear to him" by "any change on the estate, or by any sale of its valuable woods" (SS 4). The narrator regrets that the worthy Dashwood sisters could not have profited by the cutting down of some of these trees. When the John Dashwoods tear down these groves and replace them with a greenhouse, we see yet another sign of their bad taste for the artificial over the natural, not their disrespect for tradition. (Compare the praise of the woods at Pemberley [PP 245]). The love of these trees for their own sake comes chiefly from Marianne's romantic perspective, not from a traditionalist one, and Austen does not fully endorse it.[37] Austen's high regard for real taste—the sense of the right way to act in a given situation—is a sign of the way in which she, more than Burke, stresses the aspect of choice in morality. Duty is not what one makes it to be, but neither is it chiefly a matter of adherence to traditional laws and manners.

Austen differs from traditionists not from the perspective of individual rights but from that of virtue itself. She suggests that happiness can be judged, to some extent, objectively; it is *more* than just a matter of an individual's feeling of satisfaction or fulfillment. In one scene, for example, we see how Mrs. Weston "was happy, knew she was happy, and knew she ought to be happy" (E 304); her happiness consists in all this. The happiness of Austen's villains is not as desirable as the happiness of her heroes. Such characters as Willoughby and the Crawfords have the good taste to envy the better happiness they have forfeited and, as for those characters who do not, Austen gives the reader no reason to envy them. (Lucy Steele will have "some months" of "great happiness . . . for she had many relations and old acquaintance to cut" [SS 376]; Mr. Elliot will be left to the pleasures of Mrs. Clay.) In her suggestion that virtue leads to the best kind of happiness, Austen differs from Samuel Johnson, whom she admired[38]—whether it be the conservative Johnson of *Rasselas*, criticizing the vanity of choosing a best way of life, or the more "progressive" Johnson who attacks pride from (among other ways) the point of view of the powerless.[39] Austen is more accepting of pride—not the pride of self-conceit but the "better pride" (NA 244) or "laudable pride" (SS 189) that comes from demanding of oneself that one be worthy of high things. This, too, has to do with the fact that virtue is not only of service to others but leads to the perfection of the individual. Austen, too, may have believed that *perfect* happiness was not possible on earth. But "true merit" and "true love" can make happiness "as secure as earthly happiness can be" (MP 473). Austen does not denounce pride and imagination as irrational or base (as Johnson does), but shows them to be connected to a person's *choosing* to act well.

Austen's concern with happiness even more obviously responds to those who would put a concern for power in its place. Praise is implied in the novels for those who do not insist upon what is due to themselves (see P 46, where this is one of the signs of Anne Elliot's superiority to her sister Mary, or PP 316–317, where Lydia Bennet's deficiencies include her too eager assertion of her rights). The point is not that one should forsake private happiness, but rather that asserting one's rights and power does not lead to happiness but substitutes for it. Mary Crawford is enchanted by "having it in one's power to pay off the debts of one's sex," (MP 363), but Fanny is unmoved by this because she cares too much about her own happiness.

Austen always shows the fullest happiness to consist in attachment to others. The choice of a husband is presented as the most important one a woman faces, not because every woman has a duty to marry (it is clear that many, if not all, of the heroines would not marry at all if it meant accepting an inferior man), but because Jane Austen takes seriously "the blessing of domestic happiness, and pure attachment" (MP 350). It is an assumption, sometimes unstated, of those critics who have looked to Austen for politically subversive teachings that a domestic life involves submission and diminishment for women. But Austen does not portray it this way. When Emma faces a marriage grounded on mutual love and respect, she is in "an exquisite flutter of happiness—and such happiness, moreover, as she believed must still be greater when the flutter should have passed away" (E 434). Austen does not dwell on these moments of excitement because she is more interested in the signs of a happiness that will outlast and even exceed the thrill of such moments. We must look seriously at each novel's concluding forecast of *greater* happiness to come, and be wary of assuming that marriage means a decline for the heroine.[40]

Of course, marriage is a sort of assimilation—both to social expectations and, more interestingly, to what Austen seems to present as a natural human culmination. In a well-known letter to her niece Fanny, Austen laments the fact that marriage entails the loss of a certain kind of individuality:

> Who can keep pace with the fluctuations of your Fancy, the Capprizios of your Taste, the Contradictions of your Feelings? . . . Oh! what a loss it will be when you are married . . . I shall hate you when your delicious play of Mind is all settled down into conjugal and maternal affections.[41]

Still, Jane Austen continues, in a passage much less attended to, "and yet I do wish you to marry very much, because I know you will never be happy till you are." Real happiness is somehow at odds with individuality; it comes from assimilation not simply to the cultural norm of marriage (for all the heroines would reject marriage if it is not based on the love of real attachment) but to an objective standard of virtue that makes such attachments desirable and possible. Many minor characters in the novels show that Austen is perfectly aware of the problems that await ill-matched couples (as, perhaps, she thought *most* couples are).[42] But her defense of the potential happiness of marriage responds to the counterview that marital happiness is a matter of chance, a view that is held especially by those people—such as Charlotte Lucas and Mary Crawford—who defend the pursuit of *power*. Those who take the happiness of attachment as a real possibility are, in some sense, more self-sufficient than those who pursue power.

In other words, Austen does not suggest that some people are interested in marriage, while others are made for something else. Humans seem naturally inclined to couple with each other. Her best and most intelligent characters insist that it be a union of love (in this, Austen differs from the classical view), for she defends the convention of marriage on a natural ground: it follows from the genuine attachment between two people that only virtue can make possible. (Because she takes such a high view of marriage, she must allow that it cannot happen for everyone, for forming such an attachment requires not only virtue but the help of external circumstances.) Austen's own spinsterhood is not necessarily an exception to this rule. Marrying depends to a certain extent on good fortune, for getting to know and becoming attached to another person—a person who is not attached to someone else and who has virtue and cultivation (and thus the upbringing and education that produce them) and sufficient means to marry—requires certain favorable circumstances. (We need not jump to the conclusion that a happy marriage is simply a fantasy. Austen suggests that there *are* many good people in the world and that her good characters have the capacity to attach themselves.)

These considerations must raise some doubts about seeing Austen's choice of marriage as a subject as a concession to novelistic convention[43] or to the social mores of her day.[44] It has become popular recently to discuss the ''ambiguities'' of the endings of her novels, for ironic humor pervades all of them.[45] But we cannot take Austen's ironic meaning to be the *only* meaning, to deny a certain surface truth.[46] One recent critic cites the ending of *Mansfield Park*, where it is said ''the happiness of the married cousins must appear as secure as earthly happiness can be'' (MP 473).[47] It is surely true that Austen means for us to notice the incongruity of ''married cousins,'' the presence of the word ''appear'' and the qualification of ''earthly'' happiness.[48] But given all this, we are left with a prediction of unusual happiness that, if anything, gains credibility from the precision with which it is presented.[49] The nature of Fanny and Edmund's happiness and the reasons for it appear when the above quote is read in its full context:

> With so much true merit and true love, and no want of fortune or friends, the happiness of the married cousins must appear as secure as earthly happiness can be. Equally formed for domestic life, and attached to country pleasures, their home was the home of affection and comfort (MP 473).

This is quite a characteristic passage, detailing the exact reasons why their love might be relied upon. Austen cannot be accused, as she accuses Mrs. Norris, of having "never heard of conjugal infelicity in her life" (MP 203). Nevertheless, she shows that enough ("so much") of such real things as virtue ("true merit") and attachment ("true love"), along with common pleasures and the help of external goods such as fortune and friends, make *this* happy marriage quite probable.

Austen's greatest distinctiveness—and the reason she is not a "novelist of classical liberalism"[50]—is her portrayal of the intrinsic rewards of moderation. We can turn to the various virtues described in the novels to see how practicing them requires an ability to discern what is right to do, and how to feel neither too little nor too much. Virtue is not only self-restraint. Austen shows how her best characters can achieve happiness, not by deliberately pursuing it or insisting on their right to it, but rather by acting in a way that benefits others *and* perfects themselves. And maybe they will even have true love. For while a Mr. Darcy may be provided by poetic license, she also shows how there is no possibility of such an attachment without virtue and intelligence.

Notes

1. Austen defends in *Northanger Abbey* the possibility that a novel can reflect "the greatest powers of the mind" and reveal "the most thorough knowledge of human nature" (NA 37–8). This and other page references inserted in the text refer to *The Novels of Jane Austen*, 5 vols. (3rd. ed., Oxford: Oxford University Press, 1933), ed. R. W. Chapman; and to *The Works of Jane Austen*, vol. 6 (Oxford: Oxford University Press, 1954); by permission of Oxford University Press. When necessary, I will indicate titles by the standard abbreviations: NA, *Northanger Abbey*; SS, *Sense and Sensibility*; PP, *Pride and Prejudice*; E, *Emma*; MP, *Mansfield Park*; P, *Persuasion*; MW, *Minor Works* (including *Sanditon, Lady Susan* and *The Watsons*).

2. Claudia L. Johnson, *Jane Austen: Women, Politics and the Novel* (Chicago: University of Chicago Press, 1988).

3. Marilyn Butler, *Jane Austen and the War of Ideas* (Oxford: Clarendon Press [1975], 1987 ed.). On p. 298, Butler explicitly questions the author's modern relevance.

4. Butler (*Jane Austen and the War*) argues that "for at least four of her heroines, moral progress consists in discerning, and submitting to, the claims of the society around them (1)." Many critics claim that the early novels, in particular, endorse full submission to society. Jane Nardin, for example, says in *Those Elegant Decorums: The Concept of Propriety in Jane Austen's Novels* (Albany: SUNY Press, 1973), 18, that *Sense and Sensibility* "dictates strict obedience to the whole conventional code of propriety, no matter what other considerations of feeling or judgment urge the individual to set that code

aside.'' The most thoughtful argument for Jane Austen's defense of community is probably that of Alistair M. Duckworth in *The Improvement of the Estate* (Baltimore: Johns Hopkins' University Press, 1971).

5. Jane Austen could hardly be a great writer, of course, if she were truly "the mere conduit for the *status quo* that a recent critic accuses readers of thinking she is. (See Alison G. Sulloway, *Jane Austen and the Province of Womanhood* [Philadelphia: University of Pennsylvania Press, 1989], xix.) The most intelligent critics of Jane Austen have always noticed that she does not complacently defend her society. For an early and balanced view of Austen's social criticisms, see D. W. Harding, "Regulated Hatred: An Aspect of the Work of Jane Austen," *Scrutiny* 8 (1940): 346–62. Others have taken this argument much further and, in my opinion, too far. See, for example, Marvin Mudrick's influential *Jane Austen: Irony as Defense and Discovery* (Princeton: Princeton University Press, 1952) or John Bayley, "The 'Irresponsibility' of Jane Austen," in *Critical Essays on Jane Austen*, ed. B. C. Southam (London: Routledge & Kegan Paul, 1968).

6. For a good description of these contexts, see Alistair M. Duckworth, "Jane Austen and the Conflict of Interpretations," in *Jane Austen: New Perspectives*, Women and Literature New Series, vol. 3, ed. Janet Todd (New York: Holmes & Meier, 1983), 39–51.

As I indicated above in the comparison of Johnson and Butler, I would suggest that the feminist criticism of the last decade—while it reveals differences of opinion about *what* historical or ideological context to use for Austen—follows the same tendency to interpret the novels in this manner.

7. Avrom Fleishman, *A Reading of Mansfield Park* (Minneapolis: University of Minnesota Press, 1967), 80. Even Hobbes did not believe that *society* had to be a war of all against all.

8. Judith Lowder Newton, *Women, Power and Subversion: Social Strategies in British Fiction 1778–1860* (Athens, Ga.: University of Georgia Press, 1981), 62, 73. See also Mary Poovey (*The Proper Lady and the Woman Writer* [Chicago: University of Chicago Press, 1984]), who says Jane Austen considers "the model of female power inherent in the premises of romantic love" (239). For a more specific discussion of feminist criticism of the novels—all of which, to my knowledge, use the language of "power" and "autonomy"—see chapter 5 below.

9. Newton, *Women, Power and Subversion*, 81.

10. Leroy W. Smith, "*Mansfield Park*: The Revolt of the 'Feminine' Woman," in *Jane Austen in a Social Context*, ed. David Monaghan (New York: Macmillan Press, 1981), 157. See also Claudia Johnson, who says Jane Austen centers her novels "in the consciousness of unempowered characters—that is, women" (C. Johnson, *Jane Austen*, xxiv).

11. Harold Bloom, "Introduction" to *Modern Critical Views: Jane Austen* (New York: Chelsea House Publishers, 1986), 2.

12. Duckworth, *The Improvement*, 142.

13. Lionel Trilling, ''Mansfield Park,'' in *Jane Austen: A Collection of Critical Essays*, ed. Ian Watt (Englewood Cliffs, N. J.: Prentice-Hall, Inc., 1965), 138–9. The essay is reprinted from Trilling's *The Opposing Self* (New York: Viking Press, 1955). Trilling quotes John Dewey.

14. Fleishman, *A Reading*, 81.

15. B. C. Southam, *Jane Austen. Writers and their Work*, no. 241 (London: Longman Group Ltd. for The British Council, 1975), 34.

16. Gilbert Ryle, ''Jane Austen and the Moralists,'' in *Critical Essays on Jane Austen*, ed. B. C. Southam, 121, has called my attention to the frequency of her use of ''mind'' in this sense. Ryle argues that Jane Austen may have been influenced by Lord Shaftesbury: ''Shaftesbury had opened a window through which a relatively few people in the eighteenth century inhaled some air with Aristotelian oxygen in it. Jane Austen had sniffed this oxygen'' (122). He points out that Shaftesbury typically uses ''mind'' to render Aristotle's *psyche*, usually translated ''soul.'' When Jane Austen uses the word ''soul'' it is usually in the context of religious reflection. The comparisons Ryle makes between Shaftesbury and Austen seem apt, although I do not see the novels as supporting Shaftesbury's more general doctrines of natural benevolence and moral sense. Rather they seem to me more directly Aristotelian.

17. David Kaufmann, in an essay that argues for Austen's modernity, gives a good description of the way in which propriety protects one's privacy. (''Law and Propriety, *Sense and Sensibility*: Austen on the Cusp of Modernity,'' *ELH* 59 [1992], 391–2.) My reasons for disagreeing with Kaufmann's conclusions are stated above.

18. See, for example, Aristotle, *Nicomachean Ethics*, ed. Hippocrates G. Apostle (Grinnell, Ia.: The Peripatetic Press, 1984): ''But things which give pleasure to those who like noble things are by nature pleasant, and such are the actions according to virtue . . . thus the life of these men has no further need of pleasure as a sort of charm . . . but has its pleasure in itself'' (1099a13–16).

In contrast is Kant: ''The ethics of moroseness assumes that all amenities of life and all pleasures of the senses are opposed to morality,'' he says, and, after criticizing some elements of this view concludes that ''this separation between morality and pleasure must be accounted greatly to its credit.'' See Immanuel Kant, ''Introductory Observations'' in *Lectures on Ethics*, ed. Benjamin Nelson (New York: Harper & Row, 1963), 77. Such a view is implicit in his later writings as well, as when he says that everything empirical, including happiness, ''is not only wholly unworthy to be an ingredient in the principle of morality but is even highly prejudicial to the purity of moral practices themselves'' (Kant, *Foundations of the Metaphysics of Morals*, ed. Robert Paul Wolff [Indianapolis: Bobbs-Merrill, 1969], 50).

Critics of the novels have tended to follow this view of morality, and yet it is hard to conceive of any word less apt for Jane Austen than ''morose.''

19. Alisdair MacIntyre, *After Virtue: A Study in Moral Theory*, (Notre Dame, Ind.: University of Notre Dame, 1981), 223.

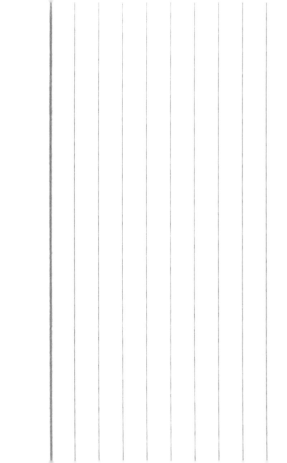

20. Kaufmann, "Law and Propriety," 397.

21. Note that "self" here is used in the traditional sense of one's welfare or interest, not in the sense of a person's essential quality or identity.

22. C. Johnson, *Jane Austen*, 164, 166.

23. Fleishman, *A Reading*, 64.

24. Trilling, "Mansfield Park," in *Jane Austen: A Collection*, ed. Watt, 140.

25. Sandra Gilbert and Susan Gubar, *The Madwoman in the Attic* (New Haven: Yale University Press, 1979), 171.

26. Aristotle says, in agreement with Plato, that the right education is to be "brought up from our early youth in such a way as to enjoy and be pained by the things we should" (Aristotle, *Ethics*, 24; 1104b11–12). To determine what virtue is, it is useful to be on guard against pleasure (1109b7–10), while yet a good man finds virtue pleasant (1099a7–21).

27. Butler, *Jane Austen and the War*, 1.

28. I make this disclaimer not to discount the moral significance of her work. She would undoubtedly laugh at such a didactic or scholarly intention. I also do not mean to suggest that her novels support Aristotle's defense of philosophy.

29. Our knowledge of what Austen read is quite sketchy and comes as much from internal evidence in the novels as from other sources. Mary DeForest has made some interesting speculations about the possibility that she had a classical education in "Jane Austen and the Anti-Heroic Tradition," *Persuasions*, 10 (1988): 14–15. Gilbert Ryle, as mentioned above, discusses the way in which she might have encountered Aristotle through Shaftesbury ("Jane Austen and the Moralists," 118–19).

30. This phrase is Butler's (*Jane Austen and the War*, 299), but the idea is shared by others who read her novels in a narrow political context. As Edward Neill puts it, "there is a sense in which 'Jane Austen' is 'Bastilled for life' by an exclusive concentration on the cultural matrix as that is defined by the concerns of the 'Revolutionary Decade' " ("The Politics of Jane Austen," *English* 40:168 [Fall 1991], 207).

31. The fact that Captain Wentworth is a sailor should not make readers miss the fact that Austen stresses the qualities in him that might be called aristocratic. It is the conceited Sir Walter who disputes, early in the novel, the right of the Wentworth family to the term "gentleman": "I thought you were speaking of some man of property: Mr. Wentworth [Frederick's brother] was nobody, I remember; quite unconnected; nothing to do with the Strafford family" (P 23). The conclusion of this speech, especially, reveals Sir Walter's provinciality, the quality which Austen thought a real gentleman could overcome. Austen tends to use the word "gentleman" to refer to a kind of upbringing, not strictly to one who owns property (for a discussion of this see David Spring, "Interpreters of Jane Austen's Social World," in *New Perspectives*, ed. Janet Todd [New York: Holmes & Meier, 1983], 59–60).

Captain Wentworth's character is marked, in the end, not only by his accomplishments (he is "no longer nobody" when he marries Anne [P 248]) but also by his cultivation—his "real taste" (47, 63), "personal grace" (179), the sense of honor that would make him marry Louisa if she wished it, and the respect for measure and moderation that he develops. He comes to share Anne's belief that "all qualities of the mind" should have "proportions and limits" (116) when he sees her mind as "the loveliest medium of fortitude and gentleness" (241).

32. This is the analysis of Edward Said (*Culture and Interpretation* [New York: Alfred A. Knopf, 1993]). One example of the fact that Austen does not see morality as dependent upon wealth is Fanny Price's younger sister Susan. Even before Susan gets to Mansfield Park, when she is living as she always has in the disorder of Portsmouth, she acts more virtuously—simply by drawing upon "the natural light of the mind" (MP 395)—than the Bertram girls do with all their advantages. Austen, of course, suggests that "a more favoured education" could lead to "juster notions of what was due to everybody, and what was wisest for herself," than Susan has managed to discern on her own (MP 396). Virtue requires cultivation, but wealth and comfort—far from *assuring* it—are not always even an advantage.

33. Winston S. Churchill, *The Second World War*, vol. 5 (Boston: Houghton Mifflin Co., 1951), 425.

34. Duckworth, *The Improvement*, 27. It will be apparent that my own work is in agreement with some chief claims of Duckworth's insightful study: particularly that the novels have a thematic unity and that they do not, in the most important ways, undermine social values.

35. Several times, Duckworth makes reference to the following passage from Edmund Burke's *Reflections on the Revolution in France*, ed. William B. Todd [New York: Reinhart, 1959], 115):

> For, taking ground on that religious system, of which we are now in possession, we continue to act on the early received, and uniformly continued sense of mankind. That sense not only, like a wise architect, hath built up the august fabric of states, but like a provident proprietor, to preserve the structure from prophanation and ruin . . . hath solemnly and for ever consecrated the commonwealth, and all that officiate in it.

(Portions of this passage are cited on pp. 46, 111, and 128 of Duckworth's *The Improvement of the Estate*.) I quote this in full only to point out how hard it would be to imagine Austen writing such a passage—about the potential "prophanation and ruin" of the "august fabric of states"—without irony. Austen is reticent to speak about the established church, the subject of this passage, but the novels do not attribute merely social and political origins and ends to religion. Edmund Bertram may not be a spokesman for the author when he defends religion as being "of the first importance to mankind, *individually* or collectively considered, temporally and *eternally*" (MP 92, emphasis added), but this statement (unlike his praise of Mary Crawford) does not seem ironic. Austen is also willing to portray a less moralistic character such as Captain Wentworth in prayer.

Duckworth, discussing Henry Crawford's ideas about improving Edmund Bertram's future parsonage, says that Edmund disagrees with Henry because he shares Burke's prejudice in favor of tradition and the established common-wealth. But Jane Austen makes it clear that Edmund chiefly opposes Henry's ideas because he cannot afford them:

> I must be satisfied with rather less ornament and beauty . . . and giv[e] the air of a gentleman's residence without any very heavy expense (MP 242).

Edmund and Henry's real differences are not over what is due to tradition but over what is due of a clergyman (MP 248).

36. Duckworth, *The Improvement*, 53–54. I would argue that only in rare romantic passages (such as comments by Marianne Dashwood [e.g., SS 27] or the description of Lyme in *Persuasion*) does Jane Austen suggest that trees represent some kind of eternal, organic continuity. More typically, the value of trees lies partly in the fact that they can be cut and sold: the novels often refer to groves as "timber" (e.g., SS 375, E 358).

37. Even in *Persuasion*, romantic beauty does not have the last word. Anne's musings about autumn leaves are interrupted by her notice of the "fresh-made path" that "spoke the farmer, counteracting the sweets of poetical despondence, and meaning to have spring again" (P 85).

38. Austen's brother remarks on her admiration for Johnson in the biographical notice attached to the 1818 edition of *Northanger Abbey* and *Persuasion* (NA 7). Among the specific studies of Johnson's influence on her novels are A. Banerjee, "Dr. Johnson's Daughter: Jane Austen and *Northanger Abbey*," *English Studies* 2 (1990), 113–24; and Peter L. De Rose, *Jane Austen and Samuel Johnson* (Washington, D.C.: University Press of America, 1980).

39. Claudia Johnson, following twentieth-century critics of Samuel Johnson who have stressed his unauthoritarian side, claims that for Austen he "legitimized the energy generated by our desire for happiness" (C. Johnson, *Jane Austen*, 80). Claudia Johnson's interpretation of Dr. Johnson seems strained, if she means to imply that he defends pleasure as the principle of morality. She quotes a passage that she says shows his belief that life is the pursuit of pleasure—"we desire, we pursue, we obtain, we are satiated; we desire something else, and begin a new pursuit"—but omits the full context. The passage (*Rambler* 6 from *The Yale Edition of the Works of Samuel Johnson*, vol. 3 [New Haven: Yale University Press, 1969], 35) concludes: "He who has so little knowledge of human nature, as to seek happiness by changing anything but his own dispositions, will waste his life in fruitless efforts."

Samuel Johnson's view here is not simply Stoic; his writings in general suggest that the proper disposition is not an attitude of detachment from the world. For Austen, however, the most important thing is not one's attitude or frame of mind, but one's actions. Emma Woodhouse is disposed to be happy (E 5), whereas Fanny Price is disposed to be solemn, but it is not their temperaments but the choices they make that determine whether they will be truly good and happy in the end. Dr. Johnson, from whatever political perspective we view him, does not allow the same latitude to free choice in determining what course of action to take as Austen allows.

40. Several critics have asserted that Jane Austen's novels end at the high point of a heroine's power (see Poovey, *The Proper Lady*, 237). Judith Lowder Newton writes that the end of *Pride and Prejudice* witnesses "a decline" in Elizabeth Bennet, "a flickering suspicion that the best is over" (Newton, *Women, Power and Subversion*, 85). Deborah J. Knuth identifies the "paradox of the courtship plot" to be that "while single women have little but marriage to hope for, marriage is the completely 'hopeless' state—whether for good or ill—because it is the state in which a woman is fixed" ("Friendship in Jane Austen's *Juvenilia* and Lady Susan," in *Jane Austen's Beginnings*, ed. J. David Grey [Ann Arbor, Mich.: UMI Research Press, 1989], 104). These opinions are true if we read from the perspective of power. But if not power over others but rather happiness is the most important business of life, we can consider the possibility that practicing virtue and enjoying happiness is a realm of action (with cares and hopes) and not a static existence.

41. *Jane Austen's Letters to Her Sister Cassandra and Others*, ed. R. W. Chapman (2d. ed., Oxford: Oxford University Press, 1952), 478 (20 February 1817).

42. Most members of what is known as the "subversive" school of criticism on Jane Austen—the school that sees an ironic attack on society as fundamental to her work—make much of the fact that the novelist shows us so many unhappy marriages. Interestingly, however, the earliest critic to see Jane Austen as fundamentally an ironist, Richard Simpson, argued from the opposite claim. He says her humor is grounded in her belief "in the possible happiness of every marriage. The most ill-assorted couples may get used to one another. . . . Thus the great coil Miss Austen makes to bring the right people together is really much ado about nothing. . . . That predestination of love, that preordained fitness which decreed that one and one only should be the complement and fulfillment of another's being . . . she treated as mere moonshine" (Richard Simpson, "Memoir," *North British Review* [April 1870], reprinted in *Jane Austen: The Critical Heritage*, ed. B. C. Southam [London: Routledge & Kegan Paul, 1968], 246). This view is more plausible than the view that she thought marriage was mostly unhappy. But Austen clearly thought that one could do better than her ill-assorted couples. She discredits the view that choice in marriage is all a matter of chance, much ado about nothing, by giving it (explicitly) to Charlotte Lucas and Mary Crawford, and then showing a counterview, that marriage *need* not be this way.

43. Wayne Booth makes this argument in "Emma, *Emma* and the Question of Feminism," *Persuasions* 5 (1983), The Jane Austen Society of America 29–40. Many critics allude to the idea in passing; for a systematic treatment see, for example, Julie Shaffer, "Not Subordinate: Empowering Women in the Marriage-Plot: The Novels of Frances Burney, Maria Edgeworth and Jane Austen," *Criticism* 34 (Winter 1992), 51–73. Claudia Johnson claims that Austen "consent[s] to conservative myths in order to ameliorate them" (C. Johnson, *Jane Austen*, 93).

44. The charge that Jane Austen succumbs to the bourgeois morality of her time—that sentiment in the novels is just a gloss on what are really marriages of economic interest—was first pointedly made by Upton Sinclair in *Mammonart* (Pasadena, Calif.: published by author, 1924), 159–62. For more extensive arguments, see especially Mudrick's *Irony as Defense and Discovery* or Mark Schorer's "Fiction and the 'Matrix of Analogy,' " *The Kenyon Review* 11 (Autumn 1949), 540–44.

45. See, for example, Robin Grove, "Austen's Ambiguous Conclusions," in *Modern Critical Views: Jane Austen*, ed. Harold Bloom (New York: Chelsea House Publishers, 1986) or the essays by Nina Auerbach ("O Brave New World: Evolution and Revolution in *Persuasion*," *ELH* 39 [1972]: 112–28) and Leroy W. Smith ("Mansfield Park," in *Jane Austen in a Social Context*, ed. Monaghan) or Booth ("*Emma, Emma*, and the Question of Feminism," 29–40).

46. Ruth Bernard Yeazell, for example, says of the conclusion of *Mansfield Park*: "with the self-conscious artifice of a novelist intent on closure, she consigns her heroine to a 'happiness . . . no description can reach' (MP 471). She would have needed no telling that this happiness was another fiction of modesty" (See Yeazell, *Fictions of Modesty: Women and Courtship in the English Novel* [Chicago: University of Chicago Press, 1991], 168.) Such a statement, by denying all the surface meaning, does not do justice to the text. Of course the novelist is "intent on closure," joking, in a way typical for her, that the book must end. The above-quoted passage continues: "Let no one presume to give the feelings of a young woman on receiving the assurance of that affection of which she has scarcely allowed herself to entertain a hope" (471). Austen suggests that there is the possibility of a happiness "beyond description," and the novel surely has prepared the groundwork for this one. Fanny's love for Edmund is the emotional center of *Mansfield Park*. The passage certainly does not support the view that *Austen* saw this as a "fiction" of modesty: the novel stresses always the inevitability, not the implausibility, of Edmund marrying Fanny.

47. Grove, "Austen's Ambiguous Conclusions," 184.

48. Austen frankly admits, in a private letter, that "pictures of perfection as you know make me sick and wicked," (Austen, *Letters*, 486–87, Letter to Fanny Knight [23 March 1817]) and, accordingly, most of her pictures of happiness are "very much a-la-mortal, finely chequered" (MP 274).

49. For another argument for "an ironic vision of the ending," this time of *Emma*, see Booth, "*Emma, Emma*," 38–39. Booth cites passages that deflate the romantic climax, such as the famous "Seldom, very seldom, does complete truth belong to any human disclosure . . . but where, as in this case, though the conduct is mistaken, the feelings are not, it may not be very material." I would argue that once again, Jane Austen's careful qualifications serve to show that, all things considered, something close enough to true love really is possible.

50. The phrase is Kaufmann's ("Law and Propriety in Austen," 403). The context is a discussion of her view of propriety, which he calls a "domesticated

notion of rights'' and sees as a way to protect ''fiercely-guarded autonomy'' with ''the exigencies of social existence'' (403). Propriety seems to be a sort of right to privacy. Others, too, take Austen's obvious concern with happiness to mean a concern with rights. Johnson says ''happiness is something many of the characters feel they have a basic right to'' (C. Johnson, *Jane Austen*, 81). Liberal phrases such as the ''right to the pursuit of happiness'' do, as Austen does, see happiness as some kind of end for man. But, for her, happiness has more positive content. Elizabeth does not reject Mr. Darcy because she has a ''right to happiness'': she, like Fanny Price, risks the loss of ''extraordinary sources of happiness'' (PP 355) because she cannot respect him at that moment. Happiness depends on a firmness of principle, which is not an insistence on one's ''rights'' but a broader conception of how to behave.

Chapter 1

Education in Virtue

Jane Austen's lexicon is full of abstract moral terms—principle, duty, truth, reason, to name a few—that can frustrate a reader, especially one expecting to see love conquer over all. Being a novelist and not a philosopher, she does not define, or systematically defend, these ideas. Nonetheless, Austen insists upon the power of the novelist to teach. In the well-known apologia in *Northanger Abbey* she says in her own narrative voice that novels display, among other things, "the most thorough knowledge of human nature" (38). Her own novels, in fact, say quite a bit about what the virtues are and how to get them. In all of the novels, true love—not to mention happy marriage—is possible only when a character recognizes and acts on his or her duty. *Emma* is a love story, but an unusual one, for Austen shows us how a concern with virtue is the ground for the deepest attachment to others and thus, in some way, of the deepest feeling.

All of Austen's works are concerned with the relationship of love and virtue, but the way in which this works is particularly evident in *Emma* and *Northanger Abbey*, which especially concern the heroine's education. Austen's indication in these novels that passion is not a guide to behavior, but rather needs to be regulated, has brought criticism from those who believe her view of love is not pure or selfless enough. One of Austen's earliest critics, Sir Walter Scott, concludes a praising review of *Emma* with the warning that the novel may teach youth "the doctrine of selfishness," by promoting "calculating prudence" in the place of romantic excess.[1] It is true that in Austen's novels love is not unreflective and virtue does not banish self-concern. Before rejecting Austen's case for reason and self-control, however, we might consider whether she can tell us something about what real unselfishness is.

The Case Against Heroism

Part of the humor of Austen's books is the way she shows each couple to be, for good or for bad, a suitable match. Most often she portrays not an antihero and antiheroine but rather a range of possibilities and deficiencies, all of which shed light on the relationship of the hero and heroine. This fine-tuning is particularly true of *Emma*, where the secondary pair threatens to steal the show. Jane Fairfax is so "cried up," to use Emma's phrase, and Emma's own failings are so evident that many critics have taken Jane to be the standard of virtue in the novel.[2] I will argue, however, that the novel makes a strong case against Frank and Jane, a case that is central to its general theme. They both lack, in similar ways, the qualities of warmth and virtue that Austen often sums up with the word "heart."

Emma's brief fancy of Frank Churchill as her lover is one of her first lessons in the wrong way to use a romantic imagination. Gallantry usually signals a lack of true feeling in *Emma* and is the telling point against that "gallant young man" Frank (298, 348, see also 229, 250, 266, 368, 369). Frank's entry into the novel and exit from it are marked by gallant and graceful bows (192 and 195, 478, cf. 206). Such gallantries are the first clue that Frank, despite his name, is disingenuous. Emma sees immediately that his warm and handsome words—say, for example, in praise of Mrs. Weston (191–92, cf. 150)—come not from knowledge of the subject but from knowledge of what would please. The selfish motive behind such gallantries slowly emerges in the novel. Frank distresses and embarrasses Jane by secretly sending her a piano, and her reaction seems to justify Mr. Knightley's opinion that it is a gift whose inconvenience might exceed its pleasure (446). Even Emma feels that Frank unfairly hurts Jane (241–43) and, when he deliberately pains and angers Jane in the game of alphabet letters, the narrator (speaking from Mr. Knightley's perspective) says that this "gallant young man . . . seemed to love without feeling" (348). Gallantry pretends to be self-sacrificing, but even Emma can perceive that "the nature of his gallantry was a little self-willed" (250). When she understands this, she first realizes she does not intend to marry Frank.

Frank can be put in the camp of other romantically appealing but essentially selfish men in Austen's novels, such as Willoughby or Henry Crawford. The interesting thing is that Austen shows how the selfishness reduces the romantic appeal. Outraged at being taken in by the mystery in which Frank has surrounded himself, and by his dishonesty, Emma exclaims that he is "so unlike what a man should be!" (397).

Mr. Knightley, of course, has come to this conclusion much ea ___, arguing that Frank is unmanly for allowing his guardians' wishes to prevent him from doing his duty: "the one thing which a man can always do, if he chuses" (146).

Mr. Knightley is not an objective observer, no doubt, but the facts of this incident are worth a close look. Mr. Knightley is angry that Frank has never yet come to Highbury to pay his respects to his new step-mother, Mrs. Weston, and that he has used the whims of the Churchills, his adoptive parents, as an excuse. This show of respect is of particular importance because Mrs. Weston, a former governess, has no high worldly claims. Emma, really in agreement with Mr. Knightley, puts forth the opposite view in order to argue with him. She says Frank could not make such a speech as Mr. Knightley suggests to the uncle and aunt "who have brought him up and are to provide for him" (147). Here she alludes not only to Frank's dependence but also to his hope for an inheritance. This is one of the first hints of a quiet but important strand of the novel, the question of Frank's posture toward this money. In a later scene, Frank goes out of his way to examine Mr. Elton's small house and insists that it is sufficient for comfort. Emma credits him with feeling that he does not need his guardians' estate "and that when-ever he were attached, he would willingly give up much of wealth to be allowed an early establishment" (204). We know that Frank has some money (he frequents resorts, can buy a piano, etc.). But if he momen-tarily entertains the idea of standing up to the Churchills and marrying Jane, he does not choose to do so.

Frank might be asked the same question that Elinor Dashwood asks Lucy Steele in *Sense and Sensibility* after hearing of her engagement to Edward: has she any plan for marriage "but that of waiting for Mrs. Ferrars' death, which is a melancholy and shocking extremity" (SS 148). In both novels, the elderly relative conveniently dies. But we must wonder whether Frank has something of Edward Ferrars' passivity and weakness. In contrast is Henry Tilney of *Northanger Abbey*, who is willing to defy his father's wishes and openly propose to Catherine Morland, being "sustained in his purpose by a conviction of its justice" (247). (Here again, duty is what "a man can always do if he chooses.") Henry, unlike Frank, spares Catherine "the necessity of a conscientious rejection" by engaging her faith before mentioning his position with his father, and he does not propose a secret engagement. We are given every reason to believe that even if the improbabilities of the ending (such as the discovery of a rich and noble lover for Eleanor) had not happened, Henry would have honored his word, whereas Frank is "too much indebted to the event for his acquittal'' (445). The general point made in *Emma* is that, despite Frank's playfulness, he does not have too *much* spirit, but too little, and this is why he seems unmanly even to Emma.

Gallantry is always a sign of weakness or affectation in the novel. Mr. Elton's gallantry is dishonest: he is nothing but gallant when he wants to please a woman (42, 49, 70, 77, 82, 111), but at heart he is calculating and somewhat disdainful of women. Speaking to men he is "rational and unaffected" but with women he must make "every feature work" (111, cf. 66) unless the woman has affronted him, in which case he cannot even show common civility (140, 327–28). Emma soon sees that "this man is almost too gallant to be in love" (49). If Mr. Elton's soft gallantry is a cover for a real hardness, Mr. Woodhouse's gallantry shows the problem with real softness. Mr. Woodhouse has "the tenderest spirit of gallantry" toward women (77); he is "gentle" (32, 81, 209) and "tender" (347, 351). His mild manners, however, go along with his "habits of gentle selfishness" (8). Gallantry, whether obsequious or mild, seems to mark a (selfish) need for the favor or approval of others.

By contrast, we are shown how Mr. Knightley's moral principle makes him capable of love. Mr. Knightley is distinguished by his lack of gallantry: as Emma says, "he is not a gallant man, but he is a very humane one" (204). He has a "downright, decided, commanding sort of manner" (34), with "nothing of ceremony about him" (57), and, unlike Frank, he hates mystery (226, 446). Emma knows of no man more likely than Mr. Knightley to do "an act of unostentatious kindness" (223). The scene in which Frank sends a piano to Jane is followed by two examples of Mr. Knightley's kindness: he sends his carriage to bring Jane and her aunt to the Coles (223–24) and he amply supplies the Bateses with the apples Jane particularly likes (238–39). His offer of the carriage is, Mrs. Weston says, "the sort of thing that so few men would think of" (223). He is Austen's version of a sensitive man—and, importantly, his sensitivity does not come (as we today would have it) from being "in touch with" and able to express his own feelings. The foundation of his sensitiveness is not sentiment but rather virtue and discernment. He is concerned with other people and is able to see what he might do for them. This respect for the feelings of others is not quite the same as the modern virtue of compassion. Mr. Knightley can be highly judgmental, for one thing, and is not afraid to impose his view of virtue on others. There is a hardness to his virtue, because, unlike Frank Churchill, making himself agreeable is not his motive.

Emma contains a careful consideration of the principles of good manners. Kindness, one of the chief of these, involves making distinctions and judgments. One of the most remarkable scenes in the novel is the one in which Austen manages to make the reader feel that Emma has committed the gravest of sins by her offhand joke at a picnic. Mr. Knightley rebukes her, and his moralizing contains a passion that is hard to resist:

> How could you be so insolent in your wit to a woman of her character, age, and situation? . . . Were she a woman of fortune . . . I would not quarrel with you for any liberties of manner. Were she your equal in situation . . . (374).

Liberties would be allowed if Miss Bates were Emma's equal or superior because then they would have no sting. The real test of cultivation is with those who *lack* the things one has, for it is the ability not to make them painfully aware of their position. This is the principle Emma has violated, and it is the same one Frank Churchill violated by his failure to pay a wedding call on Mrs. Weston. Mr. Knightley explains,

> Had she been a person of consequence herself, he would have come I dare say; and it would not have signified whether he did or no (149).

Although the first part of this sentence reflects Mr. Knightley's resentment of Frank, the final point is what is important. Good manners are not slavish, not a deference to wealth and power: it is more important to respect what is due to someone who lacks consequence than to someone who has it. The mark of Lady Catherine's bad manners in *Pride and Prejudice* is that they do not "make her visitors forget their inferior rank" (PP 162). Austen shows how the point of good manners is to protect the weak, not the strong.

One of the novel's jokes is that it is Mr. Knightley who is frank—"You hear nothing but truth from me," he says (430)—and Frank Churchill who acts like a gallant knight. Yet the novel's many comparisons of the services performed by the two men establish Mr. Knightley as the true knight. In one such pair of scenes, Frank Churchill comes to the aid of Harriet when she is accosted by gypsies, and Mr. Knightley asks her to dance after she has been rejected by Mr. Elton. Emma, true to romantic tradition, imagines Harriet must love Frank, failing again to see the romantic appeal in Mr. Knightley's less dramatic act. Harriet herself has no doubt that Mr. Knightley's action was "a much more precious circumstance'' (407). In the end, the romantic-sounding ''Emma'' is as suited to ''Knightley'' as plain ''Jane'' is to ''Frank.'' These names are a hint of how virtue can be lovable and that the Knightley marriage is more truly sentimental than the Churchill union which seems to be so.

Frank's gallantry is complemented by Jane's elegance. She has ''a style of beauty, of which elegance was the reigning characteristic'' (167, see also 194, 199, 459). The criticism of Jane Fairfax's elegance is quiet, for it is not simply artificial and unworthy. Emma admits Jane has

> elegance, which, whether of person or mind, she saw so little in Highbury. There, not to be vulgar, was distinction, and merit (167).

This praise is strikingly similar to that Emma gives to Frank Churchill when she says that even if he has nothing more than good looks and good manners still,

> he will be a treasure at Highbury. We do not often look upon fine young men, well-bred and agreeable. We must not be nice and ask for all the virtues into the bargain (149).

The elegant Jane and the gallant Frank have a distinction that is not contemptible, and yet we are shown that they both have a kind of selfishness that keeps them from being the true hero and heroine of the novel.

Just as Emma perceives that ''the nature of [Frank's] gallantry was a little self-willed'' (250), so, to some extent, the nature of Jane's elegance is a self-absorbed indifference to the people around her. Emma's dislike of Jane's ''unbecoming indifference'' (263) is not groundless. Consider, for example, the scene in which everyone except Jane engages in good-natured and harmless gossip about Mr. Elton and Miss Hawkins (174–75). When Jane, startled to find herself addressed, issues the proper comment that she must wait and see before she judges, she appears not so much fair as disinterested or distracted and aloof. Even Mr. Knightley sees Jane's extreme reserve as a character flaw: ''she has not the open temper which a man would wish for in a wife'' (289). Emma's objection to Jane's reserve is the same as Anne Elliot's to the smooth Mr. Elliot in *Persuasion:*

> Mr. Elliot was rational, discreet, polished, but he was not open. There was never any burst of feeling, any warmth of indignation or delight, at the evil or good of others (161).

The point of a ''burst of feeling'' is to indicate moral judgments, and Jane's failure to do this makes others unable to really know her character. Austen always points out the limitations of elegant manners (consider along with Mr. Elton the more obvious case of Mr. Bingley's sisters in *Pride and Prejudice*) and even Jane Fairfax is not said to have the ''elegancies of mind'' that Austen so often praises (136). Emma is right to suspect ''there being something to conceal'' (203) behind Jane's reserve. Jane later admits, ''I had always a part to act! It was a life of deceit'' (459).

Jane, however superior to other elegant and reserved characters in Austen's novels, shares with them an essential selfishness. Of course Jane has a good excuse. As Emma reflects,

> If a woman can ever be excused for thinking only of herself, it is in a situation like Jane Fairfax's. Of such, one may almost say, that 'the world is not their's, nor the world's law' (400).

This novel does not criticize the world's law—the idea that a secret engagement and correspondence is improper—but rather its applicability to one for whom the world has done so little. Jane, in other words, is not held to the same standards as other less disadvantaged members of society. Emma's and Mr. Knightley's ability to champion openness has something to do with their situations: unlike Frank and Jane, they have nothing to hide. The fact that their virtue needs a support does not make it less a virtue, however. We see Emma's openness in a typical scene in which everyone must change their expressions as they enter a drawing room and ''Emma only might be as nature prompted, and shew herself just as happy as she was'' (117). Emma's openness—as well as such things as her charity to her family, generosity with guests and friends, and general humility about her own accomplishments—all make her more than the egotist she is often claimed to be.[3] The difference between Emma and Jane is reflected even in their companions. Mrs. Elton is a caricature of Jane's elegance, ''only as elegant as lace and pearls could make her'' (292, cf. 329). The similarity between Mrs. Elton and Emma in their efforts to take control of others has often been noted, but the close companionship between Mrs. Elton and Jane— however much it might be to the latter's dislike—is worth considering:

> Mrs. Elton took a great fancy to Jane Fairfax, and from the first. Not merely when a state of warfare with one young lady might be supposed to recommend the other, but from the first (282).

The narrator goes out of her way to emphasize the affinity here. Frank's gallantry and Jane's elegance are caricatured in Mr. and Mrs. Elton, respectively. So, too, there is an affinity—again without equality—between Emma and Harriet. Emma's style of beauty is not elegant but rather fresh and healthy: she is "the complete picture of grown-up health" (39) and indeed has almost never been ill. Harriet's looks and lack of pretense are more in Emma's style than in Jane's.

In order to discuss Austen's presentation of the virtue of humanity—and to defend the novel from the charge of teaching selfishness—I have drawn out her portrayal of the selfishness of certain characters in a way that is in some sense against the spirit of the novel, for Austen does not moralize in this way. Furthermore, it is important to see how she, in criticizing the model of virtue that claims to be selfless, acknowledges the inevitability of a certain self-concern. Austen makes fun of heroism because it is improbable—it overestimates the ability of humans completely to forget themselves. (Consider Emma's mistaken fantasy of Frank as a knight-errant, rescuing Harriet from ravaging gypsies.) I would suggest she also criticizes heroism because she thinks it is a threat to virtue itself.

Emma Woodhouse's character illustrates the latter point as well as the former. Emma is not as purely good as many of Austen's other heroines. Not having had the hardships of most of them, she has the habit of having too much her own way and of thinking "a little too well of herself" (5). Importantly, Austen calls these tendencies "disadvantages," not vices. No praise or blame is attached to a disposition. Indeed, Emma's self-assurance can contribute to her virtues: we see her "delighted to see her father look comfortable, and very much pleased with herself for contriving things so well" (22). Her graciousness, coming from "the real good will of a mind delighted with its own ideas" (24), is never cold. If Emma were more selfless she could not be so thoughtful to others.

This novel is not simply about a "competition of values" between Emma and Knightley,[4] for she shares his view of what is due to others and to her own character. Mr. Knightley tells her that her "vain spirit" and "serious spirit" always correct each other (330)—and we can see that Emma usually finds a balance between being too carried away with herself and being too hard on herself. No doubt, Emma's spirit is more vain and Mr. Knightley's more grave, but Austen makes a point of showing that they both contain both "spirits." Mr. Knightley's reprimands hit home because they accord with her own sense of right. She has had "many a hint from Mr. Knightley and some from her own heart'' about her deficiency in visiting Miss Bates (155, see also 67, 291, 376, 391). The choice of the word ''spirit'' rather than, say, ''feeling'' is typical—Austen is more interested in action (and the springs of it) than in sentiment as such.

Austen seems always suspicious of sentiment alone as a *ground* for duty. Mr. Knightley is called ''humane,'' and Emma is called ''compassionate'' (86). They are praised, however, not for what they feel but for what they do. And knowing what to do requires judgment, such as being able to see that ''a narrow income has a tendency to contract the mind, and sour the temper'' (85). The narrator assures us that Emma gives personal attention as well as money to the poor (86). Emma herself says,

If we feel for the wretched, enough to do all we can for them, the rest is empty sympathy, only distressing to ourselves (87).

Here is one indication that Austen does not see compassion to be a virtue as such. In this, she is more classical than modern.[5]

Austen is highly aware of all the circumstances that can deflate heroic sentiments. For example, Emma relieves her painful sense of pity for Harriet by sending her to her sister Isabel. The difference between Harriet at nearby Mrs. Goddard's, or in London, ''made perhaps an unreasonable difference in Emma's sensations'' (452), we are told, but Jane Austen accepts this difference as a fact. The novel leaves no doubt that Emma truly feels for Harriet, and yet she cannot rise to any ''heroism of sentiment,'' any ''flight of generosity run mad'' that would make her persuade Mr. Knightley to marry Harriet instead of herself, or to insist she cannot marry him if he cannot marry them both (431). This is a typical example of Austen's use of wit to undercut a more humorless, reforming view of virtue.

Matchmaking and the Need to Educate the Imagination

Just as compassion needs to be guided by thought and judgment, in Austen's view, so she suggests in general that sentiment is not a reliable guide. Again, her perspective differs from the romantic tradition that, following Rousseau, looks to love as the means to a life in which desire and duty are in accord.[6] Morality is not so subjective for Austen. She always suggests that humans have a certain nature (this is what she says novelists can teach about) which implies certain duties that a man (or woman) can "always do if he chooses." Being able to control one's desires, to take pleasure in principled behavior, is a precondition for being capable of loving deeply, the novels show. Love is not the vehicle for moral education, but is more like the reward for it (when good fortune cooperates).

Given that Austen does not rely on sentiment as an avenue to virtuous behavior, we might well ask why she thinks love is so necessary to marriage. Why is she writing love stories? It should first be pointed out that, again unromantically, Austen does not always insist on marrying for love. Plenty of matches in her novels are made for other reasons. Mr. Knightley's declaration that "men of sense . . . do not want silly wives" (64) does not mean that they will not choose them, whether guided by sexual attraction (the "unaccountable bias in favour of beauty" of Mr. Palmer of *Sense and Sensibility* [112] and Mr. Bennet of *Pride and Prejudice*, to name two) or by economic considerations (as in the case of Mr. Elton and a host of other characters in the novels). Austen makes it clear that both of these types of matches are made for the sake of utility, for each party to get what he or she needs. They are clearly not immoral, although they may be foolish (if one is deceived about what one is getting). If husband and wife turn out to have enough in common, these marriages are not disasters. Austen delights in the negative sort of commonality that results from bad taste meeting its match. The Eltons, for example, are perfectly suited in fortune in that each does not have what he or she pretends to have (see 132, 176, 181), and in character—both have a "sort of parade" in speech and actions (82, 453) that is small-minded.

Austen, in laughing at such matches, does not suggest that they should have been made for love (the vanity that made the Eltons choose each other is presented as the only sort of love of which they could be capable). On the contrary, she points out that a matchmaker would have chosen better. Matchmaking is particularly the subject of *Emma*, for it is the heroine's favorite occupation. Even though Mr. Knightley chides Emma for trying to find a match for Mr. Elton—insisting that a man can be left "to chuse his own wife" (14), he admits in the end that she would have chosen for him better than he has chosen for himself, as Harriet is much to be preferred to Mrs. Elton "by any man of sense and taste" (331). Of course Emma's efforts offend Mr. Elton, for the reason that he had resolved to marry *her*. (A rich, attractive, unmarried young woman is not the best candidate for matchmaker.) Nevertheless, Austen takes seriously what is worthy in matchmaking. Most people do not choose well for themselves, and a more suitable match would be more productive of love and happiness.

Austen is also aware of a great middle ground between arranged marriages and marriages for "love." *Emma* opens, for example, with the wedding of the Westons, a couple Emma claims to have matched. And there is something to her defense of her efforts as "a something between the do-nothing and the do-all" (13). Mr. Weston had been for so long a comfortable and cheerful widower that everyone but Emma assumed he would never marry again. Emma plausibly argues that Mr. Knightley "must know Hartfield enough to comprehend" that, if she had not facilitated and encouraged many little matters, it would have come to nothing. The reader, knowing Hartfield and its ultra-conservative master, can see the truth in this. To give another example, we are shown how Robert Martin's mother is responsible for putting Harriet in his way. She may or may not have had such a motive in inviting Harriet for a long summer visit, but we can see how, once Harriet was there, she encouraged the match in the quietest and thus most effective manner. "Well done, Mrs. Martin!" thought Emma. "You know what you are about" (28).

The case of the Martins is especially interesting because it shows Austen's understanding of a lesser type of love, and her indication that love is not the sole security for a successful marriage. Harriet's nature is "not of that superior sort in which the feelings are most acute and retentive" (138), as is shown by the fact that she falls in love with three men in one year. That she can transfer her affection so quickly means that there is some risk she could stray from a husband. Emma implies this in her reflections on the fittingness of Harriet's marriage, which are all to the effect that she is "safe," has "security," and "stability" (482). Emma does not doubt Harriet's love for Robert. But the reason that she can be confident Harriet will "never be led into temptation" or, more passively, "left for it to find her out" is *not* primarily because her love will protect her. Her security is the appropriateness of her situation:

> She would be placed in the midst of those who loved her, [here Austen means not just Robert but his family] and who had better sense than herself; retired enough for safety, and occupied enough for cheerfulness. (482).

Again, we see how Austen does not try to derive a sense of duty from love alone, and how much she depends on external supports for virtue.

Austen is not so much prescribing the convention by which marriages are made for "love" as much as she is responding to a situation in which matches are no longer arranged. The problem with parents in the novels, as a rule, is that they are absent or have abdicated authority. Emma, Anne Elliot, and Eleanor Tilney have lost their worthy mothers; other heroines have had a worthy father die (Elinor and Marianne Dashwood) or disengage himself from her affairs (Elizabeth Bennet). The parent who does most harm—Mrs. Dashwood of *Sense and Sensibility*—does so because she is under the sway of romantic ideas. In other words, the fact that Austen deliberately creates situations in which the heroine must make her own way (which makes for the interest of the novel) does not necessarily mean she would disdain parental matchmaking. In fact, in the case of the only guardian who takes an active interest in promoting a match—Sir Walter Bertram tries to pair Fanny and Henry Crawford in *Mansfield Park*—we are told explicitly that the idea would have worked, that Fanny would have come to love and be happy with Henry if only Edmund had been married first.

Austen indicates that there is a fair amount that is ridiculous in the new convention that marriage be left to the parties involved (for most people don't really marry for love or choose well). One of Austen's youthful works, *Love and Freindship* (sic), is a witty attack on the romantic convention of opposing arranged marriages. The hero Edward is matched by his father with a woman who is "lovely and engaging," but Edward, despite preferring no one else to her, rejects her for the sole reason that "never should it be said that I obliged my father" (81). Later, Edward and the foolish wife he chooses for himself cause a young girl to reject a worthy man simply because of "the very circumstance of his being her father's choice" (93). (They do have a bit of difficulty persuading the girl that her heart must already "be attached to some other Person" than the one her father chose [95]). These characters who so "nobly disentangle themselves from the Shackles of Parental Authority" (87) are notable for being outright thieves. Austen's later work is more nuanced. But her earliest inspirations are still revealing. Edward's father attributes the "unmeaning Gibberish" that he utters in rejecting a perfectly suitable wife to the fact that he has been "studying novels" (81). The spirit of Austen's own novels is not against arranged marriages so much as against those who dogmatically oppose them.

It is not just an accident that the love of hero and heroine always turns out to be conventionally suitable in Austen's novels. Of course the truest suitability, she shows, is not *simply* conventional. The hero and heroine's respect for virtue is what makes them capable of a lasting love that is the highest justification for marriage. The goal of moral education generally, as Austen sees it, is to act in a way that both respects convention and can see beyond it. Especially in *Emma* and *Northanger Abbey* we can see how the heroines are educated in this way—in the discovery of what is proper, in matters both trivial and grave. It is an education that involves training the imagination, and fancy is "a very dear part" of not only Emma (23) but also Catherine Morland. Austen is never so fearful of imagination as is, for example, Dr. Johnson.[7]

Emma is, to use Austen's coined phrase, "an imaginist" (335) and she is surrounded by people whose lack of imagination traps them in a conventional world. There is, for example, the self-absorbed Mr. Woodhouse who is "without the most distant imagination" of other people's hearts (434), his plaintive daughter Isabella who can hear and understand "only in part" (103), her husband Mr. John Knightley, who is in "mute astonishment" when he sees a man whose habits are unlike his own (303), and Mrs. Elton, who lives by a set of ideas drawn "from one set of people, and one style of living" (272). Emma, on the other hand, being able to suppose that other people feel differently than herself, is able to be amused by "a picture of another set of beings" (27). At family gatherings, she and Mr. Knightley together help turn the conversation so as to keep the other parties from upsetting each other (e.g., 100–107), for only they seem to be able to see beyond their own concerns and opinions.

Catherine Morland of *Northanger Abbey* is not there yet, and this is both the chief reason she is inferior to Austen's other heroines and the first part of her education. Catherine, like Emma, has an "honest relish" in everyday sights and activities (79, cf. E 233) and she has the open manners Austen always praises. This goes along with an artless simplicity that is more like Harriet Smith than like Emma. Her almost hopeless naïveté, which charms Henry Tilney, but probably would not be enough to win Mr. Knightley, is due to the fact that she needs to be "more expert in the development of other people's feelings, and less simply engrossed by her own" (45, cf. 79, 132). This capacity for judgment and taste is fostered partly by her exposure to discussions of art and literature. Austen's wit always separates her from the pedant, of course. We are shown how Catherine learns to make more distinctions than is her habit—she hears that "a clear blue sky was no longer proof of a fine day"—and then becomes "so hopeful a scholar" that she "voluntarily rejected the whole city of Bath, as unworthy to make part of a landscape" (111). This progression of imagination is paralleled in the second half of the novel as Catherine forms an opinion of General

Tilney. She begins by slowly perceiving that his civil manners are no proof of his agreeableness—a moral advance for her—and then becomes so carried away in her fancy as to imagine him the murderer of his wife.

In Emma, too, we see how imagination, however necessary for perceiving the truth of matters, is easily led astray. Austen does not seem to set up a dichotomy, as is sometimes suggested, between imagination and passion on one side and reason on the other. The errors of imagination she shows us are instances of being swept away not by passion, but by false reasoning. Emma is too clever to subscribe to any genuine class prejudices,[8] but she tends to become overly attached to the ideas and doctrines she has invented for herself. (This is why she can call the idea of a match between Jane Fairfax and Mr. Knightley a "shameful and degrading connection" [225], yet can assure Harriet that there have been "matches of greater disparity" than between her and Frank Churchill [342].) Emma's own interest in Frank Churchill is even from the start quite dispassionate—the "idea" of him takes hold on her, we are told, because he (rightly) seems to suit her in age, character, and condition and because she (also rightly) believes her friends must think of and approve the match (119). Emma's ability to imagine lets her see clearly, at first, but when she mistakes her imagination for her feeling she is misled. We see how "in persuading herself, in fancying [that she loved Frank] . . . she had been entirely under a delusion, totally ignorant of her own heart" (412). Her attempt to reason her way to love is a failure because her reasoning is false, not grounded upon the truth of her heart.

Education in the novel aims at discovering and acting on truths (the word "truth" appears repeatedly in Emma), whether it be the nature of the heart or how to behave in a certain situation. This is one sign that the point of education is not the development of individuality. (Of course, Austen's characters are anything but identical. From the fact that so many different individuals populate her small, homogeneous segment of society, we can infer that she does not think individuality has to be created.) These characters know general principles of conduct because they have been told them—Austen has an old-fashioned faith in the value of speech and exhortation. "Miss Taylor gave you principles," Mr. Knightley tells Emma (462), and Jane, taking responsibility for her acts, pleads, "Do not imagine . . . that I was taught wrong" (419). It is not always obvious, however, what virtue calls for. The novels do not present morality as a set of absolute rules to be applied indiscriminately. Nonetheless, Austen is not a relativist: she makes it quite clear that in any particular set of circumstances there is a best way to act, and characters with delicacy can make these judgments. This requires taste, an ability to take pleasure in principled behavior. Taste in Austen's novels is not a substitute for morality but is used to determine the right way to act in any given situation. Her argument that there is a best way to act and that it is the most pleasant is a chief way in which Austen differs from modern moralists such as Rousseau or Kant.[9]

This is not to say that Austen suggests that pleasure determines what duties are. We see how the best characters take pleasure in the very act of resisting or overcoming their feelings. Emma, on one occasion, has "the comfort of appearing very polite, while feeling very cross" (119, emphasis added). Or, when Anne Elliot decides to go to Bath, a place she dislikes: "it would be most right, and most wise, and therefore, must involve least suffering" to go (P 33). Emma devotes herself to cheering her melancholy father, even when she is in low spirits herself, and finds in this "real pleasure, for there she was giving up the sweetest hours of the twenty-four to his comfort" (377). Austen shows us not only how pleasure can come from self-overcoming, but also how a decent person finds pain in wrongdoing. Jane Fairfax confesses that "the consciousness of having done amiss" caused "perpetual suffering" to herself and made her "captious and irritable" to Frank (419). Austen's indication that noble conduct is intrinsically pleasant is more Aristotelian than modern.[10]

Discovering What is Suitable

One way to see this aspect of Austen's thought is to look at the nature of the duties that are the subject of education. We do not see many examples of real vice in any of Austen's novels, but especially not in *Emma*. *Emma* strongly gives the sense of peace and repose that often is said to characterize Jane Austen's work.[11] It is set exclusively in one small village, with only the calmest of events, and, notably, hardly a villain to be seen. Austen assumes a basic respect for the law and for one's reputation. She concerns herself always, but especially here, with the social virtues that make living together enjoyable.

These virtues might seem less significant and her vision therefore limited. And yet, Austen does not present them simply as icing on the cake. She makes us feel acutely the injury Emma does to Miss Bates, and believably portrays the distress of Eleanor Tilney as she must tell

Catherine of the degrading way General Tilney has determined to send
her home from Northanger Abbey. Eleanor says,

> I hope, I earnestly hope that to your real safety it will be of [little conse-
> quence]; but to everything else it is of the greatest consequence; to com-
> fort, appearance, propriety, to your family, to the world (225).

In fact, *Northanger Abbey* gives the impression that Catherine's opinion
of the General's character—that he would be capable of murdering his
wife—is more than vindicated by this act of incivility. Austen indicates
that virtues such as hospitality, friendliness, courtesy, urbanity, and
openness are of crucial importance to the affairs of the human heart.

In addition, these virtues are of particular interest because performing
them requires more intelligence and taste, more of what Austen herself
often calls "delicacy," than is necessary for some more fundamental
virtues. The cultivation that is a mark of finding pleasure in virtue might
actually interfere with some parts of virtue. Such refinement would not
be an asset to courage on the battlefield, for example, or to delivering
justice to lawbreakers, and it is significant that Austen avoids these subjects. We do hear of a few petty thieves, and it is a testament to the good
character of a gentleman in *Persuasion* that —contrary to his lawyer's
advice—he makes an "amiable compromise" with a pilferer (23). A
lack of insistence on one's own claims (or "rights") seems generally
to be a part of virtue in Austen's novels. To take another example of
Austen's avoidance of the aggressive side of justice, when Mrs. John
Dashwood moves into her mother-in-law's house as soon as she has
inherited it, it is because "no one could dispute her right to come"
that "the indelicacy of her conduct was so much the greater" (6). Her
insistence on her rights is a mark that she does not have the best character. And Austen rarely punishes wrongdoers—they are rather left to the
satisfactions of their chosen lives, which they may or may not feel as
inferior. Consistent with this general attitude toward virtue is Austen's
special interest in the social virtues, which add to the pleasure of life.

These virtues are a chief part of Catherine Morland's education, as
she learns how to act in regard to "engagements" of all kinds. Most of
these engagements are purely for pleasure—such as, arrangements to
dance, to drive, to walk, to read together, to have supper—but Henry
Tilney raises the stakes by comparing the duties of an agreement to
dance with those of marriage. As always with him, it is hard to tell how
much he is in jest, for his argument makes a certain sense. Matrimony
and dance are both "a contract for mutual agreeableness," he says, in

which the man has "the advantage of choice" and the woman "the power of refusal," both parties belonging exclusively to each other "until the moment of its dissolution" (77). He implies the possibility of divorce (unusual in Austen), and it seems to be Catherine's inability to conceive of this that makes her protest the analogy. Catherine possesses good moral judgment, for her naiveté about the world is not due to lack of intelligence.

The evidence of the novel is ultimately with her and against Henry, I would suggest, for duties are not shown to be absolute in the sense he implies. That one commitment is for a lifetime and one for a half-hour makes a qualitative difference in the nature of them. The novel does not suggest that every promise, however trivial, simply must be honored, yet it does show how Isabella's view—"what one means one day, you know, one may not mean the next" (146)—is wrong. How to acquit oneself in any given case requires discernment and knowledge of the circumstances.

The many engagements of Catherine's social life in Bath afford her practice in making such decisions. To take an illustrative but simple case: Catherine, to her surprise and delight, is asked to have dinner with the Tilneys, but she turns down the invitation without hesitation because she is expected soon by the Allens. There is no struggle of duty versus inclination as she simply does not entertain the idea of breaking a dinner engagement with her guardians on a moment's notice. Other situations in the novel become more complicated because Catherine must contend with the unscrupulous John Thorpe, whose brutish character is revealed to her by his disregard for commitments made to others and his insistence on fabricated commitments to himself. One of the most passionate moments in the novel turns on the question of whether or not Catherine will take a walk with Eleanor Tilney. John, who has tricked Catherine into ignoring a previous engagement with Eleanor, then insists that Catherine give up her new engagement in order to go for a drive with him and their mutual friends. Catherine resists, and John, in essence, resorts to force; he goes himself to Eleanor and invents an excuse for Catherine. Catherine's reflections as she persists in fulfilling the promise to Eleanor reflect the careful distinctions Austen often makes:

> Setting her own inclination apart, to have failed a second time in her engagement to Miss Tilney, to have retracted a promise voluntarily made only five minutes before, and on a false pretence too, must have been wrong (101).

Several things are significant here. First, Catherine's worry about whether she should have deferred to her friends reveals that she does not think it is simply wrong to break any engagement. Under different circumstances, and in a more proper manner, an engagement to walk presumably could be postponed. Second, her distrust of herself comes because her choice coincides with her inclination. She seems to think the safest way to do right is to oppose one's own pleasure—"a sacrifice was always noble," she reflects a bit later (103). (Compare Fanny Price's similar self-doubts in regard to acting in the play [MP 135].) The context shows that even this rule of thumb, however useful, cannot simply dictate what to do.

Catherine, like most of Austen's heroines, must use her own wits to make these decisions. The chapter at hand concludes with her appeal to her guardians for their opinion, and it turns out they would have opposed her driving with a man in any case but did not bother to tell her so before. Here again, Austen points out the typical absence of parental authority, and suggests that what makes her characters real heroes and heroines is their ability to rise above their surroundings and choose for themselves a virtuous and happy life. Catherine, like the other heroines, is not *devising* a life for herself, for all the novels convey a confidence about the content of virtue. But Austen suggests that the fullest practice of virtue is only possible to those who have an ability and willingness to think for themselves. The clearest line of distinction in Austen's novels is between those who can think and those who cannot.

Now thinking for oneself does not mean being unconventional, in Austen's eyes. Austen laughs more harshly at the conventionalities of society in *Northanger Abbey* than in any of her more mature novels. (The trifling chatter of Mrs. Allen and her friends is much more empty than any of Miss Bates' speeches in Emma. There is a sort of ridicule in the narrative voice that is directed even at the heroine, as when we hear that "here Catherine and Isabella, arm in arm, again tasted the sweets of friendship in unreserved conversation" [35].) Nonetheless, even in this novel, it is clear that it is not the convention but the minds of the people involved that get in the way of truth. When Catherine and Eleanor talk they do not say anything much different than Catherine and Isabella do—probably "not an observation was made, nor an expression used by either which had not been made and used some thousands of times before" in that very place—but what is uncommon is that they are spoken "with simplicity and truth, and without personal conceit" (72). Henry Tilney especially loves to mock conventional expressions, and although this is funny, we are also led to see that this self-indulgence is not the highest kind of wit. After watching Henry engage in a long discussion with Mrs. Allen about muslin, Catherine fears that "he indulged himself a little too much with the foibles of others" (29). Mr. Bennet ultimately is not as witty as the narrator of *Pride and Prejudice* for the same reason.

Austen always shows how it is possible to work within a convention while not having one's behavior defined by it. To take one example, we can consider the convention that in marriage, as Henry points out, the man chooses and the woman has the power of refusal. *Northanger Abbey* makes fun of the idea that a woman cannot fall in love first (30), and indeed Catherine does so, for "a persuasion of her partiality for him had been the only cause of [Henry] giving her a serious thought" (243). Here is a situation in which the convention neither fully describes reality nor gets in the way of it. Even if the particular conventions of engagements served no purpose (and I will argue later that Austen thinks the one at hand is of value), a respect for them is a sign of a willingness to fulfill one's duty in matters of more weight. Isabella Thorpe's habit of making and breaking promises in an instant (e.g., 52) establishes the fact that her word means nothing, so that it is no surprise to see her double-dealing in her engagements. In the end, her disregard for duty doesn't pay. Henry Tilney points out that if she had "had a heart to lose" she would have been a different creature and would have met with better treatment (219). He implies that her habit of living for the pleasure of the moment deprives her of the best pleasures.

The heroines' ability to discern and do what is suitable in ordinary affairs is what makes them capable of discovering and loving a suitable husband. Here too, Austen suggests that doing what is truly fitting requires a certain respect for convention. She is always disarmingly frank about money and situation, and she shows that these considerations do not cease to be relevant to marital decisions when marriages are no longer arranged. In *Emma*, Austen makes a case for what is real, and not just prejudice, in the convention that class or "situation" is relevant for marriage. Austen's own lack of snobbism is as apparent here as in all of her novels; she would belittle, as Mr. Knightley does to Emma, the idea of "what you call good society" (62, cf. 23, 31–32). Even Emma is not directed by deep-seated prejudices. She might disdain the Coles for being "of low origin, in trade" (207), but then prefers their society to "solitary grandeur" (208). And Mr. Weston, who made his modest fortune by trade, and Mrs. Weston, her former governess, are among her "chosen and the best" society (20).

While the tone of the novel protests the idea that class is a guarantee of character, it does suggest that it is rightly of relevance to marriage. Birth and connections are important because Austen suggests that respectability, a certain deference to convention, is necessary for happiness and even for love. Mr. Knightley does not make moral judgments based on class; he believes, for example, that Robert Martin has "true gentility" of mind (65). Yet the chief of his harsh objections to Harriet's claims to a high connection in marriage is that she is "the natural daughter of nobody knows whom, with probably no settled provision at all and certainly no respectable relations" (61). Such a sentiment is echoed in Emma when she repents the vanity that made her stop Harriet from marrying Robert Martin, who "would have made her happy and respectable in the line of life to which she ought to belong" (413). The formula "happy and respectable" appears frequently in this novel (64, 413, 418, 482), and throughout her work Austen takes both happiness and respectability as the standard of well-being. The best life includes respect for the opinions of others, but happiness does not reside in this alone.

What Austen seems to have in mind in this discussion of respectability is the virtue that Aristotle calls "truthfulness" of speech and way of life.[12] This is different from truthfully upholding promises (someone who lies in this way—consider John and Isabella Thorpe of *Northanger Abbey*—is unjust in a stricter sense of the word). Rather, it is the habit of showing oneself as one truly is in even trivial matters, something Austen often calls "openness." For her, this quality is a mark of the good taste that is necessary for other moral actions. Mr. Knightley's speech and conduct show that his desires and duties are in accord. His estate "was just what it ought to be, and looked what it was" (358). Both parts of this praise are important, for "openness" or "truthfulness" is not the same as what we might call "sincerity." In addition to being without pretense, the estate is objectively "what it ought to be."

Truthful manners are, for Austen as for Aristotle, a mean between being boastful and self-deprecating. Mr. Knightley's attitude is akin to Anne Elliot of *Persuasion*, a novel that strongly attacks the vanities and prejudices of the gentry. Anne does not think rank is irrelevant: she criticizes Mr. Elliot, for example, for marrying a "very low woman" (202), strongly objects to a marriage between her father and the lowborn Mrs. Clay, and has a high respect for the "*duties* and dignities of a resident landholder" (P 138, my emphasis). Nevertheless, she has the gracefulness to be "easy and indifferent" about the rights due to her rank (P 46, 148). Mr. Knightley tends, if anything, to err on the side of self-deprecation. Emma praises him at a party for having arrived in his carriage, which is not his habit, and she argues that when he comes in a way he knows to be beneath him he has

> a sort of bravado, an air of affected unconcern; I always observe it when I meet you under those circumstances. Now . . . you are not afraid of being supposed ashamed. You are not striving to look taller than anybody else (214).

This interesting criticism reveals what too much disregard for the privileges of class has in common with overregard for them: both affectations are a kind of vanity, signifying the fear of being undervalued. The novel suggests in general that Mr. Knightley's tendency to understate his claims is in better taste than overinsisting on them, but there is an extreme even in this.

A question is raised in *Emma* about the extent to which privileged circumstances are necessary for the truthful manner praised here. Emma respects Mr. Knightley's estate because it has, and needs, no pretensions, and then adds that it belongs to a family "of such true gentility, untainted in blood or understanding" (358). "Untainted": Mr. Knightley has nothing to explain. This word is echoed by Emma in her reflections on Harriet's "stain of illegitimacy, unbleached by nobility or wealth" (482).[13] Even granting a certain snobbism in Emma's words, she makes a point that is borne out by the evidence in the book—having nothing to be ashamed of is necessary for real truthfulness and openness. Austen suggests here that a sense of shame, while necessary when there is a reason for it ("Leave shame to her. If she does wrong, she ought to feel it," we hear of another character [243]), in itself is not a virtue. Again she is in agreement with Aristotle, who treats shame as a feeling rather than a virtue, because one should not do anything shameful.[14] Harriet has something to hide and nothing to hide it with, nothing of consequence to make the circumstances of her birth less obvious to herself or others. Austen describes a natural reason to respect the conventional difference between Mr. Knightley and Harriet. Their lack of equality—even if it were only in a conventional sense—would impede the truest kind of open communication between them.

Now one solution to this problem would be to declare that no shame should be attached to, for example, an illegitimate birth. Why couldn't Harriet say, "This is who I am and I'm not ashamed of it"? Austen suggests it is not so easy to do away with shame. We saw a hint of this in Emma's speech on Mr. Knightley's "bravado," when she attributes his "affected" unconcern when arriving on foot to the fear of "being supposed ashamed." Even (or especially) if one is determined not to be ashamed, it is difficult to avoid being self-conscious, being aware of (and thus in some sense fearful of) what others will think. Harriet *can* carry herself without fear in a marriage that is conventionally equal; she is equivalent enough in situation to Robert to have no cause for shame.

Austen suggests, somewhat paradoxically, that real dedication to truth means *not* being motivated by a concern with the opinions of others, yet that such openness (an *unaffected* unconcern with public opinion) is difficult if one is defying conventional ideas of respectability. We see a clue of this again when Emma, reflecting on a marriage between Harriet and Mr. Knightley, finds it "horrible"

> to think how much it must sink him in the general opinion, to foresee the smiles, the sneers, the merriment it would prompt at his expense . . . the thousand inconveniences to himself (413).

Despite the fact that she is jealous and upset, Emma here presents a relatively objective and plausible picture of a consequence of such a marriage. We might be tempted to blame Emma for giving heed to this sort of public opinion. But the context of the novel seems to support her—Austen never portrays *such* an unequal match. Mrs. Weston's reflection on Emma's and Mr. Knightley's love—it was "all right, all open, all equal" (468)—could not have been made of him and Harriet. These qualities all seem to require some respect for what is thought to be right, as well as what is right. (Of course Austen is aware that the two might sometimes conflict, and what to do then requires good judgment. Henry Tilney is portrayed favorably for defying his father when his real obligation to Catherine calls for it, but Frank Churchill is criticized for *not* defying his guardians in order to make a proper social call on Mrs. Weston.) Respectability is not a cowardly conformance to social standards. The best characters in the novels can be free of the tyranny of public opinion because they—without demanding a reason—avoid doing anything disgraceful.

Austen's willingness to respect (all other things being equal) conventional notions of virtue is consistent with her acknowledgment that virtue needs political support. In *Emma*, she especially goes out of her way to suggest that the virtues she describes are particularly English. The national difference between England and France is a running theme of the novel. Austen criticizes the French character for its greater concern with politeness, its vanity, and its idleness. Frank Churchill's faults—such as, his willingness to dissemble—are said to be French. Mr. Knightley's home is a picture of "English verdure, English culture, English comfort" [360], whereas Frank Churchill declares "I am sick of England" and often uses French words in conversation [365, e.g., 220, 222]). Mr. Knightley tells Emma that "your amiable young man can be amiable only in French, not in English," for someone who can adapt his conversation to the taste of everybody, "can have no English delicacy towards the feelings of other people" (149). Presumably he means that a person who is truthful in speech and manner, being less engrossed in worry over his own appearance, has more attention for others. Montesquieu, analyzing the English character, helps explain Austen's suggestion that Mr. Knightley's humanity is particularly English. The English, always "busy with [their] own interests" have no time for "the politeness that is founded on idleness."[15] (Industriousness is a standard quality for Austen's praiseworthy characters, whereas the vanity of the villains is always blamed on idleness.) Montesquieu points out that the commerce that makes Englishmen busy also makes them more dependent on their neighbors and thus more gentle, peace-loving, and humane.[16]

Austen does not rely much upon *political* virtue, or only upon that of a relatively low order. This we see in *Northanger Abbey*, when Henry Tilney upbraids Catherine for imagining that General Tilney murdered his wife (NA 197). He first calls attention to the fact that "we are English, we are Christians." Both Christianity and the English system make people less likely to commit barbarous crimes. Education and the knowledge that comes from commercial exchange are also essential: "Does our education prepare us for such atrocities?" "Could they be perpetrated, without being known, in a country like this, where social and literary intercourse is on such a footing . . . where roads and newspapers lay everything open?" (197–98).[17] The final assurance of security, according to Henry, is that "every man is surrounded by a neighborhood of voluntary spies" (198). This phrase aptly describes how the government does not rely on the virtue of its citizens but only on their independence and watchfulness, a spirit that is somewhat suspicious and unsociable.

The conclusion of *Northanger Abbey* does not prove Henry too sanguine about the security that individuals have in England (as many critics have charged); rather, it shows how the commerce and self-interest that help assure this security can be detrimental to virtue in a broader sense. When General Tilney turns Catherine out of his home because he discovers she is not as wealthy as he had believed, he does not put her in physical danger. The reaction of Catherine's parents, when she comes home in such an undignified way, displays the same English spirit of independence and lack of vanity described above. They blame the General's behavior on his eccentricity and do not take offense— "Very unfriendly, certainly; and he must be a very odd man"—and even take comfort in the incident proving that Catherine is "not a poor helpless creature, but can shift very well for herself" (237). But even they must admit that his breach of hospitality shows a lack of honor and feeling (234). General Tilney's act is an example of Montesquieu's warning that the spirit of commerce, while being opposed "on the one hand to banditry" (as Henry Tilney argues), is opposed "on the other to those moral virtues that make it so that one does not always discuss one's own interests alone and that one can neglect them for those of others."[18] (The example Montesquieu goes on to give, in fact, is that bandit peoples are more notable for hospitality than are commercial countries.) Now Austen does not, like Catherine, suggest that this breach of hospitality is as cruel as murder (247). But in General Tilney, she shows most clearly the threat to virtue that is posed by a spirit of economic utilitarianism. General Tilney's vices are not French, but English, and such vices (seen in other novels in such characters as the John Dashwood family of *Sense and Sensibility* and even to a certain extent in Sir Walter Bertram of *Mansfield Park*) are a chief target of Austen's criticism.

Nonetheless, Austen portrays, more than Montesquieu does, the possibility that real virtue (albeit in a domesticated form) is not only compatible with a regime such as England's but also can even flourish in it. Mr. Knightley's restraint, the "true English style," buries "under a calmness that seemed all but indifference the real attachment which would have led either of them [the Knightleys], if requisite, to do everything for the good of the other" (E 100). This example of the attachment between two brothers helps make the point that Austen did not intend simply to exchange the economic foundations of society for romantic ones. The attachment she defends does not have (primarily) selfish origins, be they of economic self-interest or sexual desire. The culmination of the virtues Austen portrays (virtues such as prudence, moderation, friendliness, truthfulness, and justice) is the ability to form an attachment based on virtue. She suggests that English seriousness and lack of affectation are suited to this deepest kind of love. Mr. Knightley's "plain unaffected, gentleman-like English" (448) conveys his love to Emma better than flowery speech could do, for the fact that he says what he means even when it is not important makes her know that she can trust him when it is. Austen does not set out to reestablish republican virtue but rather portrays the virtues that find expression in "the quiet of the private life" (SS 16).[19]

An example of Mr. Knightley's taste may help illustrate how truthful manners allow for sensitivity to others. He describes his plans for a party to Mrs. Elton, who wants to plan a "sort of gipsy party" that is "as natural and simple as possible" (355). He responds,

> My idea of the simple and the natural will be to have the table spread in the dining room. The nature and the simplicity of gentlemen and ladies, with their servants and furniture, I think is best observed by meals within doors (355).

This position shows not only his lack of affectation but also his delicacy for others' feelings, for we learn a bit later that he has another reason to avoid an outdoor picnic. He wishes to invite the reclusive Mr. Woodhouse, who would be made ill by seeing anyone eat outdoors, and Mr. Knightley will not "tempt him away to his misery" (356). Mr. Knightley's own position about picnics is not fastidious but rather commonsensical, and it reflects these particular circumstances. Is his speech to Mrs. Elton just a dignified cover for what is really an act of kindness? Perhaps, in part, for Mr. Knightley has the good taste not to display his virtue. But it also shows that he is not ashamed of the dignities of "gentlemen and ladies"—he does not disdain eating indoors as unnatural.

Austen, in general, points to the natural ground for respecting convention. Even if we grant her case for the importance of suitabilities in marriage, however, we have not solved the problem of how to make the matches. What makes her heroes and heroines superior is their ability to choose lives, and marriages, that are more than just conventional. The Knightleys' marriage is both perfectly proper—"in every respect so proper, suitable, and unexceptionable," to use Mrs. Weston's words (467)—and not strictly conventional. We could say it is almost too obvious a match, and Mrs. Weston is not the only one who has been "the stupidest of beings" for not having thought of it. For by romantic conventions they are not particularly suited. Mr. Knightley is twice Emma's age, he is her brother-in-law and has acted almost as a father to her, and his particular eligibility is that he is so much a member of the family that giving up his home for Mr. Woodhouse's could work. Emma alludes to the close connection when she proposes dancing with him: "you know we are not really so much brother and sister as to make it at all improper" (331). They are almost as close to brother and sister as is possible without being so, a phenomenon Austen also makes use of in *Mansfield Park*.

Given Austen's suggestion throughout her work that love requires a sense of equality and suitability, it is not surprising that she is interested in the friendship of siblings, who can have so much in common. The narrator of *Mansfield Park* points out that common blood and upbringing are "a strengthener of love, in which even the conjugal tie is beneath the fraternal" (235).[20] Of course, it is fundamental that the couples are not *really* siblings. The question of incest has often been raised in connection with *Mansfield Park*.[21] I would suggest that Austen does not concern herself with the question of whether such love is truly disgraceful or only thought to be so; she describes a sort of virtue that would not consider it in either case. (The wrongfulness of the love between Maria Bertram and Henry Crawford is suggested, early on, by their indefatigable rehearsing of a dramatic scene in which they portray the love between mother and son in an obviously sexual way [MP 165, 168–69, 175–76].) Austen would not seem to agree with Mrs. Norris that it is "morally impossible" for children raised as brother and sister to fall in love (6)—*if* they know they are not truly siblings. Fanny feels a different kind of love for her real brother, William, than she does for Edmund. She and William can only dance because "nobody would know who [he] was here" (250). (Here is another case of Austen's willingness to consider circumstances. The conventional propriety that brother and sister not dance is worth respecting, but might not need to be insisted on if no one would take offense. Austen shows how preserving the appearance of propriety need not be seen as hypocrisy, but rather as a concern for the sensibilities of others.)

Friendship: An Education in Virtue

Austen's interest in the potential depth of familial affection seems to be, in part, an exploration of the naturalness of love. Is marriage just a conventional agreement or the fulfillment of something more natural and lasting? The narrator of *Mansfield Park* could be echoing Mr. Knightley's reflections about Emma: "What could be more natural," it is asked, than Edmund's wish to marry someone "of such close and peculiar interest" to him? (470). The friendship of Emma and Mr. Knightley is so natural—their closeness so taken for granted—that the idea of them choosing each other in marriage takes them and others by surprise. It is worth considering Austen's dual emphasis on both the naturalness of their love and on the element of choice in it, for this is a typical instance of the way in which she shows unselfish and selfish elements to be combined in virtue.

Austen goes to some length to explain the way in which Emma and Mr. Knightley have chosen each other as friends; their affection for each other is not the inevitable result of their circumstances. It should be pointed out that sexual attraction is not a sufficient reason to explain why they are drawn together. They *do*, of course, enjoy the sight of each other. Mr. Knightley, in his understated way, says of Emma, "I love to look at her" (39), and Emma reflects that his "tall, firm, upright figure . . . was such as [she] felt must draw everyone's eyes" (326). But this is presented as a *sign* of their affection, not the source of it. Their coming together reflects more involvement with each other than this alone would allow. We are shown, rather, how Mr. Knightley's project of education—his concern with Emma's virtue, and her concern with his—is the truest foundation for their friendship and love.

Mr. Knightley says (and the novel bears out his analysis), that he loves Emma because of all his efforts to improve her over the years. He says his interference may not have done her any good, but rather,

> The good was all to myself, by making you an object of the tenderest affection to me . . . by dint of fancying so many errors [I] have been in love with you ever since you were thirteen at least (462).

Austen suggests that the things we do for another person attach us to them, by making them seem a part of us. (Aristotle also stresses this aspect of friendship: "those who have conferred services feel love and affection for those they have benefitted"[22]). Mr. Knightley's love is not idealized sexual desire—he came to love Emma not because he fancied her perfect but because he fancied her imperfect. The word "fancy" is important here, for clearly Mr. Knightley would not have taken such pains over someone he did not admire. But he cannot just admire from afar. It is because he cares about her virtues that Mr. Knightley simply "cannot see [her] acting wrong, without a remonstrance" (374), even if there is a risk he will offend her (cf. 349). We can have confidence that his love for Emma is lasting because he sees and cares about the virtues she has. His capacity for what we would call "commitment" comes from a broader concern with virtue; it is not the only important duty. His concern for virtue is at the root of his capacity to love.

Austen indicates how it is natural that Emma, feeling that Mr. Knightley loved her, came to love him back. The deepest source of her love for him is gratitude for the concern he has shown her:

> he had loved her, and watched over her from a girl, with an endeavour to improve her, and an anxiety for her doing right, which no other creature had at all shared (415).

Emma does not dwell on the benefits she received from Mr. Knightley—perhaps his efforts, as he thinks, did not accomplish much or perhaps it is not pleasant to remember what she owes him. What she finds lovable are not his services per se, but the concern for her that prompted them and the character that is revealed by such concern. But it is not only Mr. Knightley's concern for her that makes her admire his virtue. Just as with Mr. Knightley, Emma's capacity to love exists in the context of a broader moral concern. We are shown how Mr. Knightley is always the standard of right behavior for her, however much she often pretends to disagree with him (e.g., 33, 145, 325–26). Like his, her love comes not from admiring him from afar but from a high degree of involvement with him, an involvement that is so all-encompassing that it is almost invisible to her. Emma fails to see how each time she tells herself that Frank has intruded into her thoughts, really Mr. Knightley is who has come first to her mind (279 cf. 363). Emma's inability to conceive of Mr. Knightley apart from herself makes her fail to notice that Harriet has always seen him as a standard of perfection (see 33, 54, 75, 337–42, 405–407). (One irony of this novel is that Emma is so wrongly convinced of her friend's bad taste [54, 180]).

Austen would seem to be describing the highest sort of friendship, a friendship that is—to borrow Aristotle's terminology, which again seems relevant—not only for the sake of pleasure or usefulness (as is the case with most of the other marriages in the novel) but is based on virtue.[23] Austen takes care to show how Emma and Mr. Knightley do not love each other *simply* for each other's virtue. Their ''precious intercourse of friendship and confidence'' is pleasant and useful as well (416). Emma has always been in danger of ''intellectual solitude'' (7), and she can hardly bear the thought of a life with no Mr. Knightley to come ''walking in at all hours'' to offer cheerful and rational companionship (6–8, 422). Still, as I have suggested, the fact that their affection for each other is grounded in a concern for each other's good is what makes it lasting.[24] They have, in Mr. Knightley's words, ''every right that equal worth can give, to be happy together'' (465). The fact that they see virtues in each other will make them stay together.

It is not inappropriate or surprising that such a friendship as Austen describes might culminate in the social convention of marriage.[25] The duties of marriage are not an affront to the kind of love she describes, which is grounded in a regard for virtue. Furthermore, the act of entering into a legal contract in a certain way only makes explicit the concern for justice that is already implicit in friendship as Austen describes it. Despite her emphasis in this novel on the *naturalness* of the friendship between hero and heroine (they are practically brother and sister), she nonetheless makes it clear that their affection is *not* simply natural or selfless. Austen never emphasizes the fact that each person wants to receive something from the other; she is always more willing to talk about giving, rather than receiving, what is due. There are hints, though, that the services of friendship are not purely selfless. We can consider the scene in which Mr. Knightley agonizes over whether to give Emma a hint of his suspicions about Frank Churchill. He knows his advice may offend and may be fruitless, but he finally decides he would rather ''encounter anything, rather than the remembrance of neglect in such a cause'' (349). On the one hand, Mr. Knightley is acting as a true friend, doing what is good for Emma for her own sake, even at the cost of unpleasantness for both her and himself. At the same time, he wants to avoid ''the remembrance of neglect;'' he is concerned about what she will feel for him in the future.

That marriage imposes a sense of duty on friendship—and that, by making clear what is owed by each person, it acknowledges that each person desires something from the other—is not shown to be a burden on love but rather a support. Emma, in the end, can look forward to ''giving [Mr. Knightley] that full and perfect confidence which her disposition was most ready to welcome as a duty'' (475). It is not onerous to her to feel that she owes him something (we have seen elsewhere her ability to be grateful). Aristotle may help us understand Austen's suggestion that issues of justice (such as the duties and legal agreement of marriage) are not an affront to love, as for example when he argues that when people have nothing in common ''there is no friendship, as there is nothing just.''[26] The love Austen describes can be fulfilled in marriage in part because it is based on real commonality or suitability. Marital vows simply will make explicit the aspect of love that Austen has always stressed—not the feeling of affection per se, but the act of choosing a friend for life.

Austen does not stress, even as much as Aristotle might, the aspect of friendship that wants something for oneself. Yet she is aware of it. The ability to sacrifice for someone, Austen shows, might even require knowing the importance of that person to oneself. Emma says, for example, that the fact she never thinks of "making a sacrifice" for Frank means that he must not be necessary to her happiness (264). She suggests a motive for giving that is neither mercenary nor selfless. The recipient's love is strengthened by being aware of such a motive, Austen shows. Emma, seeing what independence of habits Mr. Knightley is sacrificing in leaving his own estate to move in with her needy father, becomes "sensible of all the affection it evinced" (449). What makes his sacrifice lovable is precisely that it is not purely selfless—it reveals how important *she* is to him. (Similarly, his efforts to improve her make her know she is "dear to him" and possibly "very dear" [415].) Of course, it is important that Mr. Knightley does not feel his sacrifice as such. (This is what makes it not mercenary or calculating.) He is the *only* man who could have married Emma because he is the only one who could "know and bear with Mr. Woodhouse so as to make such an arrangement desirable" (467).

I have used the words "love" and "friendship" somewhat interchangeably in this discussion because the love Austen describes (we could call it "affection" if that did not imply something of lesser depth) is more typical of friends than of lovers. Love comes into being between Emma and Mr. Knightley, as I have argued, not through the sensation of looking at each other but by the act of being morally involved with each other. Of course, as we have seen, they *do* love to look at each other. Physical desire is clearly a part of Emma's love at the end of the novel, when Mr. Knightley's tenderness excites a "flutter of pleasure" in her, the expression of his eyes "overpowers" her, and she blushes at the thought of calling him by his first name (426, 430, 463). But the important fact is that Emma's happiness "must still be greater when the flutter should have passed away" (434), and indeed her reflections a bit later on the value of "such a companion for herself in the periods of anxiety and cheerlessness before her" are even more heartfelt than her first ones (450). Austen suggests, at least in this novel (although not only here, as I will argue), that sexual desire is not the most salient aspect of love.

We might then be justified in asking, as Mr. Woodhouse does, "why could not they go on as they had done?" Why do they have to get married? To a certain extent the answer has to do with the fact that they are a man and a woman. Austen suggests that it is natural for sexual desire to enter into the affection a man and a woman have for each other (assuming such desires are not immoral). Their wish to live together reflects, too, Austen's portrayal of love or friendship as an insight into one's neediness. Here we can see the chief way in which she differs from modern rationalists. Her denial of the fundamental importance of sexual desire does not come from a belief that humans are simply rational and industrious with no need for an erotic imagination. Only when Emma is shocked into imagining herself without Mr. Knightley can she see the truth about herself. Emma blames her mistakes not on imagination but on vanity (412–13), and, it is true her (understandable) tendency to think a little too well of herself has made her too attached to her own ideas. Her frequent resolves to be more humble (133–34, 142, 377–78) are to no avail until she sees that her original claim that "love is not my way, or my nature" (84) is false. This claim, it seems, was the most arrogant of all, for it presumed that she did not need anyone. Now, Emma's "humiliation" and "mortification" (411–12) are truly heartfelt: her sudden knowledge of her love is a knowledge of her lack of self-sufficiency. The fact that a scene of humiliation almost always precedes the union of hero and heroine in her novels tells us, at the very least, that love is an awareness of one's neediness and lack of independence—a point disputed by many recent critics of Austen who wish to defend love as allowing for separateness.

Emma's and Mr. Knightley's exceptional suitability for each other creates in them a oneness of mind that Austen shows to be beautiful. We see Mr. Knightley praise "the beauty of truth and sincerity in all our dealings with each other" (446), a phrase that reveals Austen's unmodern assumptions. First, there is the idea, as we have seen before, that there is an objective "truth" to be had—being sincere or true to oneself is not enough. Now Austen's ironic tone is present here as ever, for we learn that at this very moment Emma is keeping a secret from Mr. Knightley. But her irony, while making us smile, does not undercut the main point. The narrator, in a more serious mood, says

> Seldom, very seldom, does complete truth belong to any human disclosure; seldom can it happen that something is not a little disguised, or a little mistaken; but where, as in this case, though the conduct is mistaken, the feelings are not, it may not be very material (431).

She does not insist, in other words, that truth—and the possibility of real understanding between two people—is illusory. So we are told in *Sense and Sensibility* that Edward is "not only in the rapturous professions of a lover, but in the reality of reason and truth, one of the happiest of men" (361), or in *Pride and Prejudice* that Mr. Bingley, "in spite of his being a lover," has "rationally founded" expectations of happiness (347).

It is also significant that Mr. Knightley praises the "beauty" of truth, for Austen is distinguished from modern moralists by the fact that she stresses *both* the beauty and the usefulness of virtue.[27] The chief result of Mr. Knightley's education of Emma is not that it has improved her but that it has made them fall in love with each other. They will be not only respectable but also happy, for insofar as truth is possible, happiness too is not just imaginary. Having cleared away the ignorance, jealousy, and mistrust that have distressed them of late, Emma and Mr. Knightley feel something "so like perfect happiness, that it could bear no other name" (432). Such a careful phrase could not be found in a fairy tale.

Notes

1. Sir Walter Scott, unsigned review of *Emma*, *Quarterly Review* March 1816, reprinted in B. C. Southam, *Jane Austen: The Critical Heritage*, 68.

2. Many critics do see Jane Fairfax as superior to Emma and embodying the virtues Emma only achieves at the end. See Wayne Booth, "Control of Distance in Jane Austen's *Emma*," in *Emma: A Casebook*, ed. David Lodge (London: Macmillan, 1968) 198, 200; or Susan Morgan, *In the Meantime* (Chicago: University of Chicago Press, 1980), 32. Mark Schorer, "The Humiliation of Emma Woodhouse," in *Jane Austen: A Collection of Critical Essays*, ed. Watt, 107, sees Jane not as a standard of virtue but as "a woman capable of rash and improper behavior, a genuine commitment to passion, a woman torn by feeling, and feeling directed at an object not entirely worthy. . . . She stands in the novel as a kind of symbolic rebuke to Emma's emotional deficiencies." Schorer may express modern tastes, but it is difficult to see how the qualities he mentions are endorsed by the author.

3. For the claim that Emma is primarily an egotist, see John Halperin, ed., *Jane Austen: Bicentenary Essays* (Cambridge: Cambridge University Press, 1975), 202; Jane Nardin, *Those Elegant Decorums*, 109ff.; A. Walton Litz, *Jane Austen: A Study of Her Artistic Development* (London: Oxford University Press, 1965), 140. Nardin seems especially determined to dislike Emma, as when she implausibly asserts that Emma's tears and extreme remorse after the Box Hill incident are due to the fact that her image as a gracious lady has been shattered (125).

4. Malcolm Bradbury, in Lodge, *Emma: A Casebook* 222.

5. Austen's suggestion that compassion or pity is not in itself a virtue follows Aristotle, who does not discuss pity in the *Ethics*, but rather in the *Art of*

Chapter 2

Prudence, Sensibility, and Justice

Jane Austen's portrayals of three heroines with particularly strong sensibility—Anne Elliot of *Persuasion*, Fanny Price of *Mansfield Park*, and Elinor Dashwood of *Sense and Sensibility*—are evidence that she understood passion. The strong feeling of these women is not their virtue (in some instances it is even a liability), but Austen treats it with great sympathy. Most interestingly, she shows how it goes along with—and may even come from—an unusually deep sense of duty to others. These three women have in common, among other things, the loss of the homes they grew up in, and the need to make their way in the midst of family and neighbors who mostly do not understand them. This situation contributes to the inwardness of mind that they all have in some form. And yet Austen shows how their self-awareness is anything but selfish.

Before considering Fanny Price, whose sensibility is in some ways unique, I would like to look at the similar way in which the sensibility of Elinor Dashwood and Anne Elliot is joined with prudence and a respect for propriety. It is perhaps necessary, at the start, to defend Elinor as having strong sensibility. The view that Elinor learns sensibility in the course of the novel, while Marianne learns sense, can be supported only if we read through the eyes of Marianne, who only appreciates her sister's sensibility in the end. There is plenty of evidence to support the narrator's initial claim that Elinor's "feelings were strong, but she knew how to govern them" (6). (Marianne, at the same time, never lacks sense—she simply does not use it to govern her feelings [6].) From the start we are shown Elinor's deep compassion for Colonel Brandon (50, 55, cf. 211). She cares so much for Marianne that she feels "sickness at heart" when she fears Marianne is about to hear bad news about Willoughby (181). Although Marianne does not appreciate until very late that her sister has suffered disappointments in love, she never doubts Elinor's heart or her love: "I know you feel for me; I know what a heart you have," Marianne tells her (185–86).

Elinor does not dwell on her love for Edward Ferrars but it is never far from the surface of the novel. In fact, Elinor's "heart gave [Edward a connection] with everything that passed" (184). This feeling for Edward partly explains why she is left speechless when she sees Willoughby abandon her sister, or why she is too affected to speak when Colonel Brandon tells her how he found the woman he loved left poor and ruined (176, 206, cf. 55). Elinor is not given, like Marianne, to use "a voice of the greatest emotion" (176), but Austen shows how sensibility does not have to be marked by emotional rhetoric. When Lucy maliciously convinces Elinor that she is engaged to Edward, Elinor replies "with a composure of voice under which was concealed an emotion and distress beyond anything she had ever felt before" (135). When Elinor expects Edward to tell her of his marriage to Lucy, "she would have given the world to be able to speak" but she cannot (358). Edmund Wilson has asked whether Marianne's love of Willoughby is really the most passionate thing in this novel, for "isn't it rather the emotion of Elinor as she witnesses her sister's disaster than Marianne's emotion over Willoughby?"[1] The reason the reader is led to feel so strongly for Marianne may be precisely because the novel is told from Elinor's perspective and Elinor feels so deeply for her.

The sensibility of Anne Elliot is more obvious because the narration of *Persuasion* is so introspective and because—unlike *Sense and Sensibility*, in which Edward Ferrars always remains a somewhat shadowy figure—we are given quite a clear picture of Captain Wentworth and the nature of his and Anne's love. Wentworth and Anne briefly had what Marianne Dashwood dreams of and thought she had found in Willoughby. Anne reflects that of almost all the couples she knows "there could have been no two hearts so open, no tastes so similar, no feelings so in unison" (64) as between them. Their love, as is usual with Austen's heroes and heroines, makes them feel less alone in a world that is not cruel but also not fully satisfying. Since her mother's death, for example, Anne's piano-playing made her "always . . . feel alone in the world" (47), except during her courtship with Willoughby.

The similarities of the heroine of *Sense and Sensibility*, Austen's first novel, and that of *Persuasion*, her last finished one, are not usually noted. On the contrary, recent criticism of Austen has argued for *Per-*

suasion as a fundamental departure for the author, a shift that could be described—to use Austen's own terminology—as one from "prudence" to "romance." The opinion, first expressed by Virginia Woolf in 1925,[2] that in *Persuasion* Austen "is beginning to discover that the world is larger, more mysterious, and more romantic than she had supposed," is now widely held, and many have gone further to argue that *Persuasion* concerns a new alienation of the individual from society. As A. Walton Litz puts it, "the sense of community has disappeared and the heroine has found herself terribly alone . . . [Anne's] despair is that of the modern 'personality,' forced to live within itself."[3] There is surely a greater reflectiveness and sense of sadness in *Persuasion*. But to see this as representing a fundamental shift in Austen's view of the world, as a progression into romanticism, seems to me to lead to a misunderstanding of both this last work and her earlier ones.

Before discussing the reasons for Anne's sadness, it is worth noting some general ways in which the world of *Persuasion* is not a radical departure from that of the earlier novels. It is not only *Persuasion*, with its praise of the navy, that shows "utility" as "becoming a term of approval."[4] Men are always praised for utility in Jane Austen's novels. Edmund Bertram's character "bid most fairly for utility, honour and happiness" (MP 21); Edward Ferrars praises what "unites beauty with utility" (SS 97) and refuses the idleness proposed for him by his family; Mr. Knightley criticizes "a life of mere idle pleasure" (E 148) and is himself, like Mr. Darcy, the industrious manager of an estate. Austen's concern with utility is one of the most characteristic elements of her work as a whole. It is not only one of the English characteristics she admired, but also reflects, in a deeper sense, her insistence that moral virtue leads to happiness. The uniqueness, too, of the "abandonment of the estate"[5] in *Persuasion* may be less if we remember that the early *Sense and Sensibility* begins as the Dashwood sisters are cut off from an estate inherited by a modern-minded brother.

Persuasion is the novel that exalts the navy, but for the paradoxical reason that sailors are so domestic.[6] The novel's last words praise the profession for being even "more distinguished in its domestic virtues than in its national importance" (252), and we are shown how sailors make good husbands. Captain Harville's home, "the picture of repose and domestic happiness" (98, cf. the descriptions of Admiral Croft's domesticity, 128, 170) would be the envy of Edward Ferrars of *Sense and Sensibility*, whose wishes are "centered in domestic comfort and the quiet of private life" (SS 16). In fact, nowhere does Austen appear more as an advocate of marriage and domesticity than in *Persuasion*.[7]

Nor is this because she presents home as a refuge from a new world of estrangement. The charm of the Crofts' domestic life is *not* their all-sufficiency to each other: a part of their happiness is that "we are always meeting with some old friend or other . . . sure to have plenty of chat" (170), and Anne's first reflections on her happiness in marrying Captain Wentworth include her expectation of expanding her circle of friends.

Of course, all of Jane Austen's novels measure happiness on a domestic scale. The happiness for those characters who do not marry well is not outside of the home but in second-rate domestic pleasures, and such happiness marks resignation to a less-than-full life. (Consider Willoughby's version of domestic felicity in *Sense and Sensibility* [379] or the Crawfords at the end of *Mansfield Park* [350, 469] or Charles Musgrove of *Persuasion* [43] or Mr. Bennet of *Pride and Prejudice* [236].)

The Virtue of Prudence

Elinor Dashwood and Anne Elliot are both noted for their prudence. Elinor's ability to govern her strong feelings enables her at age 19 to be the counselor of her mother and contrasts her to Marianne, who is "everything but prudent" (6). *Persuasion*'s initial claim about Anne—she "had been forced into prudence in her youth, she learned romance as she grew older" (30)—might seem to imply that her nature shares more with Marianne's imprudence. But the novel does not support this view. Anne is invariably, seemingly instinctively, prudent—she feels the imprudence of Mrs. Clay's presence in her father's house "quite as keenly as Lady Russell" (34) and judges that the Uppercross style of communicating *everything*, however undesired or inconvenient, is "highly imprudent" (40, 83; see also her wish to suppress information at 107). And nowhere is she more prudent than in her slow reconciliation with Captain Wentworth. As for her being "forced" into prudence at 19, Austen examines the difficult position of someone lacking the experience or confidence to judge an important matter for herself and who gets bad advice from a counselor. Ultimately, prudence requires discerning for oneself, rather than blind adherence to a dictate of society. From the outset we are shown that prudence cannot be free of self-concern.

Prudence and True Sensibility

The characters of Anne and Elinor help illustrate what prudence *is* for Austen. It is obvious, at first, that prudence and sensibility are not warring principles. Perhaps one can be prudent without having strong feelings (Charlotte Lucas of *Pride and Prejudice* is an example), but the novels suggest that it is not possible to have the depth of feeling that leads to real attachment without also having prudence. What connects prudence and sensibility, as Austen portrays them, seems to be that both—in their truest forms—are involved with virtue. Austen shows that prudence is in some deep sense self-regarding, while yet she also shows that the direction of principle is needed to keep prudence from being mercenary self-interest. Similarly, the direction of principle keeps sensibility from being mere self-absorption.

To see Austen's belief that feeling is good or bad insofar as it is moral, we can consider Anne Elliot's oft-quoted complaint about Mr. Elliot's reserve. "He was not open. There was never any burst of feeling, any warmth of indignation, at the evil or good of others" (161). The primary deficiency of Mr. Elliot's manners is that they do not reveal his perception of good and evil. It is this doubt about his *virtue* that makes Anne not trust him. She could not "fix on any one article of moral duty evidently transgressed [by Mr. Elliot]; but yet she would have been afraid to answer for his conduct"(161). Austen often uses phrases such as "proper feeling" (PP 368) or "feel what you ought to do" (PP 373, SS 319); not *any* feeling is worthy.

Real sensibility, it follows, is not the readiness to feel any emotion but the ability to feel what is right; it is a capacity for unselfishness. No one could more wish to be unselfish than Marianne Dashwood, the champion of sensibility. Her feelings of indignation are most quickly aroused by injuries to those she loves (e.g., SS 62, 236), and "where Marianne felt she had injured, no reparation could be too much for her to make" (265, see also 98). She considers sensibility, in fact, to be a sign of virtue: she worries that Edward's eyes lack spirit and fire because these characteristics alone are what "announce virtue and intelligence" to her (17). Most importantly, she could not love someone whom she could not regard as virtuous. When she hears about Willoughby's injustice toward Eliza, she says she could never have loved him, knowing this, for "nothing could have done it away to my feelings" (350). Her sensibility is rooted in a love of virtue.

The problem with Marianne, Austen indicates, is that good intentions are not enough. Unselfishness—and thus true sensibility—requires prudence. In this suggestion, Austen differs fundamentally from Kant.[8] That Marianne is "everything but prudent" and strives for "no moderation" gives her an "*excess . . .* of sensibility" (6–7, my emphasis) that is, in fact, a kind of insensibility. More than once, Marianne's "im-

pulse of affectionate sensibility'' for Elinor leads her to actions that
unwittingly hurt her sister (235–36, cf. 34, 61); her kind intentions are
defeated by her refusal to think and to take account of circumstances
before she gives way to her feelings. Lack of prudence diminishes the
worth, too, of the good will of Mrs. Jennings. Elinor unsuccessfully
tries to persuade Mrs. Jennings that spreading unwarranted news of
Marianne's and Willoughby's engagement is "doing a very unkind
thing" (182), and the narrator points out that Mrs. Jennings's effusions
can be "distressing" (193) and even unkind in their oppressiveness
(314, cf. 215). Real kindness is not just Mrs. Jennings's "impulse of
the utmost good will" (202) but includes a beneficial *outcome* requiring
what Elinor describes as "attention to people and circumstances" (49).

Marianne is never deliberately unkind, but her readiness to indulge
her feelings makes her *in*sensible and thus unjust to others. She is often
"lost in her own thoughts and insensible" (175, 193, cf. 221); when
Lucy hurts Elinor, for example, Marianne "seemed entirely insensible
of the sting" (243). Marianne cultivates a sense of being cut off to the
point that even her romantic mother comes to hope that occupations or
company might "cheat [her], at times, into some interest beyond herself" (213). The implication is that her indulgence of feeling is selfish,
and, in the end, Marianne sees that the feelings she believed to be unselfish had unwittingly led her to injustice. She blames herself for having been "insolent and unjust" to every common acquaintance and
especially to Elinor (346), for she "scarcely allow[ed] sorrow to exist
but with [her]" (346). Her real sensibility comes in this moment of
moral awareness. In other novels, we see the "real sensibility" of
Henry Tilney's embarrassment over his father's conduct (NA 241) or
the "true sensibility" of Emma when she sees her own deficiencies (E
478).

Marianne's problem is not, as I have argued, that she doesn't love
virtue or that she does not have sense (she is "sensible and clever"
[6]); rather she refuses to consider the means to achieve the virtuous
ends she desires. She assumes that the rightness of her intentions is
enough, whereas Austen, like Aristotle, suggests that prudence is a necessary means to goodness.[9] A sign of Marianne's faith in the goodness
of her desires is the fact that she takes pleasure as a sign of rightness:
"we always know when we are acting wrong, and with such a conviction I could have had no pleasure" (68). But Austen shows how this
belief often leads her, to her dismay, into selfishness. To take one example, her "dream of felicity" about receiving a horse from Willoughby
makes her forget about the hardships a horse would cause her mother—

when she is made aware of the hardships, she quickly refuses the present (58). We see the same idea in the criticism of Louisa Musgrove of *Persuasion,* whose eagerness is similar to Marianne's. Wentworth's speeches to Louisa, which implicitly criticize Anne's prudence, allow Louisa to act not only from "the pleasure of doing as she liked" but also make her "armed with the idea of merit in maintaining her own way" (94). The tone here implies that Louisa's imprudent behavior is really selfish, and her philosophy is called into question by the life-threatening fall that follows from it.

Likewise, Marianne's lack of prudence hurts herself more than anyone because it blinds her to the selfishness of the man she loves. Marianne's chief maxim is that second attachments are impossible: love *must* be at first sight, and must last forever, for "it is not time or opportunity that is to determine intimacy—it is disposition alone" (59). She seems unselfish in her disregard for anything that would detract from the purity of love. But here, as always, Austen argues that concern for another's virtue—a sort of involvement that often takes time and always takes good judgment—is the foundation of the most lasting love. As Willoughby confesses, Marianne's eager encouragements elevated his vanity and made him try to please her with no serious intention. Now, to the credit of both, Willoughby *did,* in spite of himself, fall in love with Marianne. But Marianne's imprudent hurry to love his charms kept her from understanding the nature of his love. "Well may it be doubted," Willoughby admits, whether he really did love Marianne—for he was able to sacrifice the feelings he felt, and those *she* felt, "to vanity, to avarice" (320).

Prudence aims at the happiness we want for ourselves, Austen always shows. Yet because this happiness depends upon virtue, prudence is also always connected to unselfishness and real sensibility in the novels. This argument is not changed in *Persuasion.* It is frequently said that to justify Anne's defense of her sense of duty is to justify a decision that pulls in the opposite direction of the rest of the novel.[10] I would suggest, however, that the direction of the novel is to show how prudence contributes to the deepest romance. To be sure, in *Persuasion* we see the beauty of two persons rapidly sensing a kinship of taste and feeling. Anne's narrative voice provides all the subtle interpretation of Wentworth's character: she can read the slightest movement of his face (67, 86, 104, 114, 190, 227); it is she who "understood" him (59, 63, 77, 91). Nevertheless, as in *Sense and Sensibility,* their happiness was jeopardized because neither fully appreciated the other's virtues. Anne blames herself not for failing to put love first, but for failing to trust

enough in Wentworth's virtue and ardor[11]; he, on the other hand, refused to understand her sense of duty, and "smarting under" her rejection, was for eight years too proud to ask again (245, 247). They suffer
the fate that *almost* befell Elizabeth Bennet and Mr. Darcy of *Pride and
Prejudice.* Elizabeth, enlightened to Mr. Darcy's virtues and the
strength of her own love, chides herself for hoping he will ask again:
"is there one among the sex, who would not protest against such a
weakness as a second proposal to the same woman?" (341). Captain
Wentworth, not Mr. Darcy, has this spirit of proud resentment, which
comes from not doing Anne justice.

Anne and Wentworth's subsequent courtship testifies to the place of
prudence in love. They are more "exquisitely happy" in their reunion
even than they were at first because they are "more tried, more fixed in
a knowledge of each other's character, truth, and attachment" (241). In
other words, their confidence in the reasonableness of their love *en-
hances* their passion—again, because Austen portrays the deepest happiness to be one of composure rather than ecstasy. Also contributing to
their happiness is that they are now "more equal to act, more justified
in acting" (241); the action more than the feeling is what is important.
So we saw in *Sense and Sensibility* when Marianne, even though she
knows Edward has not offered to marry Elinor, cries out, "Edward
loves you—what, oh! what can do away such happiness as that?"(186).
Elinor's quiet reply—"many, many circumstances"— makes Marianne wild, for Marianne, as usual, considers (worthy) feelings alone to
be sufficient. Elinor is unhappy because she cannot act on her love;
unlike Marianne she realizes the need for favorable circumstances.[12]
Anne and Wentworth are equal to act in the end because they have
"maturity of mind, consciousness of right *and* one independent fortune" between them (248, my emphasis), none of which they had eight
years earlier.

The point is not simply that they are better off for having waited.
They, unlike Elinor and Edward, *could* have acted on their feelings at
that earlier time. As Austen points out, when any two young people
"take it into their heads to marry," they usually carry their point, "be
they ever so poor, or ever so imprudent, or ever so little likely to be
necessary to each other's ultimate comfort" (248). In the case of Anne
and Wentworth, such a chance would probably have succeeded. That
Anne did not feel "justified in acting" and that Wentworth refused to
understand her deprived them of eight years of happiness. But the love
they feel in the end is one typical of the heroes and heroines of Austen's
novels, one that is *not* dependent on chance for its success. For this
reason, it is deeper and happier.

Austen always suggests that emotions, rather than being a source of guidance, are in need of it, and the fact that Anne and Wentworth misjudged each other early on does not deny this. One of the conclusions that follows from Austen's general association of sensibility and prudence (as opposed to innocent enthusiasm) is that decency sometimes demands putting a check on compassion. The end of *Sense and Sensibility* analyzes this theme as we see Elinor struggle against her "softened" heart as she listens to Willoughby's confession (322, 325, 333). Austen is aware of the power of suffering itself to bring about sympathy. Still, she suggests that such compassion is not just. Long reflection finally "sobers" Elinor's judgment of justice and truth in Willoughby's case, so that she can tell Marianne only "such facts as were really due to his character, without any embellishment of tenderness to lead the fancy astray" (349). The principle here, again, is that goodness depends on actions rather than feelings. So, Willoughby's "indifference is no apology for [his] cruel neglect" of Eliza (322). Nor, Elinor says, can indifference excuse disrespect for his wife: "You have made your own choice. . . . Your wife has a claim . . . to your respect, at least" (329). Austen always indicates that it is the element of *choice* rather than the feeling of affection that is the ground for fulfilling duties in marriage (and elsewhere). This is why prudence becomes so fundamental.

Propriety and Private Life

A part of Elinor's and Anne's prudence is their respect for even conventional proprieties. The usual interpretation of this fact is to see *Sense and Sensibility* as endorsing duty to society (represented by Elinor) over freedom and personal desires (represented by Marianne).[13] Anne's willingness to respect social conventions is often overlooked by those who would rather see her as a romantic; one critic, noting it, attributes it to her being "the unfortunate victim of a formal upbringing."[14] In other words, it is often assumed that the sort of deference and discretion practiced by Elinor and Anne (and, I would suggest, *all* of the heroines) is an unnecessary and inhibiting archaism. I do not think, however, that it is an accident that Anne's and Elinor's propriety goes along with an unusual sensibility.

Austen is interested in the way in which respecting common proprieties can be liberating rather than enslaving. When we hear in *Persuasion* that "Anne said what was proper" (37, 103), it is indicated that she is not blind to the selfish or unreasonable meaning of the speech she has heard, but does not insist on pointing it out (see also 40, 82). Her modesty is not dishonest; she simply is not concerned to *convince* others of all she knows. Anne admits that no one "can expect to prove anything" on a subject such as women's constancy because the most relevant circumstances cannot be brought forward "without betraying a confidence, or in some respect saying what should not be said" (234). She is not so interested in winning an argument as in maintaining the difference between a public and a private sphere. Anne is not prudish or affectedly modest. When Louisa falls, it is Anne who takes charge and issues orders to the men (110). Or, at a concert of Italian love songs, Anne is not afraid to admit her knowledge of Italian or to translate the words into "clear, comprehensible English" (186) for her companions. She then says,

> This . . . is nearly the sense, or rather the meaning of the words, for certainly the sense of an Italian love-song must not be talked of.

By declining to discuss the "sense" of the songs, she matter-of-factly makes a distinction again between private and public subjects without feigning ignorance of the unsaid meaning.

It is important to see that the reason for distinguishing a public and private sphere is not a defensive wish to protect oneself, but rather a wish to preserve a distinction between noble and base conduct.[15] Anne's delicacy appears in the scene in which she cannot avoid overhearing Mrs. Musgrove relate in a loud whisper the financial details of Henrietta's marriage, minutiae that "even with every advantage of taste and delicacy which good Mrs. Musgrove could not give, could be properly interesting only to the principals" (230). Again, her reaction is not affected or contemptuous—it is "good Mrs. Musgrove"—but she has an innate respect for the privacy of certain matters (even in a case that does not concern herself) and she hopes the gentlemen are too occupied to hear (230). (This implies that speech among those of the same sex is somehow more private, and part of Mrs. Musgrove's impropriety is in the loudness of her whisper.) Elinor shows the same sensibility when she protests Anne Steele's relating information learned by eavesdropping. The reason for observing such proprieties seems to be that freedom from convention, in Austen's view, does not demand *rebelling* against convention and may even require preserving it. For even purely conventional rules of propriety assume a distinction between what is noble and what is base, and the existence of such a standard is what allows humans to aspire to something beyond the ordinary, beyond self-preservation.

In support of this, the novels often suggest that respect for convention is more *reasonable* than defiance of it. Austen shows that Elinor is less in the grip of convention—has more freedom of thought—than Marianne. Marianne believes that concealing her affection for Willoughby would be "a disgraceful subjection of reason to common-place and mistaken notions" (53), but Elinor denies that she has ever "aimed at the subjection of the understanding." She has tried to influence her sister's behavior, but "when have I advised you . . . to conform to their judgment in serious matters?" (94). Austen is not arguing, as Burke does to some extent, that common opinion is always wiser than that of an individual,[16] but rather that it is decent to take into account what is owed to others. Marianne allows for no distinction between judgment and behavior; her and Willoughby's "behavior, at all times, was an illustration of their opinions" (53).

Marianne objects to subjecting reason to "common-place notions," but her own opinions are "all romantic" (56) and thus "neither reasonable nor candid" (202). Elinor hopes that a few years will "settle her opinions on the reasonable basis of common sense and observation" (56). Common sense and observation are a *reasonable* standard for judging; Elinor does not slavishly follow arbitrary social rules, nor does she judge simply by her personal wishes. Her respect for propriety is a matter of discernment. Austen indicates that this quality of "delicacy" belongs to the superior characters in the novels (140, 279, 283, cf. 127; see also, for example, PP 128, 165, MP 81, E 51). The need for delicacy points to the fact that virtue is not only self-restraint, or adherence to a social code, but also requires an individual to judge and choose wisely.

Some examples of Elinor's conduct show how her standard of reasonableness allows for a freedom of thought that other characters lack. We can see, for example, how she avoids both acting unjustly and being treated unjustly. Elinor is not obsequious and therefore is not always liked (e.g., 234, 239, 247), but at the same time she does not go out of her way to offend everyone that she "thoroughly despises" (233, cf. 252). Judging on the "reasonable basis of common sense" lets Elinor avoid the "irritable refinement" that causes Marianne to take offense even at trifles (180, 201) and even the more credible refinement of her mother, whose wish not to be indebted to anyone makes her stand on ceremony and forsake even her beloved children's pleasure (40, 108, 111). (Such a wish not to be in debt, although not strictly unjust, is a kind of insistence on one's own claims that Elinor and Anne Elliot have the grace to avoid. In *Persuasion* Anne is "easy and indifferent" about respect for her rank (46) and would "never think of standing on . . .

ceremony" with people she knows as well as the Musgroves (40), however much her sister Mary does so.) At the same time, Elinor's lack of
vigilance about what is due to herself is not the extreme acceptance of
injustice that we see in Charlotte Palmer, who is not pained by anything
and laughs at her husband's abuse (112, 118), or in Lucy Steele, who
overlooks any slight in her servile wish to flatter (e.g., 120, 377). Elinor
has respect for others *and* respect for herself.

One of the drawbacks of Marianne's beliefs about the exclusive importance of feeling is, ironically, a tendency to give too much importance to manners. It is *she,* not Elinor, who is led to be unjust because
of judging by outward appearances rather than by reason. Marianne, in
fact, tends to dislike the company of anyone who is not exactly like
herself. She can "never be civil" to someone deficient in general taste
(19, cf. 35), she has "not much toleration for anything like imperti-
nence, vulgarity . . . or even difference of taste from herself" (127);
and "rapturous delight" is what "could alone be called taste" (19, 35).
She is much less ready to see others' feelings than is her sister because
she places "too great importance" on the "delicacies of a strong sensibility and the graces of a polished manner" in other people (201). (One
of the ironies of the novel is that Marianne is so unable to appreciate
the kindness of Mrs. Jennings, who, in eagerness and enthusiasm at
least, is not so unlike herself. But Marianne's "heart was hardened"
against the belief that Mrs. Jennings can feel compassion because Marianne cannot abide Mrs. Jennings's lack of grace and delicacy [201].)
Jane Austen never suggests that perfect manners are a sign of good
character (contrary to what is often thought of her), as a comparison of
the awkward Edward and the smooth Willoughby (or Mr. Darcy and
Mr. Wickham in *Pride and Prejudice* or Captain Wentworth and Mr.
Elliot in *Persuasion*) suggests.

Elinor's greater ability to do justice to others is only one advantage
of her regulation of her feelings. In addition, her propriety and composure lessen her own pain. Propriety contributes to happiness, in Austen's view, in part because happiness lies, she suggests, in a state of
composure. When Anne hears, for example, that Wentworth has found
her "wretchedly altered," she is deeply mortified, but rejoices at least
that she has heard his words: "they composed [her], and consequently
must make her happier" (61). (Of course, Anne would be happier yet
if she knew her love for Wentworth was returned; the point is that a
composure of disappointment is better than the agitation of doubt.) This
is why in each novel, after we see the heroine thrilled to be engaged to
the man she loves, we are told that her deeper happiness will come after

the excitement has passed away. Anne at that point needs "an interval of meditation, serious and grateful" to correct "everything dangerous in such high-wrought felicity" (245). Austen does not mean to praise the happiness of such people as Lady Middleton, whose composure is due to lack of thought or feeling. Rather, she portrays the satisfaction that comes from knowing that one's feelings are right and reasonable.

To put this another way, Austen suggests, in the way of Aristotle, that the pleasures of self-control are deeper than those of self-indulgence.[17] Elinor's self-control, far from being lack of feeling, *increases* with her feeling: her "exertion of spirits . . . increased with her increase of emotions" (SS 130). Such self-control lessens her own pain and that of others. Elinor does not feel "equal to support" the condemnation of Edward that would come from telling her story to her mother and sister (141). She also struggles for self-control in the face of her love for Edward because, as she says, "I did not love only him" (263): she wants to spare her mother and sister pain. Now, a show of emotion is sometimes a relief, as when Elinor discovers her sister's pain at Willoughby's desertion and herself gives way to "a burst of tears, which at first was scarcely less violent than Marianne's" (182). Elinor's tears are real but this is not the moment of her *greatest* emotion in the book (cf. 135, 264). And her tears are only "at first" as violent as Marianne's; even they are a means to composure. Elinor disapproves of Marianne's show of distress because it can only "augment and fix her sorrow" (85), and Marianne admits in the end that some of her sufferings have been self-induced: "my own feelings had prepared my sufferings" (345).

Austen also indicates that there is an intrinsic pleasure in virtuous conduct. It has been said that *Sense and Sensibility* is at root, about "the extent to which 'nature' has to be reshaped and 'pruned' to make 'society' possible."[18] Yet, I would suggest that this novel, and all of Austen's work, argues that the exercise of reason and virtue are a *fulfillment* of human nature, not a pruning of it. She suggests that virtue leads to happiness not only because it composes painful feelings but because it is pleasurable in itself. *Sense and Sensibility* cannot be said to be about "the excess of Elinor's social martyrdom."[19] Elinor, for example, finds it more *pleasant* to remember good things than bad. She can praise her new neighbors because she remembers "how many pleasant days" she has spent with them, whereas Marianne can only remember "how many painful moments" there were (88). Elinor in fact has had more cause for pain in moving to Barton Cottage than has Marianne (54), but she does not dwell on it. In another scene, we see

Marianne get her way by a rude speech to Lady Middleton, while Elinor, with a little civility, "gained her own end and pleased Lady Middleton at the same time" (145). Elinor does not seem to find what Edward calls her "plan of general civility" (94) to be painful. As David Cecil says, Jane Austen thought "intelligence and refinement add to the pleasantness of life."[20]

Propriety is no more a burden to Anne Elliot than it is to Elinor Dashwood. The social world is not primarily responsible for Anne's sadness.[21] To be sure, Anne's situation is especially sad. Without a home of her own, she must constantly adjust to a "total change of conversation, opinion and idea" that makes her feel her own "nothingness" (P 42). But Austen does not leave it at this. We are shown how Anne greets with equanimity the prospect of a visit to her querulous younger sister. She considers it "very fitting" that each little society should "dictate its own matters of discourse" (this fact is not a sign of some general disintegration of society) and she hopes "to become a not unworthy member of the one she was now transplanted into"; "she had no dread of these two months" (43). And Anne *is* soon accepted into this society: she has "the satisfaction of knowing herself extremely useful" (121) and even achieves the inconvenience of being "treated with too much confidence by all parties" (44).

Society satisfies Anne about as much and as little as it does any of Austen's heroines. Elinor Dashwood laments that she and her neighbors "could not be supposed to meet for the sake of conversation" but only for anything "sufficiently noisy" (143). John Dashwood's dinner table, for example, shows "no poverty of any kind, except of conversation," for the visitors all have

> one or other of these disqualifications for being agreeable—Want of sense—want of elegance—want of spirits—or want of temper (233).

Good conversation requires intelligence, taste, and self-control, but many of the characters in this (and the other) novels are utterly selfish and many others are good-hearted but ignorant. Emma Woodhouse's greatest fear, for example, when she thinks she cannot marry Mr. Knightley is to be left without "cheerful or rational society" in her reach (E 422). The fact that Anne's society does not fully satisfy her is less a criticism of this particular (or changing) society as evidence of Anne's superior nature. Like the other heroines, she has "resources for solitude" (37), but she neither scorns nor is unfit for social life. The chief satisfaction of Anne (and Fanny and Elinor) is, in fact, in being of use to others as a counselor or comforter (e.g., P 43–45, 221). Emma is a gracious hostess and takes pleasure in what society she can get; Elizabeth loves dances and is pained when her family is rude or ridiculous in public.

Persuasion, as much as the earlier novels, suggests that a respect for propriety is *not* an offense to romance. Anne does, at times, have apprehensions about the restraints imposed by her social situation. She wonders at one moment,

> How was the truth to reach him? How, in all the peculiar disadvantages of their respective situations, would he ever learn her real sentiments? It was misery to think of Mr. Elliot's attentions. Their evil was incalculable (191).

The exaggerated tone here suggests some irony at Anne's expense, indicating the agitation produced by her newly awakened hopes. Certainly, Anne must be less miserable now than at any previous point in the novel, and her acknowledgment of her misery is one sign of this happy agitation. Feeling able to indulge her fears—not to strive, as usual, for composure—shows that now she really has more hope than fear. The narrator makes this very point in a later scene in which Anne worries about how to speak to Wentworth and is "deep in the happiness of such misery, or the misery of such happiness" (229).

Austen's novels always assume that people of sense and sensibility can eventually find a way to communicate their feelings. Real love does not fall sacrifice to the requirements of convention. Anne's worries are natural and yet they are hardly ever presented without a smile. To cite one more example: when Anne has read Wentworth's proposal and then fears she will not be able to give him the sign he asked for, she thinks "this was dreadful . . . worse than all . . . her heart prophesied some mischance" (239). Then we see her discover, anticlimactically, that, even if she doesn't see Wentworth, all she need do is "send an intelligible sentence by Captain Harville" (239).[22] Anne puts forth an "argument of rational dependence" that, even if *she* cannot always trust in, the reader can: "Surely, if there be constant attachment on each side, our hearts must understand each other ere long" (221). We might note, in this regard, how Elinor and Edward are perfectly aware of their love for each other—almost from the start—despite the fact that neither has ever explicitly acknowledged it (SS 21–22, 139, 366). In a letter of Frank Churchill we are shown how a subject can be "just enough touched on to shew how keenly it was felt, and how much more might have been said but for the restraints of propriety'' (E 266). These restraints do not keep the meaning from being conveyed.

To conclude, prudence does not mean denying love and sensibility in favor of social and mercenary concerns. Rather, we are shown that the kind of love that is deep and lasting can meet the test of prudence. Such love is grounded in a love of virtue that might reasonably be expected to contribute to each person's well-being. Elinor's half-brother has told her she has "too much sense" not to see that marrying Edward is impossible, but he is wrong (224). As long as Edward is single—as long as there can be *any* hope—Elinor cannot overcome her love for the sake of prudence. Indeed, her love is not finally imprudent; her and Edward's "intimate knowledge of each other seemed to make their happiness certain" (369). As for Anne and Wentworth, not only do we see how their confidence in each other's merits makes their love deeper as well as more prudent, we also are shown how their respect for propriety contributes to the beauty of their love. In the end—in a phrase that perfectly captures Austen's spirit—they show "a most obliging compliance for public view, and smiles reined in and spirits dancing in private rapture" (240). The thoughtful respect for propriety of Austen's best characters is a sign of their regard for noble behavior in general and a sign of what distinguishes their love from mere sexual attraction.

Prudence and Marriage

Just as Austen does not derive high sentiments of love from lower physical pleasures, neither does she derive loyalty and commitment from lower desires for money and security. It is important to see that the prudence Austen is defending is not basely self-serving. We can ask the question that Elizabeth Bennet asks of her aunt in *Pride and Prejudice*: "what is the difference in matrimonial affairs, between the mercenary and the prudent motive?" (153). She is trying to defend Wickham, who *had* been paying attention to *her*, from the charge that he has chosen his new love, a Miss King, for her money. Her patient aunt replies, "If you will only tell me what sort of girl Miss King is, I shall know what to think" (153), for the monetary facts of the case are not enough to settle the question.

Elizabeth's exasperated comment notwithstanding, Austen clearly does not equate being prudent with being mercenary. The context of this conversation shows that Elizabeth is arguing against her true opinion, and we can compare her statement about Wickham to one she makes a bit earlier in reaction to Charlotte's marriage to Mr. Collins.

She tells Jane not to "endeavour to persuade yourself or me, that selfishness is prudence" (PP 134). So was Wickham selfish or prudent? What about Charlotte Lucas's successful attempt to lure Mr. Collins, or Lucy Steele's capture of Edward Ferrars's brother in *Sense and Sensibility*? Austen shows enough facts to allow a judgment in each case, while indicating that prudence is something that cannot be decided by abstract principles alone.

Wickham's and Lucy Steele's motives *are* mercenary. Mrs. Gardiner points out the "indelicacy" of Wickham's pursuit of Miss King so soon after she came into a fortune. Elizabeth replies that a man "in distressed circumstances" does not have time for "all those elegant decorums" (153), a statement that, if in some sense true (what is proper in an emergency is not the same as in ordinary affairs),[23] clearly cannot apply to this case. There are hints, in Elizabeth's frustration, that she is arguing against her real opinion, and later she comes to see the truth of Mrs. Gardiner's analysis. It is important not to be misled by Elizabeth's dismissive reference here to "elegant decorums" or by her lack of fashion to fail to see that she herself is highly observant of even conventional propriety and is pained by the lack of it in those she cares about (see 98–101 and 292); her younger sisters can complain that "formality and discretion" are typical of her (220). As Mrs. Gardiner argues, Miss King's not objecting to Wickham's indelicacy only shows "her being deficient in something herself—sense or feeling" (153).

Not just feeling but *sense* is wanting, for the novels suggest that selfishness is often imprudent. Lucy Steele's pursuit of Robert Ferrars, which begins when it appears that Robert will inherit Edward's fortune, shows "selfish sagacity" (SS 375), "earnest self-interest" (376), and "self-provident care" (357), but it notably is *not* called prudent. We see the "impolitic cruelty" of Mrs. Ferrars in cutting off Edward (SS 282), as well as a long account of how Fanny Dashwood's "cold-hearted selfishness" (229) makes her inadvertently promote a match for Edward (with Lucy) that she regards as even worse than the one she is trying to prevent (232–33, 248, 253, 259). Austen's defense of sense or prudence is not an endorsement of the selfish characters in the novel over the benevolent ones.

In fact, Austen never seems to distinguish what is imprudent from what is immoral.[24] Elizabeth, exclaiming over Charlotte's imprudence in marrying Mr. Collins, says she lacks "principle" and "integrity" (136). We especially are shown how imprudence leads to injustice in the case of Marianne Dashwood. Marianne's refusal to control her own hopes and fears injures herself—when her "ecstasy of more than hope" on one occasion is disappointed, she feels as if "till that instant she had never suffered" (202). This lack of self-control is also unjust to others, however, for we see Marianne imagining that Mrs. Jennings, who delivered the letter that disappointed her, had *intended* to hurt her—"the cruelty of Mrs. Jennings no language . . . could have expressed" (202). Whether calculating or thoughtless, Austen shows imprudence to be selfish.

Charlotte Lucas's marriage is a more complicated consideration of the difference between prudent and mercenary motives to marry. Austen indicates that it is not a lack of romance but rather a lack of prudence that makes a match immoral, and, as we have seen, it is prudence that Elizabeth accuses Charlotte of lacking. (She tells Jane that Charlotte's action is *selfish*, not prudent, and her first reflection is on it being "so *unsuitable* a match" [125].) The question is whether it is ever prudent to marry without love. A case, at least, is made that Charlotte's marriage is not wholly imprudent. Here, as often with Austen, it is helpful to consider Aristotle, who says a prudent man is thought to be one who can "deliberate well concerning what is good and expedient for himself, not with respect to a part . . . but for living well in general."[25] Charlotte's action is prudent rather than mercenary because she is not led by avarice to forget all other considerations. Rather, after considering her own character and circumstances ("I am not romantic you know") and his "character, connections and situation in life" (125), she decides that this is the best course of action for her happiness as a whole. It is significant that Austen so often stresses Charlotte's chances for happiness. Charlotte manages her household and husband in such a way as to make her husband happy and to find happiness herself, even if it is not in his society (156–57, 178, 216). The friendship between them begins in utility, but they both have reliable virtues—Charlotte's "prudent, steady character" and Mr. Collins's "respectability"— that make it likely to last (135–36). Her marriage is not presented as dishonorable.[26]

Among the facts that Charlotte considers, undoubtedly, are that she has no fortune, and that, unlike Elizabeth, she is 27 years old and has never been pretty (123). Elizabeth's hasty criticism is presented as somewhat unfeeling. In fact, it is only on this occasion that we hear the (much-quoted) statement that Elizabeth "overcome[s] . . . the bounds of decorum" (124). Elizabeth's impropriety is not in teasing Mr. Darcy but in making her friend mindful of her inferiority to herself (for *Elizabeth* would not accept Mr. Collins). Charlotte had forseen that "her feelings must be hurt" by Elizabeth's disapproval (123). The novel's sensitive portrayal of Charlotte is an example of Austen not always insisting on marriage for love.

We can conclude from these examples that prudence is, on the one hand, *not* selfish or mercenary, and yet, on the other, that in being directed toward individual happiness it cannot be free of self-concern. Another way to put this is that for Austen, selfishness is not the best route to happiness. Prudence is necessary to the fullest happiness, she suggests, and yet it loses its substance if it is conceived of as a *means* to this end. When in *Persuasion* Mrs. Smith says of Mr. Elliot that " 'To do the best for himself,' passed as a duty" (202), it is implied that this is not where real duty begins; as Anne believes, Mr. Elliot "never had any better principle to guide him than selfishness" (208). Prudence is shown to be not the pursuit of *any* desired end, but the pursuit of the truly best end.

This account is borne out by the case of Anne Elliot. There is a question, as I have suggested, about whether Anne's early rejection of Wentworth *was* really prudent. Her decision to reject him was not made for the selfish reason of wanting to make a better match for herself. She was not led by "selfish caution" (27)—she is consoled chiefly by the belief "of being prudent, and self-denying principally for *his* advantage" (28). It seems that Anne's self-denial may have been partly responsible for the decision. And it is a decision that is somehow imprudent: Anne realizes later that she would have been happier maintaining the engagement, even with all its worries and disadvantages. In fact, Lady Russell's fear that Anne be put in a state of "youth-killing" anxiety by her engagement is exactly what comes true by cancelling it. Austen lets us see this fact while not yet decisively criticizing Anne, who to the end defends "a strong sense of duty" as "no bad part of a woman's portion" (246). Anne dislikes those "ambitious feelings which have led to so much misconduct *and* misery, both in young and old" (218, my emphasis), suggesting that *both* virtue and happiness require the habit of controlling one's desires. Again, Austen implies that real prudence would not have made such an unhappy choice, yet she does not defend a selfish *motive* for prudence (Anne's habit of self-denial is not simply ill-judged).

Perhaps the chief reason Austen can allow for a place for prudence in decisions to marry is that she never portrays love as irrational. She is aware of many types of affection (some of them deep and moving) and many ways for it to begin, but she can always *account* for it. Even love that is rapid—as with Anne Elliot and Frederick Wentworth—is not at first sight. Their romance is carefully explained. It is inevitable given their situation ("he had nothing to do, and she had hardly anybody to love") and their real merit ("such lavish recommendations" of mind as well as beauty). They were "gradually acquainted" and only then fell in love (26). This love does not arise in the manner criticized in *Pride and Prejudice*, "even before two words have been exchanged" (PP 279). And even love as warm as theirs loses its force when it is not fulfilled. Captain Wentworth may be surprised by Captain Benwick's "untaught feeling" for Louisa, after the recent death of his beloved wife, but even *Persuasion* argues that second attachments are a "thoroughly natural, happy, and sufficient cure" for lost love (28). We are told that "perhaps nearly all of particular attachment" to Wentworth has vanished for Anne, over the years; her constancy owes much to the fact that she has had no change of place or novelty, and that no one in the "small limits" of her society could satisfy her mind and taste (28).

The fact that love is not inexplicable, and that desires and sentiments do not direct behavior but are themselves in need of guidance, helps us see how prudence can bear upon love. First of all, Austen believes that it is often possible to control the development of love. A character like Mr. Darcy's friend Colonel Fitzwilliam in *Pride and Prejudice*, who is both worthy and charming and clearly takes pleasure in Elizabeth's company, guards against forming in himself, or encouraging in her, any *particular* attachment. He points out that Mr. Darcy's wealth gives him more power of choice in marriage than he himself has, for as a younger son of an earl—with "habits of expence" but no fortune to inherit—he cannot marry "without some attention to money" (183). Similarly, Mrs. Gardiner urges Elizabeth to be on her guard with Willoughby: "Do not involve yourself, or endeavour to involve him in an affection which the want of fortune would make so very imprudent" (PP 144). She is not, like Lady Russell to Anne, asking her to sacrifice her love for prudence, but rather is urging her not to *develop* affection for him. Austen's point is precisely not that love is a feeble passion, but rather that it is something powerful and not to be toyed with. Still, the deepest love does not come in an instant; reason has power over its development.

The difference between sacrificing love for prudence and prudently trying not to develop affection is apparent in the difference between Edward Ferrars and Willoughby of *Sense and Sensibility*. Willoughby is a knave *and* a fool (318), for doing exactly what Mrs. Gardiner warned against: he has tried as hard as possible to win Marianne's heart (53, 71, 80) while having no intention of marrying so imprudently. And in involving her he comes to involve himself in love, so that the marriage he makes (to another woman) for fortune turns out to be not so prudent, not so productive of his best happiness. Edward is less a scoundrel for he has tried, in the manner suggested by Mrs. Gardiner, not to involve himself and Elinor in affection that could not end in marriage. That his efforts did not succeed is a testimony to the power of love—his previous engagement (imprudent not only in fortune but because it was not based on real love) was not enough to guard his heart (368). In both cases we see how prudence means not ignoring desire, but on the contrary taking it seriously. Edward's case illustrates the reason Austen frequently criticizes long engagements: she is aware of the temptations that can arise to love someone else. In *most* cases, at least, faithfulness requires the external support of conventions such as marriage.

A comparison of the similarities of the surprising matches in *Sense and Sensibility* (Marianne Dashwood and Colonel Brandon) and *Persuasion* (Louisa Musgrove and Captain Benwick) shows how imprudence leads to a greater dependence on such conventions than does prudence. These marriages have in common the fact that they at first seem highly unsuitable and yet, at second glance, seem natural to the parties involved and to onlookers. The "high-spirited, joyous, talking" Louisa Musgrove wholeheartedly transfers her affection from Captain Wentworth to the "dejected, thinking, feeling, reading" Captain Benwick in a matter of weeks (166). The two at first seem "everything that would not suit the other," yet Anne, on reflection, thinks their union is perfectly natural (P 166–67). Their situations have thrown them together, and he—though he has just lost his wife—has the type of heart that "must love somebody" (167).

The eager Marianne Dashwood meets the same fate, marrying the older, more somber Colonel Brandon. This marriage has been frequently attacked by critics of Austen, who charge her with betraying Marianne—burying her "burning heart" in the "coffin of convention,"[27] or choosing "dull conformity to social conventions" over "personal commitment."[28] The fact that Colonel Brandon soon has Marianne's "whole heart" as much as Willoughby ever did (379), for Marianne "could never love by halves" (379), might raise some question about whether she sacrifices love for convention. Marianne's marriage is presented hurriedly and even jokingly,[29] and I would like to consider the possibility that this comic scene reveals something about Marianne.

Marianne's marriage to Colonel Brandon is not a "gross overcompensation for her misguided sensibility"[30] but a match with a man with the *same kind* of romantic sensibility. His marriage to Marianne is *not* a marriage of reasonable suitability. Just as Anne's first reaction to the match between Louisa and Captain Benwick is that it is "everything that would not suit," so Elinor first feels that the fitness of Marianne and Brandon for each other cannot be based "on an impartial consideration of their age, characters, or feelings" (236). Nevertheless, with a confederacy of good reasons against her, "what could [Marianne] do" but transfer her affection (378)? Of course, while it is funny to see Marianne overcome her self-proclaimed "irresistible passion" so quickly, Austen does not mean this scene to be improbable. The reason she can love again is not *simply* because her first love was not as substantial as she believed. All the novels show gratitude for being loved by someone else to be a plausible motive for love (consider Henry Tilney of *Northanger Abbey* or Elizabeth Bennet of *Pride and Prejudice*). Not only is Marianne grateful, she also has found a man with her own sort of mind. Colonel Brandon comes to "talk to Elinor" whereas he comes to "look at Marianne" (169); "he was a lover" (55). He has fallen in love at first sight (336) and his melancholy air is due to his love (309, cf. 50, 173). He loves Marianne for her faults (unusual in Austen): "there is something so amiable in the prejudices of a young mind, that one is sorry to see them give way" (56, cf. 236). Like Captain Benwick, who reads Scott and Byron, Colonel Brandon (and not Willoughby) is the true romantic.

Marianne's marriage is not a betrayal by Austen but a necessary service, for her eager enthusiasms require more conventional supports than does her sister's firm mind. Marianne's fate is summed up in one sentence: her expectations have changed from "falling a sacrifice to an irresistible passion" to "finding her only pleasures in retirement and study," to submitting to the duties of a wife, mother, and patroness, all in a matter of months (378). It seems impossible not to take Austen's extravagant language to be ironic here.[31] Marianne still knows "no moderation"; when she is cured of the "languid indolence and selfish repining" caused by her "excess of sensibility," she replaces it by "introducing excess into a scheme of rational employment and virtuous self-control" (6, 343). Part of the comedy of this ending is that Colonel Brandon has exactly as much money as Marianne thinks is necessary for marriage, even though she denies that wealth is important at all. Marianne has protested to Elinor that wealth is not necessary for happiness, and the ensuing debate reveals that Marianne's idea of "competence" is twice as much as Elinor's idea of "wealth" (91). Marianne's greater need for money, despite her professions, is one sign of her greater need for a happy and suitable marriage. Colonel Brandon compares Marianne to the disgraced Eliza and hopes that she will not share her fate: she will be "guarded by a firmer mind or a happier marriage" (208). This phrase is typical of Austen's thought. A happy marriage can make up for the lack of a firm mind in guarding against sexual temptations (consider also Harriet Smith of *Emma*), whereas someone with principle and prudence is less in need of conventional protections.

Sensibility as Love of Virtue

Mansfield Park is not the only novel in which Jane Austen chooses moral and religious principles over sophisticated charm, but it is unique in its sober and urgent tone and its unusually intense heroine. Fanny Price is a heroine of sensibility, and this novel studies her acute and retentive feelings in a curiously unsentimental way. Fanny is not portrayed as pitiable. Her sufferings are not due to the tyranny of others, nor is her horror at wrongdoing calculated to evoke sympathy. As David Lodge writes,

> Everything . . . depends on our identifying with the heroine, but Jane Austen endows her with few of the attractive and endearing qualities which the novelist is licensed to dispense.[32]

Many readers object to Fanny's frequent passivity[33]; Tony Tanner remarks that "even sympathetic readers often find her something of a prig."[34] Some readers, in fact, fervently dislike Fanny, charging her with self-righteousness and complacency.[35] This last criticism seems to me to overlook the problem of what unrequited love does to Fanny's character, for many unpleasant qualities in her are aroused by her jealousy of Mary Crawford and are striking because they are so unlike her general disposition. Nevertheless, Fanny is not *charming*, and yet the remarkable thing is that it is extremely difficult to read *Mansfield Park* without rooting for her in some way. I would suggest that this testifies not only to Jane Austen's narrative magic, but also to the insights of her presentation of sensibility. *Mansfield Park* explores how Fanny's two most important qualities, an "affectionate heart, and strong desire of doing right" (17), may explain her unusual capacity to love. Here we see an extreme version of Austen's typical presentation of the way moral virtue *goes along with* the deepest sensibility.

Fanny's sensibility is the most romantic of any of Austen's characters. Barbara Hardy has shown how she is "one of the most complete

Romantic heroines,'' one whose romanticism is, like Rousseau's, "grounded in sense and science."[36] Fanny's keen observation and curiosity about nature contributes to her ''delicacy of taste, of mind, of feeling'' and contrasts her, throughout the novel, to Mary Crawford, who ''saw nature, inanimate nature, with little observation'' (MP 81). In one important scene, Edmund is on the point of going out to gaze at the stars with Fanny (an activity she is fond of) when he is drawn instead toward the group surrounding Mary who is singing and playing the piano (113). Mary's performing and Fanny's star-gazing suggest their different sources of strength. Gazing at the stars, Fanny feels that there ''certainly would be less [wickedness and sorrow in the world] if the sublimity of Nature were more attended to, and people were carried more out of themselves by contemplating such a scene'' (113). Fanny's taste for natural beauty is presented as a sign of her moral disposition.[37] Austen's point here is similar to Kant's: ''we have reason for presuming the presence of at least the germ of a good moral disposition in the case of a man to whom the beauty of nature [not art] is a matter of immediate interest.''[38] Fanny's love of nature shows her longing to be a part of something greater than herself. *Mansfield Park* explores in a very precise way the *source* of Fanny's sensibility.

Fanny's Inwardness

Fanny in general is anything but complacent, anything but sure that she is virtuous. Her primary characteristic is in fact her acute sense of her own insignificance and sinfulness (e.g., 13, 20, 26, 176, 221, 274, 276). Her unusual inwardness has to do with her having been taken from her home at an early age and raised in a home in which she feels she does not belong. Only in this novel does Austen give a significant amount of space to a heroine's childhood, for it is important for Fanny's shy and reflective nature. We meet Fanny at age ten, ''longing for the home she had left'' and ''ashamed'' of her inability to fit in at Mansfield Park (13). To compound the manifest differences between Fanny and her more cultivated cousins, her uncle Sir Thomas and her aunt Norris have impressed upon her that she is not her cousins' equal (10–12, 220–21). Austen does not sentimentalize Fanny's situation: for one thing, the Bertrams have not been knowingly unkind to her (14, 17), and occasional hints of self-pity in Fanny (as when she claims ''I can never be important to anyone'' [26]) do not make her appear more sympathetic. The author seems less interested in evoking sympathy for a helpless victim as in exploring the kind of inwardness of mind such a person might have.

The excesses of sensibility in Fanny that come from her sense of insignificance and timidity are not presented as her virtue: Austen is not prescribing passivity and meekness for women.[39] (Here, as usual, she does not portray feeling as virtue.) One of Edmund's projects is to "conquer the diffidence" in Fanny that hides her merits from others (21, 27, 198). Austen often shows how excessive diffidence, like excessive vanity, shows too much fear of others' opinions of oneself. Austen's comments in a letter about the "disease" of shyness are relevant:

> What is become of all the Shyness in the World? Moral as well as Natural Diseases appear in the progress of time, & new ones take their place.[40]

Mansfield Park also portrays some new moral diseases—such as the easygoing confidence about one's own goodness seen in the Crawfords—but Austen does not forget that Fanny also has a sort of disease. It is the understandable result of being kept back by everyone else (e.g., 22, 48, 221).

The author's tough-minded analysis of Fanny goes so far as to present her situation as *advantageous.* Just as in *Emma* we see that the "real evils" of the heroine's situation are the power of having too much her own way, and the disposition to think too well of herself (E 5), so here Austen points out the advantages to be gained by the opposite situation. Credit for Fanny's "excellence" in the end is given to "the advantages of early hardship and discipline, and the consciousness of being born to struggle and endure" (473). She has had the unusual situation of being raised (yet not indulged) in wealth, comfort, and order, coupled with the consciousness of no natural claim to such things. At Mansfield Park, Fanny sleeps in the smallest attic room, has no fire in the old schoolroom that she makes her own, and her will is rarely consulted. In part through such privations, she has learned "the necessity of self-denial and humility" that her cousins never have known (463). Yet Fanny's room, however cold and small, is a quiet and private retreat. There she has books of poetry, travel, and biography (156, 398) from which she often quotes by heart. This "nest of comforts" (152) helps foster Fanny's highly developed inner life. Fanny has a warm imagination and curiosity about foreign places and former times (e.g., 85, 197–98) as well as about the nature around her (56, 80–81, 113, 208–209, 409, 432, 447). Such reflectiveness could not have been possible in her father's house, where there is "incessant noise" (391), where "a stifling, sickly glare'' takes away the pleasures of spring (439, cf. 431–32), and where there are no books (398).

All of Austen's heroines of sensibility have experienced the loss of a home. Elinor as well as Marianne Dashwood was ''deeply afflicted'' at being cast out from the estate her family had had for generations (7). Anne, too, upon the renting out of her family estate, feels for her ''beloved home'' and ''precious rooms and furniture, groves and prospects'' (47); in addition, she sighs that her father ''should see nothing to regret in the duties and dignity of the resident land-holder'' (138). The attachment these women have to the places they have known seems to be a sign of their general capacity for caring. For Fanny, leaving her home is particularly important because she is a child when it happens. Eight years after leaving Portsmouth she feels ''emotions of tenderness that could not be clothed in words'' at the idea of seeing her mother and father again (369–70), and the story of Fanny's return to Portsmouth and the disappointment of all her hopes is one of the saddest passages Austen wrote. Yet even here the author does not pull at our heart-strings: she avoids both an emotional reconciliation of the heroine with her true parents, and a pitiable scene of a neglected child. Fanny's hopes are understandable and yet unreasonable, as she comes to see.

Fanny's shyness and passivity are not her virtue. But Austen is interested in the source of her sensibility, which does Fanny credit: she has an unusual *love* of virtue, of doing the right thing for others and for herself. Fanny's sense of not deserving what she has been given—for she is fully conscious that Mansfield Park is *not* her home—helps explain her longing for virtue. She retains a childlike innocence, despite her tough spirit, throughout the novel. The impression lingers of her as a ''little cousin'' (12, 15, 17) with a ''constant little heart'' (14, 27). Mary Crawford finds her at age 18 to be ''as good a little creature as ever lived'' and says she will be ''a sweet little wife'' (231, 292). Even in the end, Edmund calls her ''dear little Fanny'' (342). There is something childlike in a mind so unreconcilable to wickedness in herself or in the world (113, 441).

Fanny is not at all convinced she is good, but has a deep desire to be so. Her lack of smugness appears when she is afraid of appearing to set herself off as better than others (198) or when she cannot bear to be in ''what might seem a state of triumph'' (222). The difference between Fanny and her cousins is not so much that she is virtuous and they are not, but that Fanny knows she is *not* always virtuous, and takes this deeply to heart. Arriving at Mansfield Park as a child, her misery is increased ''by the idea of its being a wicked thing for her not to be happy'' (13). She is as relieved as her cousins when Sir Thomas leaves for India, but her ''more tender nature suggested that her feelings were ungrateful, and she really grieved because she could not grieve'' (33). She has feelings so akin to envy at one point ''as made her hate herself for having them'' (413). Fanny is not free from ungrateful or petty feelings, but she cannot reconcile herself to them. ''Her heart was almost broke'' when Sir Thomas accuses her of ingratitude for refusing Henry Crawford: ''selfish and ungrateful! to have appeared so to him!'' (319, 321). She is pained by the very possibility of the truth of these charges. In general, Fanny is slow to take offense. She is mortified by the way her cousins treat her, but ''thought too lowly of her own claims to feel injured by it'' (20, cf. 221, 274).

Fanny is interesting not as someone with extraordinary virtue but as someone who takes seriously the possibility that virtue is not so easily known or achieved. For it is not Fanny but Mary Crawford and the other worldly characters in the novel who are certain they possess virtue. Mary, like the Bertram sisters, is quite confident of her respectability. Her philosophy is ''it is everybody's duty to do as well for themselves as they can'' (289; see also 38–39, where a similar position is attributed to Maria Bertram). Mary's belief that self-concern is a moral duty lets her treat selfishness lightly, saying, ''I depend upon being treated better than I deserve'' (433), or, ''selfishness must always be forgiven you know, because there is no hope of a cure'' (68). This easygoing attitude makes her as forgiving of others as she is of herself. In the character of Fanny, Austen raises some questions about the modern philosophy that the most important thing is feeling good about oneself: Fanny is intriguing because she is more desirous of *being* good than of feeling good.

Austen can laugh at Fanny's excessive fears for Mary's soul, but she does not completely dismiss them. Mary is kind, having ''really good feelings by which she was *almost* purely governed'' (147, emphasis added) but such things are not enough. Fanny uses religious language to describe Mary's mind as ''led astray and bewildered, and without any suspicion of being so; darkened, yet fancying itself light'' (367). Austen, in her own narrative voice, is not so ominous, pointing out that Fanny

> may be forgiven by older sages, for looking on the chance of Miss Crawford's future improvement as nearly desperate. . . . But as such were Fanny's persuasions, she suffered very much from them (367).

Fanny's inexperience makes her too hopeless about the possibility of overcoming wrongdoing. But what is important is that her judgments do not make her self-satisfied but rather make her suffer. The subsequent account of how Mary has treated Edmund justifies some of Fanny's fears. Mary is led away from the truth about her own happiness by her confidence that she (and others) are doing just fine. She can believe, for example, that marriage is always a "take in" (46) while yet not questioning the motives that might make it so (359–60).

An extraordinary sensibility lies behind Fanny's wish to be good. Almost any glance at this novel shows that Jane Austen tends to think of sensibility and virtue together. Henry Crawford has qualities that "ought to have made him *judge* and *feel* better" (45, emphasis added), and the Bertram sisters have "not *affection* or *principle* enough" to be truly friends (63, emphasis added). So it may not be surprising that someone who desires virtue as much as Fanny does has deep feelings. Her longing for her family is only one clue that "her feelings were very acute" (14); her reunion with her brother reveals to Henry a "sensibility which . . . illumined her countenance," her "feeling, genuine feeling" (235). Fanny's strong sensibility can be subject at times to the author's irony, as, perhaps, when we hear that her heart is so "completely sad at parting" from Mansfield Park that she had "tears for every room in the house, much more for every beloved inhabitant" (374, cf. 359). Fanny sometimes seems to feel more than is called for: "My dear Fanny, you feel these things a great deal too much," Edmund says on one occasion (262). This "tender-hearted cousin" feels regret for the absence of her cousins much beyond what they have done to deserve it (204, see also 359, 428).

But Fanny's feelings, if sometimes excessive, do not detach her from the world around her, as Marianne Dashwood's so often do. Rather, they reflect an exceptional degree of involvement: she has made the people and things around her—even ones she isn't fond of—a part of herself. Fanny, more than anyone, is loyal to the things and people she knows—she is "of all human creatures the one, over whom habit had most power, and novelty the least" (354). Her sensitivity to change is a sign of her hope of devoting herself to something lasting. Changes in her own state of mind and in the world are the most frequent subject of her reveries (208, 374, 393, 432, 446–47), and she fervently believes in the importance of constancy (156, 159, 343).

Fanny's "purity of mind," "purity of . . . principle," "purity of . . . intention" (468, 428, 324) make her unusually disturbed by wrongdoing. Her response to the news that the man who has professed to love her has committed adultery with her cousin is perhaps the most striking instance of sensibility in any of Austen's novels:

The horror of a mind like Fanny's, as it received the conviction of such guilt . . . can hardly be described. At first it was a kind of stupefaction . . . she passed from feelings of sickness to shudderings of horror; and from hot fits of fever to cold. The event was so shocking, that there were moments even when her heart revolted from it as impossible (441).

Fanny is not absorbed in condemning the sinners (although she does not excuse them), but in horror at the sin itself. "A mind like Fanny's"—one so convinced of the importance of good conduct— can hardly comprehend it. Fanny can scarcely believe that high and noble feelings could so completely vanish, and she is utterly desperate about the state of affairs if they have. Again, her fears, if naive, are not self-satisfied: far from leading to complacency, they make her physically ill. Her horror comes from the purity of principle that makes her take her own shortcomings so seriously.

One positive result of Fanny's extreme sensitivity is that she cannot forget kindness that has been done to her or to those she loves. She can "never receive kindness without wishing to return it" (26); her disposition is "peculiarly calculated to value a fond treatment" (365) from having known so little of it. She knows the worth of the "blessing of affection" (397), and, despite her shyness, shows her own affection to others. She has "pity and kind-heartedness," "kindness and patience," "kindness and sympathy" (166, 224, 270), is a "kind, kind listener," a "very courteous listener" (164, 268). She does work of charity for the poor (151, 396, 404). She has "habits of ready submission" in attending to the wishes of the household (356, cf. 145, 281) and behaves, as Henry Crawford observes, "with such unpretending gentleness, so much as if it were a matter of course that she was not to have a moment at her own command" (296). When people leave she is reminded of missed chances to have performed services for them (282). This sort of sensitivity has a less appealing side, which Austen does not cover up—Fanny is easily pained (although not angered) by slights to herself.

Fanny is remarkable for being capable of real gratitude. She is humble enough not to resent being indebted to a benefactor and clear-sighted enough not to assume that those who have done good for her are of good character generally. Unlike Marianne Dashwood, whose insensibility makes her not appreciate the imperfect kindness of Mrs. Jennings, Fanny cannot resist *any* sort of kindness in others, even the "apparent affection" of Mary toward herself (365, cf. 147, 199). Fanny is more alert than Catherine Morland of *Northanger Abbey*, who is de-

ceived by Isabella's professions of friendship; Fanny sees Mary's insincerity (208, 433) while yet being grateful for even the *appearance* of
kindness. The point is that, while Fanny can be critical of others (she
cannot approve, for example, of how Mary Crawford speaks of her
uncle, Admiral Crawford, for "whatever his faults may be, [he] is so
fond of her brother, treating him, they say, quite like a son" [63]), she
is anything but hard in her virtue. She can be softened in an instant.
She is aware of Admiral Crawford's faults but still can be extremely
grateful to him (and to his nephew Henry) for getting her brother William his lieutenancy. Her gratitude keeps her from disdaining Henry
"in all the dignity of angry virtue" (328).

Fanny's Love

Fanny's love for Edmund is a thread running through and tying together the entire novel. It is a peculiarly unromantic kind of love in a
heroine of such romantic sensibility. The love defended in all the novels
is characterized by mutual involvement (doing favors for each other,
being concerned for the other's good) rather than by admiration from
afar. No one is less susceptible to being swept off her feet, less apt to
love what is novel, than is Fanny Price. As Edmund puts it, "the man
who means to make you love him . . . must have very up-hill work"
because she will have all her early attachments "in battle array" (348).
Fanny's love of what is good is mingled with, and inseparable from,
her love of what is her own.

"Battle" aptly describes what Henry Crawford comes to wage. In
defending herself against his advances, Fanny's love of principle and of
Edmund make her unmoving. But even here she is not smug. The test
of Fanny's right-mindedness is whether she can forgo even her most
noble pleasures for the sake of duty. Fanny withstands what is most
painful to her—the charge of selfishness from everyone she knows and
loves (e.g., 318, 333, 347). Her wish to be grateful to Sir Thomas, to
Edmund, and even to Henry, and to be able to offer a home to her
younger sister, are the greatest inducements on the side of marrying
Henry. Fanny does not worry about never again being "addressed by a
man of half Mr. Crawford's estate, or a tenth part of his merits" (319),
as much as about following the dictates of her principles and her heart.[41]
Austen seems to suggest that doing one's duty requires thinking seriously about one's happiness. Fanny does not think *only* of herself, as
Sir Thomas has charged, and yet she *does* think about herself and her
duty very deeply. It is simply not "possible . . . to do otherwise" than

to refuse Henry (320), because she is so convinced she cannot love him and that it is *"wicked"* to marry without love (324, emphasis added). What she leaves unsaid is that it is wicked to marry one person while loving another.

For Fanny might have come to love Henry, we are told, if Edmund had married first and if Henry had persevered uprightly (467). But Fanny's long involvement with Edmund has made her love him in a way that no attractive newcomer can overcome. She loves him in part out of gratitude: she gives him large credit for even the formation of her mind (470, cf. 22, 355, 398) and considers him as "entitled to such gratitude from her, as no feelings could be strong enough to pay" (37, cf. 16, 66, 79, 261–62). She has felt Edmund's kindness "with all, and more than all, the sensibility which he . . . could be aware of" (79). She loves him, too, because she has invested many hours and emotions in him, becoming his all-important confidant and adviser (155, 270, 345). The rightness of her love seems to be confirmed by the fact that Edmund's chain, not Henry's, fits through the gold cross that is the only ornament she has ever desired to wear.

Fanny feels, in sum, that her love for Edmund is unselfish, that he deserves any sacrifices she could make for him. Yet this sort of love becomes problematic. The more Fanny feels her love for Edmund, the more unpleasant qualities, such as envy, suspicion, impatience, and even self-pity, are aroused in her. As Fanny slowly becomes aware of these things, she resolves to purify her love of Edmund:

> It was her intention, as she felt it to be her duty, to try to overcome all that was excessive, all that bordered on selfishness in her affection for Edmund (264).

But it turns out not to be so easy to purge love of its selfishness. Fanny cannot give up the wish for Edmund to be *hers*. After making her good resolutions she seizes a scrap of paper on which Edmund had been writing "as a treasure beyond all her hopes," for in addition to "all the heroism of principle" she also has many "feelings of youth and nature" (265). Austen is careful never to portray Fanny as a saint.

Fanny does, of course, have fears that loving Edmund is wrong, but for conventional rather than moral reasons. She reflects that marrying Edmund would be

> a *presumption*, for which she had not words strong enough to satisfy her own humility. To think of him as Miss Crawford might be justified in thinking, would in her be insanity (265, emphasis added).

The context makes it clear that Fanny is not thinking of incest here, as some have argued. The thought of marrying Edmund is presumptuous not because she is his sister, but in fact because she is *not* his equal. In addition it would be presumptuous because Fanny cannot "be justified in thinking" that Edmund has encouraged her to love him, as Mary Crawford might be. Sir Thomas would consider such a match unsuitable for his son in terms of fortune and rank (6, 11), and Fanny has not "any idea of classing herself with his children" (176, cf. 10, 221). Fanny is an example of a heroine, forecast in *Northanger Abbey*, who loves a man before he loves her, but if propriety cannot regulate her feelings, still her "high notion of honour," "observance of decorum," and "propriety of mind" (294, 223) make her try to regulate her thoughts and behavior. Incest is not the issue for Sir Thomas, who comes to support a match between Edmund and Fanny only when he sees her as his daughter (see 431, 444) and becomes "sick of ambitious and mercenary connections" (471).

Such unrequited love inevitably involves Fanny in certain petty and selfish feelings. Perhaps the most prominent of them is jealousy, which cannot be ignored in evaluating her reaction to Mary Crawford. It must be understood, too, in considering the "debility" that is often attributed to Fanny by critics of Austen. It is Mrs. Norris who blames Fanny's headache on cutting roses in the sun[42]; the chapter makes it clear that Fanny is, in fact, suffering from the disappointment of seeing the proof of Edmund's preference for Mary over herself—"the pain of her mind had been much beyond that in her head" (74). In fact, the point is made that such illness is unusual for Fanny (71). The health of Fanny's full-grown looks is often mentioned (e.g., 178, 197, 198, 230, 272, 294). Austen goes out of her way to say she is *not* sickly; she tires easily but this is always attributed to her lack of freedom to exercise, be it because of the stifling conditions of her early childhood or because of her aunt's demands later.

Fanny, in general, is diffident and not prone to self-pity (e.g., 20, 221, 274), to the point that her "favourite indulgence" is "being suffered to sit silent and unattended to" (223). But she cannot watch Edmund with *Mary* without feeling sorry for his lack of attention to herself: "she wondered that Edmund should forget her, and felt a pang" (67), she is "feeling neglected" by him (74), she would have thought "it was impossible for Edmund to forget her so entirely" (100). She tends to become judgmental on such occasions. When she watches Mary ride Edmund's mare while she awaits her turn, she begins to think it "rather hard on the mare to have such double duty; if she were forgotten the poor mare should be remembered'' (68).[43] And when Edmund and Mary have left her alone on a bench in the woods, and Henry and Maria similarly abandon Mr. Rushworth, Fanny reflects ''that [Mr. Rushworth] had been very ill-used'' (101). Fanny does feel for the mare and Mr. Rushworth, but her ''self-denying tone'' (217) on such occasions is not appealing. Jealousy has put her in the untenable position of feeling at once that she is unlovable and yet that she deserves love. We might even wonder if Fanny's conviction that kindness is deserving of love from her (''she had never received kindness from her Aunt Norris, and could not love her'' [25]) also makes her feel that *her own* kindness deserves love.

But jealousy in Fanny is a more sad than bitter passion, and one that somehow reflects her virtues. Fanny's suffering is particularly acute because her love is so serious. We can contrast the nature of Julia's jealousy when Henry begins to court Maria. Julia loves Henry herself, and she suffers

> with a strong sense of ill-usage. Her heart was sore and angry, and she was capable of only angry consolations (162).

Fanny is the only one who feels sorry for Julia because only she notices her jealousy and knows what it is like. She cannot think of her ''as under the agitations of *jealousy* without great pity'' (136, emphasis in original). They are ''two solitary sufferers, or connected only by Fanny's consciousness'' (163). But while Julia is ''not superior to the hope'' of a distressing end for her sister and Henry (162), Fanny is not capable of such angry consolations because she cares too much for Edmund. She does not want revenge, but rather feels ''disappointment and depression'' (103).

In this sort of mood, Fanny can even momentarily lose her concern about doing the right thing. She has been distressed about whether she should act in the play or not, but when she sees proof of Mary's influence over Edmund, ''this deeper anxiety'' swallows up that care: ''things should take their course; she cared not how it ended'' (157). She feels immune to the claims of others (although this feeling is not lasting [159]), for nothing seems important anymore if Edmund is Mary's. The terms used to describe Fanny's suffering are quite violent for Jane Austen. When Edmund tells Fanny that she and Mary are his two dearest objects, she can hardly tranquilize herself:

> She was one of his two dearest—that must support her. But the other! the first! She had never heard him speak so openly before. . . . It was a stab. . . . It was a stab (264).

No matter that she has long expected him to marry Mary Crawford, she is not prepared for confirmation. The thought that he has proposed to Mary "turned her too sick for speech" (268).

Fanny's moral judgments of Mary reflect jealousy much more than smugness, and yet perhaps not only this. This novel of sensibility makes a case against feeling as a guide to behavior. Fanny is anything but complacent when she finds the prospect of a marriage between Edmund and Mary to be "most sorrowful to her—independently—she believed independently of self" (367). Her fears seem to be substantiated, for the novel indicates that Edmund's love is even more partial than Fanny's jealousy. With the "ingenuity of love," Edmund often dwells on or invents warm and obliging motives for Mary to explain actions or opinions in her that seem objectionable (129, cf. 63, 111). He has "satisfactions very sweet, if not very sound" in thinking himself right to oblige Mary's feelings at the expense of his judgment (159). In these cases, it is indicated that Edmund is wrong in thinking that Mary's improprieties are a credit to her strong affections. *Mansfield Park* suggests not only that sensibility is a quality in need of moral guidance—Henry Crawford has "no principle to supply as a duty what the heart was deficient in;" his "*feelings*" have "been too much his guides" (329, 351)—but also that true sensibility is a strong desire to do right. Fanny can only relieve her "dejection" over Edmund's being deceived in Mary ("he gave her merits which she had not") by the influence of "fervent prayers for his happiness" (264). She cannot glory in the unhappiness she foresees for him but is left to find consolation in prayer.

Perhaps the most startling change that love brings about in someone as gentle as Fanny is impatience. She frequently wants to tell Edmund various criticisms of Mary but keeps them to herself, "lest it should appear like ill nature" (66, 115, 170, 199). She can be "quite impatient" and "full of jealousy and agitation" when he is with Mary (103, 159). Now her smiles are sometimes forced (354) and there is "perpetual irritation" at knowing Edmund's heart (370), to the point that it is a relief to be apart from him (285, 370). Finally Fanny becomes almost angry in her impatience that Edmund has not written to her to announce his marriage: "Oh, write, write . . . Let there be an end to this suspense. Fix, commit, condemn yourself" (424). Such feelings are too near resentment to guide her for long (425), but her love makes it hard for her to be passive.

All of Austen's novels suggest that the love that will last through marriage must somehow be reasonable, and grounded in virtue, gratitude, and esteem. Nowhere, however, does she show sexual attraction to be of such little importance as in *Mansfield Park* (although even here it is not absent).[44] The love between Fanny and Edmund, originating in their relations as teacher and student and protector and confidant, is a more spiritual than physical attraction. Fanny is offended when Mary Crawford praises Edmund's good looks: "The woman who could speak of him, and speak only of his appearance—what an unworthy attachment!" (417). By the end of the novel Edmund comes to believe, and to persuade Fanny, that her "warm and sisterly regard for him" is foundation enough for "wedded love" (470). With such a conviction of his and Fanny's importance to each other, it is said to be a small matter that he "learn to prefer soft light eyes to sparkling dark ones" (470). In other words, sexual attraction will come; there need not be much worry over it. Edmund has long loved *both* Fanny and Mary. What he comes to learn—and this is the startlingly unmodern point of *Mansfield Park*—is not just that the type of love he feels for Fanny is more reasonable, but also that it is deeper and more heartfelt, than the romantic attraction he has for Mary. Austen rarely makes this point so sternly, but the idea that the truest sensibility is found in moral involvement and not flights of emotion is common to all her work.

Notes

1. Edmund Wilson, "A Long Talk About Jane Austen," *Classics and Commercials: A Literary Chronicle of the Forties* (New York: Farrar, Straus & Cudahy, Inc., 1950), 203. Good discussions of the way in which *Sense and Sensibility* is told through Elinor's eyes are given by Duckworth in *The Improvement*, 110–11, and by Stuart Tave in *Some Words of Jane Austen*, 1973), 96–98. Barbara Hardy argues persuasively that *Sense and Sensibility*'s failure to "move as fully into Marianne's track of feeling as in Elinor's" is one of the novel's difficulties (Barbara Hardy, *A Reading of Jane Austen* [New York: New York University Press, 1976], 47).

2. Virginia Woolf, *The Common Reader* (New York: Harcourt, Brace & Co., 1925), 204.

3. Litz, *Jane Austen*, 153–54. See also Marilyn Butler, who argues that "marriage, the aim of romantic womanhood, becomes structurally more marginal to the last three novels," which concern "a new general theme, society at large" (Butler, *Jane Austen and the War*, xliii). Anne lives in a society of "changes, alienations," one that is "no longer truly a society in any meaningful sense," one showing a "general dissolution of the institution of the family," says Tony Tanner (*Jane Austen*, 214, 221, 227). In Alistair Duckworth's words, *Persuasion* is about "the total alienation of the individual from society, friendship and love" (Duckworth, *The Improvement*, 180). One of the very few

counterarguments is put forth by the historian David Spring ("Interpreters," in *Jane Austen: New Perspectives*, ed. Todd) who examines the class structure of Jane Austen's day with care and precision and concludes that "major turning points have been found [in Austen's novels] in what in fact was the same old story" (65). I would suggest that the argument Spring makes from historical data can be made equally strongly from the ideas expressed in the novels themselves.

4. Tanner, *Jane Austen*, 231.

5. The title of the chapter on *Persuasion* in Duckworth's book *The Improvement of the Estate*.

6. Perhaps it should not seem odd to see sailors as chiefly domestic. A similar comment is made by another sea-loving novelist, Joseph Conrad, describing how Marlow is different from his class: "most seamen lead, if one may so express it, a sedentary life. Their minds are of the stay-at-home order, and their home is always with them—the ship" (Conrad, *Heart of Darkness* [London: Pan Classics edition, 1976], 11).

7. Contemporaries of Jane Austen were quick to see this, if not always to approve. The novelist Maria Edgeworth concurred with the judgment of a friend about *Persuasion*: "One grows tired at last of milk and water even tho the water be pure and the milk sweet." Marilyn Butler, who quotes this exchange, plausibly says that this criticism has "an ideological rather than aesthetic charge" (Butler, *Jane Austen and the War*, xli, xlii).

8. "The good will is not good because of what it effects or accomplishes or because of its adequacy to achieve some proposed end; it is good only because of its willing, i.e., it is good of itself" (Kant, *Foundations*, 12). Austen judges more by results. Thus, we see her refer to the class of "those well-meaning people, who are always doing mistaken and very disagreeable things" (MP 332). This phrase, in Sir Thomas's narrative voice, refers to Mrs. Norris, whom we are given evidence to believe may not even be well-meaning. Nonetheless, Austen believes such a class of people exists, and she does not call them good in a strict sense.

9. Aristotle, as opposed to Kant, insists that goodness requires prudence. "[T]here can be no right intention without prudence or virtue; for the one [i.e., virtue] posits the end while the other [i.e., prudence] makes us do those things which bring about that end" (Aristotle, *Ethics*, 1145a4–6).

10. The point is put nicely by Nardin, *Those Elegant Decorums*, 144. Many commentators on the novels agree that *Persuasion* defends romance over prudence.

11. David Cecil persuasively says that "Anne is declared mistaken in her early renunciation of Wentworth, not because love should override all other considerations, but because Wentworth was virtuous and intelligent enough for a reasonable woman to risk poverty with him" (David Cecil, *Jane Austen* [Cambridge: Cambridge University Press, 1935], 40–41).

12. Aristotle stresses that virtue is neither just intending to do good nor the

capacity to do good: it is, rather, *acting* well, and "it is impossible or not easy to *act* nobly if one is not furnished with external goods" (Aristotle, *Ethics*, 1099a32–33).

13. Ian Watt suggests that Austen saw society in *Sense and Sensibility* as an "unalterable given," to which submission is an unpleasant but necessary chore (Watt, *Jane Austen: A Collection of Critical Essays*, 50). Tony Tanner more recently presents a very similar view in *Jane Austen*, 101. See also Duckworth, who says that Jane Austen endorses "social principles" over "freedom" and "individual inclinations" (Duckworth, *The Improvement*, 113); and Nardin, *Those Elegant Decorums*, 18. Susan Morgan gives a thoughtful dissent to this almost universal view, arguing that Elinor's civility is not reasoned conformity in *In the Meantime*, 113, 127.

14. Nardin, *Those Elegant Decorums*, 144.

15. Kaufmann, arguing from a belief in the radical individuality of Austen's thought, sees the point of propriety (he is speaking of *Sense and Sensibility*) to be "a protective secrecy" ("Law and Propriety, *Sense and Sensibility*," 391).

16. Nardin suggests in *Those Elegant Decorums*, 146, 152–53, that Austen's view in *Sense and Sensibility* is that social rules of propriety contain more wisdom than can be achieved by fallible individuals. I believe this overstates the case. Doing what is proper actually requires a high degree of discernment on the part of the individual: her novels are not a manual of manners prescribing what to do in every instance (she would deny that there could be such a thing). Austen stresses not so much the inherent wisdom of custom (although she often does defend the common sense of "the world") as the need to pay attention to other people and circumstances to determine what is called for in any particular case.

17. "Now things which give pleasure to most men are in conflict with each other because they are not by nature such [pleasurable]. But things which give pleasure to those who like noble things are by nature pleasant . . . thus the life of these men has no further need of pleasure as a sort of charm, to be attached like an appendage, but has its pleasure in itself" (Aristotle, *Ethics*, 1099a11–16).

18. Tanner, *Jane Austen*, 102.

19. Nardin, *Those Elegant Decorums*, 36–37, see also 27, where Nardin says the novel argues that conventional rules must be upheld even when they are repugnant to feeling. Yet there are few signs that such rules *are* repugnant to Elinor's feelings.

20. Cecil, *Jane Austen*, 35.

21. This is often claimed to be the case, as when Litz says that "the social world of *Persuasion* seems cruelly unhelpful" (Litz, *Jane Austen*, 155).

22. Many commentators take Anne's fears at face value. Duckworth concludes that "Society, the arena of most previous *ecclairissements*, becomes in *Persuasion* a bar to the truth being conveyed" (Duckworth, *The Improvement*, 204). The truth in fact *is* conveyed in this novel through crowded rooms and

public streets, and such statements do not account for the humorous tone in the descriptions of Anne's worry.

23. Consider, for example, how Elizabeth, in shock over the bad news she has just heard about Lydia, encounters Mr. Darcy and has no time to think of ceremony or reserve; he, in turn, replies "with more feeling than politeness" (*PP* 276).

24. In this, again, she is Aristotelian. See Aristotle *Ethics*, 1144b30–32: "a man cannot be good in the main sense without prudence, nor can he be prudent without ethical virtue."

25. Ibid., 1140a25–28.

26. The careful undermining of Elizabeth's initial charges against Charlotte makes it hard to say Charlotte is "immoral," as is argued by Tave (*Some Words*, 136–37) and Morgan (*In the Meantime*, 94–96). When the narrator says that Charlotte has married "from the pure and disinterested desire of an establishment" (122), a certain truth as well as irony is intended. Charlotte's choice of a useful, social role for herself (and one that benefits her family) is not simply selfish. If the need often to overlook her husband is one that "diminishes her life" (Tave, 137; Morgan, 95), there would be other diminishments, perhaps greater ones, in a dependent life of poverty. The poor and single Jane Austen, herself fulfilled by writing novels, seems aware that not everyone is capable or desirous of such a solitary life.

27. Mudrick, *Irony as Defense and Discovery*, 91. See also Tanner, who argues that Marianne's romance is "vengefully stamped out" (Tanner, *Jane Austen*, 100); and Henrietta Ten Harmsel, *Jane Austen: A Study in Fictional Conventions* (The Hague: Mouton, 1964), 47.

28. Duckworth, *The Improvement*, 104. See also A. Walton Litz, who says that when Austen gives Marianne the choice between "Willoughby's weakness and Colonel Brandon's flannel waistcoat," she confesses her inability to transform the conventions she inherited from other writers. (See Litz, *Jane Austen*, 81.) It is only through Marianne's eyes that Colonel Brandon's flannel waistcoat looks feeble (and Marianne silently admits that if the Colonel had complained of a violent fever she would not have despised him) and it is only Marianne who ("on the strength of her imagination") decides he has "neither genius, taste, nor spirit" (51).

29. This opinion is widely held. See, for example, Watt, *Jane Austen: Critical Essays*, 49.

30. Duckworth, *The Improvement*, 104.

31. All of the commentators on this novel that I have read think that Marianne has been converted to "sense." I think that Jane Austen's ironic language here at least suggests a problem with this. Marianne has always been eager and always will be, in romance or in rationality or in motherhood—and this is part of her charm—but she lacks moderation and the strong inner control of her sister.

32. David Lodge, *Language of Fiction* (London: Routledge & Kegan Paul, 1966), 97.

33. Litz (*Jane Austen*, 129) says Fanny is "a girl who is essentially passive and uninteresting." See also Tanner (*Jane Austen*, 143) or Nardin (*Those Elegant Decorums*, 106) who argues that the narrator must defend Fanny so that we do not dislike her *too* violently, or Morgan (*In the Meantime*, 164) who says Fanny is "a character not particularly gifted by nature who becomes better than she was."

34. Tanner, *Jane Austen*, 143.

35. See Kingsley Amis's claim that Fanny is "morally detestable" and "a monster of complacency and pride" ("What Became of Jane Austen," *Critical Essays*, ed. Watt, 142, 144). Mudrick (*Irony as Defense and Discovery*, 161) also sees in Fanny "complacency and envy, perhaps; certainly an odd lackluster self-pity." See also Joseph Duffy, "Moral Integrity and Moral Anarchy in *Mansfield Park*," *ELH* 23 (March 1956): 71–91.

36. Barbara Hardy, *A Reading*, 64, 61. Hardy points out the similarities between Fanny's rhapsodizing and Rousseau's *Les reveries du promeneur solitaire* and speculates that Austen's fondness for the term "reverie" comes from Rousseau. I would suggest that despite this similarity, Austen ultimately does not see solitude as a desirable human option. As Hardy herself shows, the "life and progress of feelings are essentially social in the novels of Jane Austen"; "passion always moves into the public world, and in many ways" (43, 53).

37. Hardy also makes this point, noting that "Fanny's celebration of nature has a moral significance that is more than a superior act of penetrating imagination. It is part of her capacity to ask, see, and judge, to appreciate, spontaneously, creatively and genuinely" (Ibid., 63).

38. Kant, *The Critique of Judgement*, trans. James Creed Meredith (Oxford: Clarendon Press, 1952), 160.

39. For a good discussion of Austen's criticism of the qualities in Fanny that were often recommended in conduct-books for women, see Margaret Kirkham, "Feminist Irony and the Priceless Heroine of *Mansfield Park*," *Jane Austen: New Perspectives*, Women & Literature New Series, vol. 3, ed. Janet Todd (New York: Holmes & Meier, 1983), 231–32.

40. Austen, *Letters*, 178–179 (8 February 1807).

41. Alisdair MacIntyre has pointed out that in refusing Henry Crawford, Fanny "places the danger of losing her soul before the reward of gaining what for her would be a whole world. She pursues virtue for the sake of a certain kind of happiness and not for its utility" (MacIntyre, *After Virtue*, 225).

42. This example is frequently cited as evidence of Fanny's weakness; see, for example, Janet Todd, *Women's Friendship in Literature* (New York: Columbia University Press, 1980), 254.

43. Fanny's jealousy is almost never discussed by the critics who point out her coldness toward Mary. One exception is David Cecil's insightful analysis of the scene about Edmund's mare (Cecil, *Jane Austen*, 28–29).

44. On Fanny's side, at least, sexual attraction is suggested by her jealousy of Mary or by her prizing of a scrap of Edmund's writing as a treasure beyond

all her hopes. Knowing what we do of Fanny's feelings, we see that the scene in which Edmund comes to Portsmouth and immediately presses her against his heart, striking her speechless, has a sexual as well as emotional charge. Mudrick goes too far when he says that Fanny's victory shows that "frigidity becomes the standard of sexual conduct" (Mudrick, *Irony as Defense and Discovery*, 180).

Chapter 3

Proper Pride and Religious Virtue

For a Christian, Austen talks a surprising amount about the merits of pride. Far from considering pride the chief human vice, it is not clear that she considers it, when justified, to be a vice at all. She does not, of course, defend the idea that one can be completely self-sufficient. Love is a humbling experience for all her heroes and heroines, one that shows them their neediness. But such humility is presented as more necessary than praiseworthy. All her best characters, even in the end, have a sort of generous pride that the novels defend. Of course, there are many types and degrees of pride, which Austen is careful to distinguish. Many of them are blamable. Nonetheless, one of the chief signs of the classical bearing in her writing is her suggestion that the point of virtue is not only to aid others, but also is to perfect one's own character. A proper pride is ideally the result of such virtue.

Aristotle's account of the high-minded man could be seen as a model for Mr. Darcy of *Pride and Prejudice,*[1] and one that is defended by the novel as a whole. Mr. Darcy is a man who has great things—not only good birth, fortune, and beauty, but also, and more importantly, virtues of character—and he considers himself worthy of them. It is his possession of virtue that is essential; we see in his companions, Mr. Bingley's sisters, how having advantages such as wealth and good luck without virtue leads to a general show of contempt for those without such things. Like Mr. Knightley, Mr. Darcy cares for truth more than for reputation. He does not gossip, wishing to talk neither about himself nor others "as he cares neither to be praised by others nor to blame others, and he is not given to praising others."[2] Mr. Darcy does not tell Elizabeth his opinion of Mr. Wickham because, as Aristotle puts it, "he

will speak no evil, not even of his enemies, except when insulted.''[3]
Even his movements are those of this high-minded man. He moves
slowly and deliberately (174, 257), writes slowly (47), and does not
raise his voice.

Pride and Prejudice is not so much about Mr. Darcy coming to re-
nounce his pride as about Elizabeth coming to understand it. Austen's
portrayal of prejudice is an example of her general theme: it is a feeling
not grounded on reason, a feeling that is in need of guidance. Under the
influence of Wickham's story, Elizabeth is convinced Mr. Darcy has
the "worst kind of pride"—pride that is no more than prejudice, that
cares more about a friend's connections than about his sense (187).
Elizabeth agrees to marry him after, gradually, "all her former prejudices had been removed" (368) and she sees that "indeed he has no
improper pride" (376). Just as Aristotle says that high-minded men
"seem" to be disdainful and that good luck "is thought" to contribute
to high-mindedness, but that these qualities really belong to those who
imitate the high-minded man,[4] so Austen points out the prejudice in the
common view of a proud man.

For the negative picture of Mr. Darcy is due more to others' prejudice
than to his pride. Mrs. Bennet's retelling of the "shocking rudeness"
of Mr. Darcy at Mr. Bingley's ball shows "much bitterness of spirit
and some exaggeration" (13), and in general his rudeness at this dance
is exaggerated (19, cf. 175). Mr. Darcy's insulting comment about Elizabeth is due more to his general unsociability than to contempt for her
social status, for as soon as he meets her he makes no secret to his
friends of his admiration and is "perfectly indifferent" to the ridicule
of Miss Bingley (27, 36, 53). Similarly, the Gardiners discover that the
townspeople of Lambton, the village near Pemberley, acknowledge that
Mr. Darcy is a liberal man and have nothing to accuse him of but pride,
which, even if he did not have it, "would certainly be imputed by the
inhabitants of a small market-town, where the family did not visit"
(265).

Austen presents Mr. Darcy's pride as a mean between two extremes,
the excessive modesty of Mr. Bingley and the vanity of Mr. Collins.[5]
Though Elizabeth blames Mr. Darcy for persuading Mr. Bingley not to
marry Jane (39, 141), she must admit that it is Mr. Bingley, if anyone,
who deserves anger and contempt for "that easiness of temper, that
want of proper resolution which now made him the slave of his design-
ing friends" (133; see also 16, 199, 371 for Bingley's lack of confidence in himself). To be sure, Jane, too, is modest and has not openly
displayed her feelings to him (208, 21), but it is Mr. Bingley's diffidence that makes him so persuadable and that deprives him of a woman

of whom he was worthy. If Bingley has too little pride, Mr. Collins clearly has too much, despite his show of humility. He is a "mixture of servility and self-importance" (64), "self-importance and humility" (70). Austen always suggests a connection between excessive vanity and excessive servility. Even the overly modest Mr. Bingley has more vanity than does Mr. Darcy: Mr. Darcy teasingly points out that Mr. Bingley's "appearance of humility" about his carelessness of writing is really "an indirect boast" (49), for he is secretly proud of his quickness and carelessness as being highly interesting if not estimable.

Moral Virtue and Good Manners

Austen does not hide the fact that there is a somewhat unsocial aspect to Mr. Darcy's virtue: his motive is not to make himself agreeable. It is almost always assumed by critics of *Pride and Prejudice* that Mr. Darcy represents society, and Elizabeth is a champion of individualism.[6] Before considering Mr. Darcy's asocial side, it is helpful to look at Elizabeth's sociability. That Elizabeth is lively and playful does not mean she is not respectful of social standards. Mr. Bingley's jealous sisters accuse her of "conceited independence, a most country town indifference to decorum" (36) and of a "self-sufficiency without fashion, which is intolerable" (271), insults which sound more like praise. Elizabeth does not have the fashions of the city. Her tastes and manners are rustic: she quotes a country saying about porridge, she considers pigs in the garden more interesting than a visit by Lady Catherine, she prefers a plain dish to a ragout (24, 35, 158). Mr. Darcy admires the brilliancy that country air and exercise give to her looks (33, 36). Elizabeth has the "sturdy independence of . . . country customs" that Mary Crawford makes fun of in *Mansfield Park* (58). Just as *Mansfield Park* presents Mary's city tastes and education as connected to her lack of real principle, we should not be surprised to find in *Pride and Prejudice* that country independence is a sign of sturdiness of conviction, including a respect not for fashion but for propriety.

Elizabeth is an unreliable narrator, and her statements about herself must be weighed against her actions. She claims to love to laugh at people: "follies and nonsense, whims and inconsistencies *do* divert me, I own, and I laugh at them whenever I can" (57). Such statements have led to a general perception of her as a detached observer.[7] But in truth she *fails* to laugh at a surprising number of things. She has no delight in the absurdities of Sir William Lucas for she has known them too long (152), she is not diverted by the evening entertainment at Lady Catherine's but only finds it "superlatively stupid" (166). That she is not as detached as her father is clear when Mr. Bingley abandons Jane. Elizabeth listens "in silent indignation" (133) while Mr. Bennet only laughs, saying "a girl likes to be crossed in love a little now and then" (137).

Elizabeth's own manners, if not fashionable, are reserved. She dismisses the waiter when her sister begins to talk about Wickham, and Lydia says the action "is just like your formality and discretion" (220). When Elizabeth gets home after Lydia has eloped, she asks whether there is "a servant belonging to it, who did not know the whole story" and Jane must explain how difficult it is to be guarded at such a time (292). Elizabeth does not need Mr. Darcy to point out the improprieties of her own family: at a ball, for example, she is "deeply . . . vexed," feels "inexpressible vexation," and finally "blushed and blushed again with shame and vexation" at her family (98–100). She is "in agonies" over her sister Mary's pedantic singing and then regrets her father's improper way of putting an end to it (100–101). She is clearly not, like her father, enjoying this display of folly (103). As usual, Jane Austen leaves an ambiguity about Elizabeth's motives, for while her shame attests to her respect for propriety it also reveals her unacknowledged wish for Mr. Darcy's good opinion. That Elizabeth laughs "when she can" does not indicate her indifference to society but rather her attempt not to "increase her vexations, by dwelling on them" (232). Elizabeth's pursuit of happiness means that she makes the best of things, and must make us wonder if she really is "the outspoken champion of . . . individual desire."[8]

As for Mr. Darcy, from the first we see not that he has great respect for social conventions but rather that he does not always observe social rules. The servile and self-important Mr. Collins strictly adheres to the forms of civility: his manners are "very formal" (64, 107, 155) and "solemn" (66, 90, 105), his formality is marked by his incessant gratitude and apologies. Mr. Darcy is never apologetic and is disliked precisely because he does not pay much attention to social forms, such as making polite conversation or asking an unattached girl to dance (see 10–19). This indifference to social opinion exposes him to ridicule. Elizabeth, although hardly endeared to Mr. Darcy by his refusal to dance with her, can find his action "ridiculous" instead of upsetting (12), for it indicates that he does not know (or care) what social rules require. Even his friends laugh at his aloofness (11, 51, 55, 175, 180). Just as his neighbors assume he is contemptuous of them, so they assume he cannot be laughed at. Elizabeth, for example, several times *thinks* "she could perceive he was rather offended" and therefore checks her laugh (51, cf. 57, 371), but there is no real evidence that she is right.

In fact, Austen indicates that Mr. Darcy's behavior is not due to a general contempt of his social inferiors but rather to his virtue. Unlike less worthy men, he is not motivated by a desire to be liked by others. Austen, as usual—and contrary to common opinion about her[9]— suggests that good manners are *not* always a sign of virtue: Mr. Darcy, for example, is "sure of giving offense" everywhere (16). Mr. Darcy is unyielding and determined (324, cf. 58) and capable of anger (73, 94, 190): good manners involve a softening of all these traits. (This is why Hobbes attacks the Darcys of the world.) Elizabeth reflects that if she married Mr. Darcy, "by her ease and liveliness, his mind might have been *softened*, his manners improved" (312, emphasis added). To be lively is what, Mrs. Gardiner says, "if he marry prudently, his wife may teach him" (325). It is Elizabeth who will socialize Mr. Darcy, not the other way around.

Austen is always somewhat suspicious of inviting manners, for she recognizes that virtue has a hard and even disagreeable side. We are allowed to compare Mr. Darcy not only to the servile Mr. Collins but also to the more charming Mr. Bingley and Mr. Wickham, just as in *Emma* the somewhat harsh Mr. Knightley is contrasted to the more agreeable Mr. Churchill. Now, Austen gives agreeableness its due. A talent at conversation is a part of good breeding, when it is used to put others at ease. Mr. Bingley has a captivating ease (9, 10, 14, 15, 16) that makes others like him. Colonel Fitzwilliam "entered into conversation directly with the readiness and ease of a well-bred man" (171), and the endeavors of Miss Darcy's companion "to introduce some kind of discourse, proved her to be more truly well bred" than Mr. Bingley's sisters (267). Mr. Darcy claims he does not have the "talent" of "conversing easily with those I have never seen before" (175). He cannot "catch their tone" or "appear interested in their concerns," he says, and Elizabeth and Colonel Fitzwilliam seem right to point out that this is because he won't take the trouble. His manners suffer for his high-mindedness and self-sufficiency.

Austen never suggests that all good things go together. She does not defend Mr. Darcy (or Mr. Knightley, similar in this respect) on the score of agreeableness, but she does defend their virtue. And to some extent she discounts the importance of inviting manners. There is a fine line between using conversation to make others feel more comfortable and using it to call attention to one's own ease. When Emma says her idea of Frank Churchill is "that he can adapt his conversation to the taste of everybody" (E 150) (here she echoes the foolish Mrs. Bennet, whose idea of good breeding is to have "always something to say to everybody" [PP 44]) Mr. Knightley exclaims that, if so, he will be insufferable: "What! at three-and-twenty to be the king of his company . . . to make everybody's talents conduce to the display of his own superiority" (E 150). In Mr. Wickham, we see how good manners are self-serving. Even after Elizabeth understands Wickham's real character, she can still admit that

> his manners were always so pleasing, that had his character and his marriage been exactly what they ought, his smiles and his easy address . . . would have delighted them all (PP 316).

Wickham's "vicious propensities" are not signaled by his manners but are only visible to one who "had opportunities of seeing him in unguarded moments" (200). The problem is that the deepest vanity can *most* master social graces: the Bertram sisters are among those whose "vanity is in such good order that they seemed quite free from it" (MP 35).

A mastery of conversation and manners is in fact something to be condemned in certain people, for too much ease of speech seems to call into question steadiness of character. Austen first pointed this out in her youthful *Lady Susan*, whose heroine's vices cannot at all be guessed from her manners. Mrs. Vernon had expected that "an impudent address will necessarily attend an impudent mind," but she is wrong; Austen never so closely connects manners and character (MW 251). In addition to Lady Susan's utmost propriety of manner (251, 255), she "talks very well, with a happy command of Language, which is too often used I believe to make Black appear White" (251). Language can be used to deceive, which is why too much ease of it is often suspect. It is Wickham's agile conversation that makes him captivating to Elizabeth (76): he is dangerous because he has "every charm of person and address that can captivate a woman" (284). Mr. Darcy concurs that Wickham is "blessed with such happy manners as may ensure his *making* friends—whether he may be equally capable of *retaining* them is less certain" (92, emphasis Austen's). Again we could compare Lady Susan. Wickham in fact has no close friends (297), while Mr. Darcy has "very steady" (16) friendships with Mr. Bingley and with Colonel Fitzwilliam. Skill at conversation, it seems, is a kind of acting, the ability to sum up a stranger by catching his tone of speech and instantly to pretend intimacy with this person. (The acting metaphor is suggested again when Elizabeth compares Mr. Darcy's slowness to converse with her lack of practice on the piano, and he says, "we neither of us perform to strangers" [176].) There is a suggestion that Mr. Darcy's lack of social ease (his manners are "well-bred" but not "inviting" [16]) is a sign of integrity, of his inability to pretend to be someone he is not.

Austen's treatment of these matters is relatively consistent throughout her novels. One critic, quoting Anne Elliot's speech in praise of openness—of the display of anger or delight "at the evil or good of others" (P 161)—says that "to get some idea of the change in Jane Austen's values . . . just think how a Darcy or a Knightley would appear if tested by these criteria."[10] But it is Mr. Knightley who so often criticizes Emma, who makes known to her his praise or blame of many of their acquaintances, who disapproves of Jane's excessive reserve, and who marries a woman who declares "how much I love every thing that is decided and open" (E 460). Mr. Darcy, while his love may make him taciturn, is equally confident to appear as he is, never concealing his admiration for Elizabeth or his disapproval of Wickham. That these two men are not motivated by a desire to be agreeable is precisely what makes them different from Mr. Elliot, and is a sign of their real truthfulness.

The same criticism of ease at conversation appears in the contrast between the manners of the inward Fanny Price and the worldly Mary Crawford in *Mansfield Park*. Fanny is incapable of the kind of easy sociability that Mary Crawford so often uses to put others at ease. She is not a good conversationalist (223, 369), in part because "her own thoughts and reflections were habitually her best companions" (80). Preoccupied by her thoughts, she is apt to interject comments "very much to the purpose of her own feelings, if not of the conversation" (111). But *Mansfield Park* indicates that such inwardness is not necessarily a sign of selfishness. The novel, in fact, reveals the vanity in Mary's sort of banter. Mary is a master at telling others what they wish to hear (82, 143, 169, 276–78), and while such attentions often promote the enjoyment or ease the situation of others, her motive is also "a prevailing desire of recommending herself" (276). Her charming manners and general pleasantness are often taken as signs of deeper virtues. Mrs. Grant, for example, finds Mary and Henry "lively and pleasant . . . and immediately gave them credit for everything else" (42), and Edmund does the same when he looks in "an ecstasy of admiration of all [Mary's] many virtues, from her obliging manners down to her light and graceful tread" (112). It is implied here that Mary is not truly virtuous, and the novel indicates that one cannot count on her kindness. Mary is polished and agreeable, but the narrator says she "had none of Fanny's delicacy of taste, of mind, of feeling" (81).

In other words, Fanny is not defended simply as being morally supe-rior to Mary. She also is said to have better taste and feeling. We should not be surprised to see that those men who are gruff and even disagree-able turn out to be wonderful dancers, for Austen's criticism of easy sociability does not deny the fact that she loves real graces. When Mr. Darcy initially disdains dancing, we are told he is fastidious (10–11, 16), which is different from being awkward or unable to please. Mr. Darcy is ashamed of the rudeness of Mr. Bingley's sisters (53) and his aunt (173). His worst transgression of manners is in his proposal to Elizabeth. Here he commits a sin akin to the one Emma commits with Miss Bates: he calls Elizabeth's attention to her inferiority to himself. His proposal shows her "his sense of her inferiority—of its being a degradation" (189). Austen always indicates that the point of good manners is not to serve the strong, but to protect the weak. This is why Elizabeth is not condemned for all her impertinences to Mr. Darcy (380); rather, on the only occasion on which we hear the (much-quoted) statement that Elizabeth "overcome[s] . . . the bounds of decorum" (124), she is unfeelingly criticizing a friend (Charlotte, for accepting Mr. Collins) whose situation is more difficult than her own. Mr. Darcy later tells Elizabeth that her suggestion that he did not behave as a gen-tleman has "tortured" him beyond what she can conceive (367).

Now, to some extent this proposal and its aftermath are a challenge to Mr. Darcy's pride. He himself says his love for Elizabeth "properly humbled" his pride (369). Austen diverges from Aristotle's account of the high-minded gentleman as she takes more seriously the importance of love.[11] First attracted by the intelligent and beautiful expression of Elizabeth's eyes, as well as by observing her conversation with others, Mr. Darcy finds he cannot help falling in love: "I was in the middle before I knew that I *had* begun" (380), he says. Others can attest that he "knew what it was to love" (262, 264, cf. 339, 381). In this novel, at least, Austen portrays love that has its origin in *looking* at the other person.[12] When Elizabeth rejects him, for the first time Mr. Darcy has reason to doubt his self-sufficiency, and for the first time he must ex-plain himself: his "character *requires*" the letter he writes to her (196); "no *obligation*" less than this would have him make these personal revelations (201). The style of his letter to Elizabeth is haughty, but the act of giving it is humbling. Mr. Darcy asks her to read it because "I demand it of your justice" (196): he lets her judge him.

The need to explain himself to Elizabeth makes him treat her as an equal, and Austen suggests that love must be a relation of equality. (This is one reason she insists on making her characters conventionally suitable, as even Mr. Darcy and Elizabeth are, if just barely.) Elizabeth sees this, for when he goes out of his way at Pemberley to treat her and her relations as friends (inviting them fishing, and to meet his sister) she knows that ''to love, ardent love, it must be attributed'' (266). The problem with Mr. Darcy, for Elizabeth, was never his pride as such: ''I could easily forgive *his* pride, if he had not mortified *mine*,'' she says after the first ball (20), and he suggests the same after she rejects him (192). She is herself too proud to accept love that is offered in defiance of reason, prudence, and common sense, too proud to be loved for her charms alone. Her pride reflects her belief in her own virtue and her determination to act in a way that is worthy of it.

Mr. Darcy is ''properly humbled'': he is, remarkably, made neither resentful nor servile by Elizabeth's conduct. This is shown by his not being ''in a humour to wait for any opening'' of Elizabeth's to renew his offer of marriage (381). This declaration has been used by one commentator as evidence of a ''criminal'' assault on Elizabeth's right to happiness.[13] I would suggest that this sentence is typical of Austen's idea of a proper sort of pride. A more common pride would have refused to renew his offer. As Elizabeth says, there is ''no indignity so abhorrent'' to men's feelings as to make a second proposal to the same woman (341). Austen shows us this sort of resentment in Captain Wentworth of *Persuasion*, who was ''too proud to ask again'' (P 247). A man of less pride would have backed away, lacking confidence to renew the subject. We see this in Mr. Bingley, who, despite his love for Jane, allows himself to be persuaded by his friends that she does not return his love.

In Mr. Darcy (and also, to some degree, in Mr. Knightley), Austen makes a case for pride that might offend our modern sensibilities, for the novel implies that Mr. Darcy is superior not only by convention. ''Pride,'' says Hobbes, is the breach of the law that ''every man acknowledge other for his Equall by Nature.''[14] Mr. Darcy does not accept that all humans are by nature his equal—which is not to say he is insolent—nor is it suggested that he should. Elizabeth's father, not one to respect mere wealth or stateliness, says that Mr. Darcy is ''the kind of man, indeed, to whom I should never refuse anything, which he condescended to ask'' (376).

When Mr. Darcy shows contempt it is not due to the prejudice of class but to a justified pride.[15] Elizabeth's shock at Mr. Darcy's affability to the Gardiners says more about her prejudice than about any change in his pride, and she finally admits to herself that he cannot behave before her mother as he does before her aunt, for her mother does not deserve the same respect (335). The "vulgarity" of some of Elizabeth's relatives mortifies and taxes Mr. Darcy to the end (384), but Elizabeth, if anything, feels the shame even more keenly. His lack of simple class prejudice is also revealed by his shame throughout the novel at the rudeness of some of his own wealthy connections (e.g., 53, 56, 173), and by the fact that his best friend, Mr. Bingley, has a fortune acquired through trade (15).

Unlike the pride of most proud people in her novels, Mr. Darcy's pride is generous and humane. His is not the "proud resolve" of Maria Bertram of *Mansfield Park*, who deliberately sacrifices her happiness by marrying one man in order to deprive the man she really loves of a triumph (201). (Captain Wentworth narrowly misses the same fate.) The novel, in general, defends him from the pride of "arrogance and insolence" seen in Mrs. Churchill of *Emma* (E 310) and in Darcy's own aunt, among others. Nor does he have Mr. Churchill's "quiet, indolent, gentlemanlike sort of pride" that harms nobody and "only makes himself a little helpless and tiresome" (E 310). Austen shows us that Mr. Darcy's is a pride that leads him to action *for others* simply because it befits himself.

Love and the Pride of Virtue

We see Austen's willingness to distinguish good from bad forms of pride also in *Northanger Abbey*, when General Tilney's "pride could not pardon" Catherine for being poorer than he thought she was, a sentiment "which a better pride would have been ashamed to own" (NA 244). General Tilney should not have been more humble, but more properly proud, more willing to consider what conduct became himself. Elizabeth Elliot's "strong family pride" (P 8)—a pride not so much of wealth but of ancestry—makes her solicit the acquaintance of a noble cousin who has so little real merit that she "would never have been tolerated in Camden-Place but for her birth" (150). Anne, watching her sister and father in Bath, wished that "they had more pride" (148); as for herself, she has "more pride than any of [them]" in wishing not to pursue a relationship that is "a matter of perfect indifference" to the other party. She repeats, "I certainly am proud, too proud to enjoy a welcome which depends so entirely on place" (151). The author's sympathies are clearly with Anne. We see the same spirit in the "much higher tone of indifference for everything but justice and equity" that makes Anne want her father and sister to cut back their expenses and pay their creditors (12–13). Her attitude shows *greater* pride than theirs. As Lady Russell says, Sir Walter's "true dignity" will be "very far from lessened, in the eyes of sensible people, by his acting like a man of principle" (12). Austen always defends the pride that is founded upon principle.

Mr. Darcy's pride is shown, in fact, as a sign of his "heart," a word Austen often uses to incorporate virtue and feeling. Mr. Bingley's fondness for dancing leads young women to "hopes of his heart" (9) but the sensible Mrs. Gardiner sees "something of dignity in [Mr. Darcy's] countenance, that would not give one an unfavorable idea of his heart" (258). Austen herself praises his dignity as heartfelt in a letter in which she tells of having searched unsuccessfully for a portrait of Elizabeth in various British museums:

> I can only imagine that Mr. D. prizes any picture of her too much to like it should be exposed to the public eye. I can imagine he would have that sort of feeling—that mixture of Love, Pride & Delicacy.[16]

Despite his ungallant first appearance, Mr. Darcy has a strong wish to protect those he loves. Even Wickham acknowledges that Mr. Darcy's "brotherly pride" is connected with some "brotherly affection" in making him "a very kind and careful guardian of his sister" (82). Wickham should know, for he is the one against whom Darcy must protect first his younger sister, and later Elizabeth's youngest sister.

In the latter case, too, we see the generosity of Mr. Darcy's pride: he is willing to undergo the trouble and indignity of seeking out Wickham in order to rescue Lydia's reputation. In part, his stated reason may be a true one—he feels it his duty to rectify an evil that he might have prevented if he had exposed Wickham's character to the world. Because Jane and Elizabeth, too, had concurred in the opinion that there was no reason to destroy Wickham's reputation, this reason seems chiefly to be a way to conceal the better motives that it would not be in good taste to proclaim. He also simply likes to be of service to others—"he had liberality, and the means of exercising it," reflects Elizabeth, and in this case he knew he was the *only* person who could help (326). And, of course, despite his efforts at concealment, Elizabeth knows he did it for her. His "generous compassion" (366) lets him form for himself a connection to Wickham from which Elizabeth fears "every kind of

pride must revolt'' (326). The point is not that Mr. Darcy has abandoned his pride—this whole episode demonstrates his dignity—but
rather to show how humane his pride is. The same warm sort of pride
appears in Elizabeth when she, reflecting on Mr. Darcy's compassion
and honor in this case, "was proud of him" (327).

Pride and Power

Mr. Darcy's estate is a sign of his superiority, revealing not only his
wealth but also his taste, mind, and character (Mr. Knightley's estate
serves the same function in *Emma*). Elizabeth dates her love for Mr.
Darcy from the day she first saw Pemberley, and this is only partly a
joke, for it is only then that she fully appreciates his consequence.

> As a brother, a landlord, a master, she considered how many people's
> happiness were in his guardianship!—How much of pleasure or pain it
> was in his power to bestow!—How much of good or evil must be done by
> him! (251).

Elizabeth sees how much good Mr. Darcy *has* done and feels that "to
be mistress of Pemberley might be something" (245). We can see that
not only money and power establish the importance of this estate by
comparing it to that of the richest man in Austen's novels, Mr. Rushworth of *Mansfield Park*. Mr. Rushworth admits that his Sotherton
"looked like a prison—quite a dismal old prison" (MP 53); its "tall
iron palisades and gates" (MP 85) are repeatedly mentioned and bode
ill for Maria's happiness in this marriage (MP 97, 99).

Pemberley is an original, not fashionable but natural in its beauty.
Mr. Bingley tells his sister he "should think it more possible to get
Pemberley by purchase than by imitation" (38), acknowledging that
neither are in the realm of possibilities. Nature is in fact increasingly
present in *Pride and Prejudice*, as we move from the drawing rooms
and ballrooms of volume one, to the action of volume two at the Collins's home in Kent, with its extensive park and woods in which Elizabeth and Mr. Darcy have frequent private walks (182, 195). Volume
three is set primarily at Pemberley: there is no place "for which nature
had done more, or where natural beauty had been so little counteracted
by an awkward taste" (245). The word "noble" as well as "natural"
is often used to describe it (we see "a nobler fall of ground" [253]; it
is "a noble place" [38, 77]). The naturalness appears even in the food
that is served: "all the finest fruits in season . . . beautiful pyramids of

grapes, nectarines and peaches'' (268). Elizabeth is not the one to introduce a socially rigid Darcy to nature. Her natural tastes suit his.

Pemberley's master, as well as the estate itself, is shown to be superior not only by wealth and situation but by his virtues and character—his nature. Elizabeth has never seen Mr. Darcy so much the gentleman as when he is at home, never ''so desirous to please, so free from self-consequence, or unbending reserve'' (263). She now sees his real taste, not only in the development of the grounds but also in the furniture, which is ''neither gaudy nor uselessly fine; with less of splendor, and more real elegance'' (346) than she had expected. Such a phrase sums up her eventual view of Mr. Darcy's own character. Even his housekeeper is ''much less fine, and more civil'' than she had feared (246).

The novel suggests that Mr. Darcy enjoys being virtuous for reasons other than having power over others. Elizabeth's uncle hesitates to take up Darcy's offer of fishing, for ''perhaps he may be a little whimsical in his civilities . . . your great men often are'' (258). Elizabeth, too, associates Mr. Darcy's pride with capriciousness (186, cf. 133). Thinking, perhaps, of Mr. Darcy's actions regarding her sister, Elizabeth tells his friend Colonel Fitzwilliam that she knows no one who ''seems more to enjoy the power of doing what he likes than Mr. Darcy'' (183), to which Colonel Fitzwilliam gives the measured reply: ''He likes to have his own way very well. But so we all do. It is only that he has better means of having it than many others'' (183). In other words, the office shows the man—the fact that Mr. Darcy has power does not mean that he does not live up to it. The tone here seems to capture Austen's general attitude toward the importance of power in the governing of human affairs. She calmly acknowledges its place—none of her desirable characters are martyrs—while not reducing everything to power. The desire for power characterizes such lesser people as Mrs. Norris of *Mansfield Park* or Lady Catherine of *Pride and Prejudice*, to whom nothing—even the way a neighbor's visitor packs her trunk—is beneath her attention if it can give her an ''occasion of dictating to others'' (163).

Austen's serious treatment of pride is one sign that she does not share the Hobbesian view of human inclination as the perpetual desire of power after power.[17] Her best characters are not motivated by the fear that they will lose what they have if they do not seek for more. Elizabeth and Mr. Darcy's love affair, for example, cannot be reduced to a matter of power relations. To Elizabeth's friend Charlotte, always a utilitarian, ''it admitted not of a doubt, that all [Elizabeth's] dislike would vanish, if she could suppose [Mr. Darcy] to be in her power'' (181). But as is often the case, Austen indicates in the novel that Charlotte's opinion, while it might apply to most of the world, is not completely true. (Consider also Charlotte's view that "happiness in marriage is entirely a matter of chance" [PP 23], another idea Austen understands but tries to disprove.)

Elizabeth's dislike of Mr. Darcy is not simply due to her belief that he dislikes her—or even to a desire not to encourage herself in the belief that he likes her. Now, Mr. Darcy's insult to her plays a part in her initial prejudice against him, as she later admits (208), and Wickham's attentions toward her help her believe the story that seems to confirm Darcy's selfishness. Nonetheless, it is because she does think him selfish that she cannot like him. She tells him, for example,

> Had [my own feelings] even been favorable, do you think that any consideration would tempt me to accept the man, who has been the means of ruining, perhaps forever, the happiness of a most beloved sister? (190).

The reason why this is true is not only that she is a loyal sister but also that she could not love a man she did not respect as virtuous. When all is known, Elizabeth is as distraught for mistaking Mr. Darcy's pride for selfishness as Marianne Dashwood is in *Sense and Sensibility* for mistaking the charm of Willoughby for virtue. Elizabeth, like Marianne, trusted Wickham, without having witnessed an act of goodness because his looks and manner had "established him at once in the possession of every virtue" (206, cf. 81, 86). Also, she overlooked the evidence given by her knowledge of Mr. Darcy's habits that he is not "unprincipled or unjust" or possessing "irreligious or immoral habits" (207). Reading Mr. Darcy's letter she is oppressed by a sense of "horror" that she might have misjudged which man was truly just and unselfish. Elizabeth's *dislike* of Mr. Darcy vanishes with "the respect created by the conviction of his valuable qualities," as distinct from her belief that he is in her power (265).

Gratitude and Love

Respect and esteem are not in themselves a ground for Elizabeth to love Mr. Darcy, the narrator says, but on top of this Elizabeth feels something more: gratitude. The most frequently stated ground for love in Austen's novels is "gratitude and esteem," and in *Pride and Prejudice* the narrator sharply defends this. If this sort of love seems unnatural, she says, compared to "what is so often described as arising on a first interview with its object," well then all that can be said is that, because Elizabeth did not have much success with the latter method, she might be allowed to try this "less interesting mode" of attachment (279). The narrator of *Northanger Abbey* uses the same defensive tone in defending the origin of Henry Tilney's love for Catherine (NA 243). Austen obviously feels strongly about this subject and sees it as something that makes her novels different from others—"it is a new circumstance in romance, I acknowledge" (NA 243). This mode of attachment is fundamental to Austen's general view of love.

Gratitude (the goodwill felt for someone who has taken an interest in oneself), combined with esteem (for it would be difficult to return the love of someone one could not respect) are put forth as a way of falling in love that is not just prudent or sensible but is also more natural than the more romantic mode of immediate sexual attraction. Of her trial of love at first sight with Wickham, Elizabeth concludes, "vanity, not love, has been my folly" (208). Austen seems to think that there is a kind of gratitude that is *not* just vanity—a love of being loved—that is thus a more real ground for attachment. Of course, Austen is aware that esteem can be an illusion, not based on the other's real worth but rather on his or her services to oneself. As Elizabeth reflects about Mr. Collins: "I suspect his gratitude misleads him, and that in spite of her being his patroness, [Lady Catherine] is an arrogant, conceited woman" (84). But if Austen suggests that not all benefactors are truly good, she also indicates that all good men and women are also benefactors, and that it is possible to appreciate their virtues apart from the fact of their goodness to oneself. Elizabeth carefully distinguishes her respect for Darcy from her gratitude to him (265), and (contrary to Charlotte's opinion) the compliment of Darcy's proposal in itself does not convince Elizabeth of his virtue.

Austen explores in some depth the question of what makes someone lovable. Esteem for another's virtue does not seem to be enough, nor even is gratitude, simply. To some extent there seems even a tendency *not* to find one's benefactor *lovable*. When Elizabeth has suspicions that Mr. Darcy might have done something to help Lydia, she tries not to encourage them, partly because she fears it is too great an "exertion of goodness" to hope for, but partly also "from the pain of obligation" (326). And when she finds out what he has done, she tries to minimize his virtue: "He had to be sure done much . . . But he had given a reason for his interference" (326). She as well as Mr. Darcy has a natural pride that makes it painful to receive benefits beyond what can be repaid.[18] Still, Austen portrays the relationship of a benefactor and recipient as not just cold or calculating.

Elizabeth's gratitude and esteem for Mr. Darcy are a motive of goodwill to him that can grow into love. She does not love him because of the knowledge of her power over him. When she first senses that she has such a power, she wonders "how far it would be for the happiness of both" that she employ it (266); power is never as important as happiness for Austen. In fact, it is only at the moment she senses "her power was sinking" that Elizabeth begins to think "she could have loved him" (278). She *could* love him: actual love will take more time to know him and to become involved with him. Both Elizabeth and Mr. Darcy come to love each other after realizing that each has been humbled by the other—even beyond what seems to an outsider to be reasonable (311, 369). Love is a sense that one has come to need another person; it has developed from their mutual involvement. Darcy has described to Elizabeth "feelings, which, in proving of what importance she was to him, made his affection every moment more valuable" (366). His affection is valuable, or trustworthy, to her because she knows *she* is important to *him*: the way in which she has made him a part of herself has attached her as much as what he has done for her. So Mr. Darcy (in the manner of Mr. Knightley) can ask, despite all the services he has done Elizabeth, "What do I not owe you?," for these services have made him realize his need for her.[19]

Austen does not portray life as an endless struggle for mastery over others because she believes that there can be happiness—not just the drudgery of duty—in living a life of virtue. What distinguishes the heroines of Austen's novels from most of the women around them is that they are not in the business of getting husbands—their very capacity to love and appreciate a worthy man has to do with their having virtues that could sustain them even if they never found such a man. (Elizabeth Bennet, Fanny Price, and Anne Elliot all prove, by turning down one or more eligible suitors, that they will risk the loss of material and domestic satisfactions rather than risk their happiness with a man they do not love.) Of course, Austen always uses the novelist's magic to bring them the luck of meeting a man they could love. There is an element of good luck in the happiness Austen describes—Anne Elliot in the beginning has had bad luck—and yet Austen indicates that her heroines' happiness does not fully depend on chance. Even Anne Elliot is not despondent; like the author herself, these women have resources for happiness. To say that *Pride and Prejudice* is "shamelessly wish fulfilling,"[20] a dream that will only make women more helpless,[21] is to vastly underappreciate the strength of mind in these heroines, as well as the intelligence of Austen's female readers.

Virtue and Happiness

Mr. Darcy's pride indicates, I have suggested, that he is virtuous not only because it is useful to others but also because he considers it fitting for himself. Austen's suggestion that such a pride is proper—and Mr. Darcy is by no means the only character who displays it—follows from her view that virtue contributes to an individual's happiness. It is this view, especially, that makes Austen's moralism more classical than modern. She would not say, with Kant, that an action lacked moral worth if it was done out of inclination, and not purely from duty.[22] (Consider the scene in *Northanger Abbey* in which Catherine Morland worries about just this point. Because she *wants* to fulfill her promise to Eleanor Tilney, she wonders if this *is* the right thing to do. The passage suggests that she need not distrust her desires so much [NA 101–4].) At the same time, of course, Austen does not judge by happiness alone: virtue has a content that is independent of desire. Mary Crawford's philosophy, that one's first duty is to oneself (e.g., MP 289)—an idea in accord with modern philosophers *other* than Kant—is not endorsed by the novel. Austen gives self-concern its due while not reducing morality to a matter of rights.

We can see that her morality is not Kantian in her indications that unselfishness does not require self-forgetting. No criticism seems implied in *Persuasion* when we hear that "neither Charles Hayter's feelings, nor anybody's feelings, could interest [Anne], till she had a little better arranged her own" (P 81). The same understanding tone appears in such statements as "what wild imaginations one forms, where dear self is concerned!" (P 201), or "self will intrude" (P 208, cf. 53, 115). Austen never portrays pure selflessness, and yet the inevitability of self-concern does not mean that it is impossible to feel and act for others. When Elizabeth hears of Lydia's crisis, for example, "self, though it would intrude, could not engross her" (278), and this seems to be all Austen hopes for from virtue.

Indeed, the suggestion that desires should be regulated by reason and reflection seems to acknowledge the importance of some concern for one's own true good. Austen sees "sense" as something that moderates selfishness by making one aware of one's *truest* good. Elinor Dashwood, for example, can hope that Lucy Steele's sense will moderate her avarice if she marries Edward: "Lucy does not want sense, and that is the foundation on which everything good may be built" (263). Elinor seems too optimistic, for we see that Lucy's avarice overcomes her sense. The problem seems to be that Lucy is "naturally clever" but does not have the cultivation to make her really prudent (127). She is not only uneducated, for which Elinor pities her, but also lacks "delicacy, rectitude and integrity of mind" for which Elinor has "less tenderness of feeling" (127). Austen manages to suggest both that education or cultivation is needed for the fullest development of virtue and that people are at least somehow responsible for their vice.[23]

Austen's suggestion that virtue requires cultivation is a sign that she sees it as contributing to individual perfection. Emma's lack of "romantic expectations of extraordinary virtue from those, for whom education had done so little" (E 86) is implicitly supported by the author, who shows us no examples of such virtue. In fact, *Mansfield Park* makes it clear that Fanny Price's virtues would never have developed had she been raised in her father's home. Her sister Susan, brought up "in the midst of such negligence and error," nonetheless—unlike Lucy Steele—has "delicacy" and generally "proper opinions" (397–98). Susan sees what is wrong at home, and wants to set it right, without knowing how. There is no ironic tone in the narrator's comment that Fanny wished to show Susan "the juster notions of what was due to everybody, and what would be wisest for herself," which come from her own "more favoured education" (396). (Again note, as always, the dual purpose of virtue: for others and for oneself.) The duties imposed by virtue, as Austen presents it, are not always easy to discern; knowing what to do requires what she often calls "delicacy." As Anne Elliot puts it, "all . . . qualities of the mind" should have their "proportions and limits" (116). Virtue is always a kind of moderation in her novels, and, as Aristotle puts it, "it is easy to miss the mark but hard to hit it."[24]

There is an emphasis in *Persuasion* not only on Anne's fundamental virtues (she has, for example, a "high tone of indifference for everything but justice and equity" regarding her father's debts [12]), but also on her refinements of virtue—her elegance, gracefulness, and decorum. We repeatedly hear of the "fastidiousness of her taste" (28), of her "elegance of mind" (5), the "nice tone of her mind" (28), her "cultivated, elegant mind" (41), her "elegance, sweetness, beauty" (131); she is an "elegant little woman" (153). Her elegance "of mind" is not a concern with elegant fashion and manners; it is joined with a "sweetness of character" (5) that makes it nothing like the "heartless elegance" of her sister Elizabeth (226).

The graces the novel defends are not substitutes for virtue, but refinements of it. *Persuasion*, like the other novels, criticizes the "ceremonious grace" that is typical of the Elliots and that Captain Wentworth displays in his annoyance with Anne (72). Captain Wentworth's capacity for "natural grace" (e.g., 68)—the fact that it is natural does not mean that it did not require a certain amount of cultivation—makes him one of the superior characters in the novel and contrasts him to Charles Musgrove, whose lack of "powers, or conversation, or grace," makes Anne not regret not marrying him (43). Austen seems to take the view that such intelligence and refinement are necessary for the fullest moral life, for virtue is not only something society demands of everyone (and assumes they are capable of), but also aims at the highest individual fulfillment.

The propriety of such heroines as Anne Elliot and Elinor Dashwood is not only a sacrifice to society, but a means to get along peacefully with others. Austen stresses even more the way in which virtue is good for the doer. Virtue and self-control are presented as desirable for their own sake. We see an example when Edward visits Elinor in London and is startled to find her with Lucy. Lucy only has to look demure, but Elinor has more to do "for his sake and her own" (241), and forces herself to welcome him. Now Elinor is no saint, and she is fully conscious here and elsewhere of "some injustice to herself" from Edward (241, see also 140). She forces herself to overcome this feeling because she does still love and respect him and because she knows he loves her and has compassion for his situation. This warm sensibility, rather than cold smugness, makes her be decent "for his sake and her own": her virtue and reserve are not only useful to others but are becoming to herself.

Despite the humility and compassion apparent in Elinor's treatment of Edward, there is a certain amount of pride in her wish to act as if she was never *particularly* attached to him and her wish to behave in the most becoming manner. This is especially clear in Elinor's relations with Lucy. Elinor thinks that it is a "reasonable and laudable pride" to wish to appear composed in the face of triumphant enemies (189). This feeling lets her endure "the persecution of Lucy's friendship" (302) and to respond to Lucy's meanness and insincerity "as every principle of honour and honesty directed" (142). Her pride is a decent kind of revenge, for Elinor "could not deny herself the comfort" of trying to convince Lucy that her heart is unwounded (142). Elinor's refusal to acknowledge her own attachment to Edward deprives Lucy of the enjoyment of her triumph.

Part of Elinor's pride is the gentler satisfaction of knowing she has done no wrong, a consolation of which Marianne deprives herself. Although angry and puzzled at Edward's treatment of herself, Elinor resolves to treat him "as she thought he ought to be treated from the family connection" (89). She wishes to be as decent as possible (again for her own sake as well as his ease) and is aided in acting this way by regulating herself not by her (possibly unfounded) expectations of love but by their "family connection." There is a comfort in having a rule to which to appeal. Elinor's prudent reserve in her relations with Edward lets her have later the benefit of knowing she has not done anything to merit her unhappiness (140)—for the pain of misconduct would add to her misery—and she is further consoled by her belief that Edward only deserted her because of his respect for duty (141). Her chief consolation—the greatest "softener of the heart"—is that Edward "certainly loved her" (140). None of these consolations is really available to Marianne, whose peace of mind is threatened both by her knowledge of Willoughby's lack of virtue and her doubts about her own role in encouraging him (see also 179).

Virtue is not only a consolation. Austen separates herself from the thought of her age by indicating that virtue and its refinements—such as good conversation—are a *height* or end of human nature. It is not necessary to make her into a philosopher to see that her novels reflect certain assumptions about human nature, and a clarity about these helps us understand the character of her work. What Austen's heroines long for most is not a grand sexual passion but lasting friendship with someone who is good and who can talk to them. The author does not rely on the desire to possess another person (or even his or her money) to overcome a natural asociality. Unlike such thinkers as Hobbes, Locke, or Rousseau, she does not portray humans as compelled by their passions (or the calculations upon those passions) into society with others, but rather as naturally attracted to human companionship.

The first clue of this is the great amount of talk in all the novels about conversation itself. Ordinary society neither fully satisfies nor disgusts her better characters; it seems rather to point to what might make for the best society. We see Austen's good-spirited analysis of what makes for good conversation in her critique of the dinner party given by the John Dashwoods. It shows "no poverty of any kind, except of conversation," and then Austen humorously describes how most of the guests had one or another "disqualifications for being agreeable": "want of sense, either natural or improved—want of elegance—want of spirits—or want of temper" (SS 233). By so fully displaying what is wanting, even this hopeless party reveals an inkling of what true conversation would be.[25] There is, similarly, no bitterness in *Emma* when the narrator describes a party's conversation as being "nothing worse" than "everyday remarks, dull repetitions, old news, and heavy jokes" (219). Austen's irony here is reconciling rather than subverting: there is a certain satisfaction to be had in being able to laugh at the deficiencies of the company, a satisfaction that then helps one recognize that there really could be many worse things. Nevertheless, her heroes and heroines are attracted by the possibility of something more.

Austen suggests that real connectedness with others is possible, given good conversation and unselfishness, although, of course, such speech and virtue are rare. We see this again in the fact that she portrays genuine friendship as being characterized by these qualities more than by the *feeling* of affection. When Elinor first meets Lucy she realizes she will have "no lasting satisfaction" in her company, because Lucy's lack of education "prevented their meeting in conversation on terms of equality" and her conduct toward others "made every show of attention and deference to herself perfectly valueless" (127). Their friendship cannot last without equal conversation and virtue, for the reason—Austen is strikingly explicit about this—that Elinor will not get enough out of it. Now, the narrator is quite capable of using an ironic tone toward Elinor, but there is no particular sign of it here. Elinor is not mercenary in her calculations. That services to Lucy are "perfectly valueless" does not mean that she might have expected some material reward, but rather that there is no possibility of becoming attached to her—Lucy would not return the affection. In other words, Austen suggests that it is not enough to think of friendship as a matter of feeling or giving affection: there must be a motive for it. That motive (even in friendships of virtue) is its pleasure or usefulness, which will only last (the "satisfaction" will be "lasting") if there is equal conversation and virtue.

The same considerations affect even the friendship of Elinor and Marianne. Elinor and Marianne have unusually great feelings of affection for each other (see, for example, Elinor's constant efforts to protect Marianne: 86, 167, 174, 177, 181, 214; or the happiness Marianne's happiness gives her: 168, 155. The fact that Marianne, in turn, "could not bear to see a sister slighted in the smallest point" leads her to actions that, though misguided, show her goodwill [236]). It would seem that their friendship has grown less from common interests and opinions than from their natural bond as sisters (a phenomenon that always interests Austen), and perhaps this alone is enough to make it lasting. But even this friendship is not free from the need for reasonable and virtuous behavior. Elinor does not tell her most important secret to her mother and sister in part because of her promise to Lucy, but also because she "is stronger alone" (141). She cannot expect assistance from their "counsel or their conversation" and their extreme affliction would increase her distress. Again we see the reference to speech and virtue, and Marianne cannot offer the kind of conversation or fortitude that would help her (141). Elinor, it is true, also finds it "a relief to her" to spare her sister and mother pain. But we see that the natural affection she feels for her family is not by itself enough to let her turn to them as friends.

It is consistent with Austen's emphasis on the natural attractions of conversation and virtue, which are what make her best characters seek to marry, that she does not have much to say about children. I have argued that she does not present people (at least ideally) as being compelled to society by their passions—and that means, among other things, that her heroes and heroines do not marry because of the desire or need to have children. (That children are not the point of marriage and that she does not take her bearings from sexual desire and its consequences, explains how she can portray women—at least her heroines—as less in *need* of marriage than can Rousseau or the romantic writers he inspired.)

Austen's hints about the incompleteness of virtue in children again gives evidence of what real virtue is for her. She is quite aware that children have charms. Their "cheerfulness" can "add a relish to . . . existence" (3), the narrator of *Sense and Sensibility* says, and we see this in the scene of "joy and kindness" when the young Gardiner children run to meet Elizabeth (PP 152) or on another occasion in the "joyful surprise that lighted up [the children's] faces, and displayed itself over their whole bodies" (PP 272). Such a sentence could not be written by someone who disliked children. Emma Woodhouse and Anne Elliot, in particular, take pleasure in their nieces and nephews and are good with them. Nevertheless, Austen's fondness is not blind. She points out the irony of children being rewarded for their very lack of conversation and virtue. The Dashwood sisters and their mother are forced to leave the home that has been their family's for generations, because their great-uncle has left it instead to their 4-year-old cousin. The boy won over his uncle

by such means as are by no means unusual in children of two or three years old; an imperfect articulation, earnest desire of having its own way, many cunning tricks, and a great deal of noise, as to outweigh all the value of all the attention which, for years, he had received from his niece and her daughters (SS 4).

Austen objects to the idea that imperfect speech and intemperance could be a claim greater than long-standing attentions. (The elder Mr. Dashwood's seeming ingratitude may again indicate the fact that virtue is not always lovable.) The author seems to particularly object to children's *noise*, for it not only indicates their inability to converse but "put[s] an end to every kind of discourse except what related to themselves" (SS 34). And Lady Middleton is not the only mother who assumes that the "impertinent incroachments and mischievous tricks" of her sons must be a delight to her visitors (120).

The happiness of Austen's couples comes from their being able to find true companionship with each other, friendship that includes both good talk and the doing of favors for each other. Mr. Knightley is the solution to Emma's fear of "intellectual solitude" (E 7, cf. 422), and Elizabeth's marriage to Mr. Darcy will remove her from the society "so little pleasing to either" in which good conversation is impossible (PP 384). Of course these couples are not expected simply to talk to each other. Austen stresses how much they will *care* for each other— she defends the superiority of her mode of attachment on the grounds that it is more *loving*. Emma admits, even early on, that it is

> objects of interest, objects for the affections . . . the want of which is really
> the great evil to be avoided in *not* marrying (86).

She goes on to insist, somewhat unconvincingly, that she will be content to have always a niece with her. Austen, however, would seem to agree with the point that people (even or especially virtuous people) need someone they can do good for.

Of course, we see how children contribute to the happiness of the most appealing couples—the Gardiners in *Pride and Prejudice*, the Westons in *Emma*, the Harvilles in *Persuasion*. Children are objects for the affections. The childless Allans of *Northanger Abbey* miss Catherine when she leaves, for "promoting her enjoyments had greatly increased theirs" (NA 154). Without children, Mrs. Norris has become a small-minded miser—her strict economy is for her "an object of that needful solicitude, which there were no children to supply" (MP 8). Even so, Austen cannot resist gently mocking the excesses of motherly absorption in such people as Lady Middleton or Isabella Woodhouse, for children cannot make up for the lack of mutual involvement of a couple with each other.

Humility and Religious Virtue

Austen's defense of pride—to repeat, Mr. Darcy has "no improper pride," Elinor Dashwood has a "reasonable and laudable pride"—indicates how she differs from the Christian moralists of her time, however much she admired them. She could not define pride, as does Johnson in his Dictionary, as simply "an immoderate degree of self-esteem, or an over-value set upon a man by himself."[26] Many of her characters do have this sort of improper pride, but Austen also shows us characters who are generous because they demand of themselves that they be worthy of their virtues. Her novels do not support Johnson's opinion that "*All* pride is abject and mean."[27]

I have suggested that Austen argues that virtue is necessary in order to be capable of real happiness, as in the affecting scene in which Miss Bates is "so truly respectable in her happiness" (E 418), or when we are told that it would be an insult to compare the nature of Anne Elliot's happiness of "generous attachment" to her sister's happiness of "all selfish vanity" (P 185). Anne's virtue makes her more completely happy. Nonetheless, Austen seems ultimately to think that the perfection or completeness aimed at by virtue is not available in this life. Although the novels are generally quite reticent about religion, certain topics—such as the need for good luck or hope or a kind of humility—show that a religious belief underlies them.

Happiness and Good Fortune

Austen is fully aware of the role of good luck in achieving happiness, and she is more apt to present this as a kind of divine providence than as random chance. This is particularly true in *Persuasion,* which has a surprisingly religious tone in many places. The role of "luck" in the naval successes of Captain Wentworth is insisted on (27, 29, 65, 66, 67). Wentworth's merits are rewarded at sea, and Anne's virtues are rewarded in the end with a good husband, but these things are not inevitable but rather owe something to good fortune.[28] Yet good fortune in this novel is never presented as unaccountable—that is, simply chance. Rather, luck seems to be influenced by effort and by divine grace. Wentworth says in seriousness, "I felt my luck . . . I assure you" (65), implying that he owes gratitude for it. At the same time, his luck is presented as predictable. His own effort is partly responsible for it: "his genius and ardour had seemed to foresee and *to command* his prosperous path" (29, emphasis added, see also 27). But such an effort has included a certain trust, to use Anne's words, in Providence as well as exertion. In contrast is Anne's father, who "had not principle or sense enough to maintain himself in the situation in which Providence had placed him" (248).

Given this idea that human effort is necessary but not sufficient for well-being, it is not surprising that religious faith is particularly important in this novel. Here, for example, Austen explicitly shows us someone in prayer. When Wentworth sees that he has again been lucky and that Louisa has survived the fall which he occasioned, we are told of his "deep and silent" rejoicing "after a few fervent ejaculations of gratitude to Heaven had been offered" (112). Furthermore we see how Anne is moved by his appeal:

> The tone, the look, with which "Thank God!" was uttered by Captain Wentworth, Anne was sure could never be forgotten by her; nor the sight of him . . . overpowered by the various feelings of his soul, and trying by prayer and reflection to calm them (112).

This is one of five times in the novel that the word "soul" is used with moral or religious significance.[29] As we see Wentworth trying to order and calm his soul, by prayer and reason, it is obvious that Austen—in a very unmodern way—believes that there is some source of truth outside oneself toward which one ought to conform. Wentworth is not taking his bearings from his own, or other people's, desires and opinions.

The descriptions of Anne's frequent meditations have a similarly religious tone. After great emotion she is "in need of a little interval for recollection" (185, see also 81, 89, 175, 238); "an interval of meditation, serious and grateful, was the best corrective of everything dangerous in such high-wrought felicity" (245). This posture is perhaps more pious than rationalist. Anne is not subjecting love to critical analysis as much as she is calming herself by the thought of what she has been given. Her new fearlessness does not come immediately with her "joy, senseless joy" (168), but rather with the reflection that her hopes are well-founded. Even Emma, along with her dancing and laughing spirits, is "serious, very serious in her thankfulness" (E 475). Marianne Dashwood may reveal typical over eagerness in her wish "to have time for atonement to my God" and to regulate her thoughts "by religion, by reason, by constant employment" (SS 347), but the general idea (and one held by classical thinkers)—that humans have a soul that calms and orders (bodily) desires—is one that underlies the actions of all the heroines.

Austen's discussion of humility must be understood in this context. She seems to look at the world with a basic posture of gratitude, as opposed to one that begins from considering one's desires and rights, and there is something inherently humbling about this. Wentworth tells Anne that she has taught him that his happiness may not be owing to himself alone: ''I have been used to the gratification of believing myself to earn every blessing that I enjoyed'' (247), he says, but he can no longer feel this. So Mr. Darcy tells Elizabeth that she has ''properly humbled'' him by showing him the insufficiency of his ''pretensions to please a woman worthy of being pleased'' (369).

It should be pointed out that there is a difference between believing oneself to have *earned* every blessing and believing oneself *worthy* of them. Austen suggests that proper pride is not basking in glory but rather requiring high things of oneself because one thinks highly of oneself. It is this sort of quality that, at least partly, explains how Captain Wentworth *commanded* his luck at sea: instead of being humbly unassuming, he felt himself worthy and set his sights high. And this sort of pride explains why Mr. Darcy and Mr. Knightley maintain such beautifully appropriate estates and do so much good in their neighborhoods. We see Mr. Knightley's good deeds and are told of Mr. Darcy's by reliable sources. It is generally acknowledged that he is ''a liberal man'' and ''did much good among the poor'' (PP 265, 249); the trustworthy praise of an intelligent servant tells us he was the ''sweetest-tempered, most generous-hearted'' boy and has never given her a cross word (248–49). Mr. Darcy's self-criticism in the end should not be taken at face value any more than we can rely on what most of the characters profess about themselves; certainly it runs counter to the evidence in the novel. At any rate, both his actions and his confession establish the need for pride to be grounded on virtue. These heroes (and heroines) are humbled into a recognition of the need for gratitude, of the fact that they did not earn all their blessings, but this does not affect the fact of their dignity. To take just Mr. Darcy, not only does Elizabeth praise his pride in the end, but we see evidence of it in his confident plan to renew his proposal to her and his understandable pain at the vulgarity of Elizabeth's relatives.

Religion and Mansfield Park

In *Mansfield Park* it is clear that the gratitude and need for reflection that Austen so often speaks of are religious (it was this book that convinced one of her earliest commentators that she was a Christian[30]).

Fanny Price, of course, is a Christian heroine: meek, poor in spirit, pure of heart, merciful, seeking for righteousness. Her only fine dress, which she wears on all important occasions in the novel along with the sole ornament of a gold cross, is all in white. There is even a religious tone in her rhapsodies on the wonders of nature, as if she is praising their creator: "We are to be sure a miracle in every way," she says about humans (209). We are told that what Henry Crawford praises in Fanny is due to the fact that she is "well principled and religious" even though he is "too little accustomed to serious reflection to know [such principles] by their proper name" (294). "Serious reflection," then, is one's thought about duties and God. In a well-known letter to her favorite niece who is trying to decide whether to marry a certain man, Austen associates wisdom with piety:

> Wisdom is better than Wit, & in the long run will certainly have the laugh on her side; & don't be frightened by the idea of [this man] acting more strictly up to the precepts of the New Testament than others.[31]

Wisdom, like serious reflection or "serious subjects" (87, 350) is some kind of knowledge (or faith) about God.

The general atmosphere at Mansfield Park is religious. The house has a general character of "soberness" (194), a word which appears over and over in the novel (e.g., 196, 240, 254, 279, 329, 358, 369, 394), often in connection with Sir Thomas, the master of the house. There is never much laughing in his presence (197). During his two-year absence the seeds of future calamities are sown, and his return is that of a god. November is the "black month" fixed for that return, which is to "achieve mighty things" (107, 161). His arrival is a moment of horror as every heart sinks "under some degree of self-condemnation or self-alarm" (175). Fanny almost prays for mercy for her beloved Edmund: she "knelt in spirit to her uncle" to spare Edmund (185). Language of religious purification is used to describe Sir Thomas's decision to cure Fanny's soul by sending her home to Portsmouth: she is "exiled" and "in a state of penance," marking the days until Easter, the (not insignificant) date set for her return (393, 430).

Sir Thomas takes his responsibility as a parent more seriously than does anyone else in Austen's novels, and even Mary Crawford, in a serious mood, says of him, "he is just what the head of such a family should be" (358). He has faults, of course—particularly in worldly prejudices for status and wealth—but they do not simply rule him. He offers, for example, with "solemn kindness" to release his daughter

Maria from a long-standing and public engagement that would create
an advantageous alliance for himself (200), because he fears she does
not love her fiancé. Perhaps he does not push the point far enough, but
he does show himself to be a "truly anxious father" (19) who has
"principle as well as pride" and a "general wish of doing right" (4).
One point of the Portsmouth episode is to show the worth of his lawgiv-
ing at Mansfield Park (383, 391–92). It is Fanny who finally teaches
him to question his worldly aspirations and to "prize more and more
the sterling good of principle and temper" (471), yet we are told that
Fanny's very right-mindedness is a sort of vindication of Sir Thomas.
His "charitable kindness" rears this comfort for himself; his "liberality
had a rich repayment," and it is a repayment he is said to deserve (472).

Austen takes some pains to analyze what went wrong with his other
daughters. The main point is that they lack the habit of virtue: they had
not been taught to "govern their inclinations and their tempers" by that
"sense of duty which can alone suffice" (463). As usual Austen presents passions to be in need of control, and here virtue is clearly seen as
religious. Maria and Julia had never been required "to bring [their reli-
gion] into daily practice" or to learn "the necessity of self-denial and
humility" (463). Now, the novel suggests that Maria and Julia's improper pride is understandable: they have had wealth, comfort, and position, and, unlike Fanny, they have been led to assume they deserve
them. (Whereas the good Miss Taylor gave Emma principles, Mrs. Norris simply flattered them.)

Perhaps Sir Thomas should have done something about Mrs. Norris,
whose "excessive indulgence and flattery" has forever contrasted unfavorably with his severity (463), but it is hard to know what. Thanks to
his charity she has been installed at Mansfield Park for over 30 years,
and even when it is obvious she is an hourly evil, "she seemed a part
of himself, that must be borne forever" (465–66). If Sir Thomas has
the authority of a god, Mrs. Norris functions throughout the novel as a
very believable kind of devil. (Her great dislike of Fanny certainly
works to Fanny's benefit. Even Julia, less Mrs. Norris' favorite, was
"less flattered," and ultimately has not "so very hurtful a degree of
self-consequence" as her sister [466].) Ultimately, *Mansfield Park* indicates the limits of a father's rule of law and suggests that his children
are themselves responsible for their vice (467). None of the points here
are contradicted by the other novels, although Austen rarely makes
them so soberly or harshly.

Mansfield Park features an aspiring clergyman who takes his religious duties seriously, more so, say, than Edward Ferrars in *Sense and*

Sensibility or Mr. Collins in *Pride and Prejudice*. Edmund believes a clergyman has "the guardianship of religion and morals," and thus of the manners "that might rather be called *conduct . . .* the result of good principles" (92–93). There are signs of the evangelical movement in Edmund Bertram's speeches, as when he praises the new "spirit of improvement abroad" for more energetic preaching and reading (339, cf. 242, 248). This is a movement that we know interested Austen herself. She writes critically of it in 1809,[32] and a close acquaintance of hers writes that, although Austen always had "the deepest and strongest" religious convictions, "a contact with loud and noisy exponents of the then popular religious phase made her reticent almost to a fault."[33] Nevertheless, in 1814 she writes in a letter that she is "by no means convinced that we ought not all to be Evangelicals, & am at least persuaded that they who are so from Reason and Feeling, must be happiest & safest."[34] Henry Austen, Jane's favorite brother, began a new career at this time as "an earnest preacher of the evangelical school."[35]

Whatever Austen's denominational preferences, there is no doubt she was a Christian. And it seems that her interest in religion that comes from "reason and feeling" rather than dogmatic obedience—whether we call it evangelical or not—is an impetus for *Mansfield Park*. For the novel surely is a defense of the idea that religious actions should not be an outward show of respect but rather should be justified by "reason" as well as "feeling," because this makes one "happiest" as well as safest. Even here, reasonableness and happiness are the highest standards for her. This helps us see how humility (however necessary at times) is not the highest virtue for Austen. The Bertram girls are made "miserable" by their lack of "that higher species of self-command" (91), whereas Fanny's self-command goes along with her taking the requirements for happiness with the utmost seriousness. She will not humbly submit to even Sir Thomas when principle and happiness are at stake. Religion, we see here, is supported by reason *and* feeling, for Austen always portrays the deepest feeling to be in those capable of reason and virtue. Henry Crawford loves Fanny for the "warmth of heart," that makes him feel he could "so wholly and absolutely confide in her" (294), and his sister later echoes him, praising the extraordinary "heart" in Fanny and Edmund that gives her "a feeling of being able to trust and confide in [them]" (359).

Austen is almost completely silent about what we might think would be the ultimate reward for virtue—the salvation of one's soul—but it is not hard to imagine that her faith in this at least partly explains why she can talk so frankly about happiness as an end or reward of virtue.

In *Mansfield Park* it is clear that Fanny, at least, believes in an afterlife. When she reflects about the possibility her cousin Tom will die, we are told:

> her tenderness of heart made her feel that she could not spare him; and the purity of her principles added yet a keener solicitude, when she considered how little useful, how little self-denying his life had (apparently) been (428).

It is clearly implied that she fears he will not go to heaven. Fanny is not passing a sentence on Tom, but is keenly worried about the fate of someone she cares about; she fears that there is a divine as well as a natural punishment for selfishness. When Fanny says such things as "as far as this world alone was concerned" (442), she implies that there is another world. The narrator is more reticent, describing events "without presuming to look forward to a juster appointment hereafter" (468). But if knowledge of a hereafter is presumptuous, it is always assumed that perfect happiness is not possible on earth (MP 274, 473).

Hope and Pleasure

This idea is reflected in the frequent discussions of the need for *hope* in the novels. The narrator at one point says of Mrs. Dashwood that no one could possess in a greater degree "that sanguine expectation of happiness which is happiness itself" (8). Perhaps Mrs. Dashwood has *too* great a degree of hope (like all sentiments, hope is not strictly speaking a virtue for Austen), for the narrator goes on: "But in sorrow she must be equally carried away by her fancy, and so far beyond consolation as in pleasure she was beyond alloy." Nevertheless, it is the narrator's voice that declares that the hope of happiness *is* happiness. Such a belief is also attributed to Jane Bennet (who has a "sanguine hope of good" [PP 287]), and Emma Woodhouse (see E 18, 137–38). Elinor Dashwood is one character who is shown sometimes to forget this. In fact, a close examination of how the author presents Elinor's attitude toward pleasure may give a more complete picture of her idea about how to arrive at virtue. I have argued that Austen is more severe in *Mansfield Park* about such things as the importance of self-denial than she is elsewhere, although there is a strand of it in all her work, and her suggestion of the need to hope helps illustrate this.

Sense and Sensibility indicates that Elinor is sometimes more self-denying than is necessary and that she has more hopes for pleasure than she will admit. Elinor's mother claims that Elinor will never "condescend to anticipate enjoyment," and in general she has a point (157). For Marianne, "to wish was to hope, and to hope was to expect" (21), but Elinor tries to guard against her pleasure and wishes in the belief that they might cloud her judgment. Now the author certainly stands behind Elinor's belief that pleasure cannot be the standard of good behavior. Marianne's readiness to take pleasure as a sign that she is not acting wrong—"we always know when we are acting wrong, and with such a conviction I could have had no pleasure" (68)—is implicitly criticized. This faith in the rightness of her pleasures (such as her visit to Willoughby's house) can lead her unwittingly into selfishness (as when her "dream of felicity" about being offered a horse makes her unable to see "the unhappy truth" that accepting it would cause hardship to her mother [58]). Or in another case, when Marianne is struck by Edward's reserve with Elinor, she "could easily trace it to whatever cause best pleased herself, and was perfectly satisfied" (243). Her search for a pleasant explanation is partly what makes her not recognize her sister's pain, about which, if she saw it, she would be concerned. Marianne's desire to be unselfish is deeper than her wish for her own amusement, but she is put off the track to her own happiness and to real sensibility by her imaginary pleasures and hopes.

Given this, it must also be seen that Elinor's tendency to always be on guard against her pleasures is gently laughed at in the novel. The author suggests, for one thing, that it is impossible to do away with hope. This is hinted, again humorously, when Elinor begins to suspect that Marianne will not die from her illness: encouraging distrust in herself, she "told herself likewise not to hope. But it was too late. Hope had already entered" (314). It is implied here that hope is not always unreasonable. Elinor's frequent attempts to avoid hoping for pleasure are an occasional subject of the author's irony. Martin Price's comment about the narrator's attitude toward high-minded virtue could apply to Elinor as well:

> the mockery is not turned upon Fanny's morality but upon the tense, vigilant heroism which might crack and shatter if it were not for the mitigation of unacknowledged pleasures.[36]

When a "party of pleasure" is formed, for example, to visit the grounds of a nearby estate, Elinor silently thinks it "rather a bold undertaking," considering the time of the year and the recent rain (62). The narrator's laugh at this position is apparent when we hear on the next page that

Elinor "was prepared to be wet through, fatigued, and frightened; but the event was still more unfortunate, for they did not go at all" (63). In other words, Elinor has more hopes than she realizes, and she might do better to see that reason does not require *such* vigilance against pleasure.

In fact, we are shown that Elinor has quite deep hopes for the happiness of herself and others. An underlying irony of the novel is that she, supposedly "Sense" personified, can so often let her hopes and fears mislead her. It has usually been assumed (even by those who do not like Elinor) that she "is totally shielded from her author's irony."[37] By failing to see Jane Austen's gentle criticisms of Elinor, we will miss the point that her mistakes are in falling into conduct like Marianne's. This happens, for example, when Elinor anxiously awaits news of Edward, and "though uncertain that anyone were to blame, she found fault with every absent friend. They were all thoughtless or indolent" (358). Misled by her hopes, she has fallen into Marianne's typical error of determining others' motives by the effect of their actions on herself (see 202). In another scene, Elinor notices that Edward is wearing a ring with a lock of hair, which later turns out to be Lucy's. "That the hair was her own, [Elinor] instantaneously felt as well satisfied as Marianne," despite the fact that she has no idea how he got it (98). Soon after, when Edward mysteriously leaves the Dashwoods' home with no stated purpose, Elinor is quick to think up excuses for his behavior, even though she was too clear-sighted to do the same for Willoughby when he left in similar mystery (101, cf. 78). Elinor "had always admitted a hope," while Edward was single, that something would prevent his marrying Lucy, and when she hears that they have married "she condemned her heart for the lurking flattery, which so much heightened the pain of the intelligence" (357). Love always contains hope (of requital, but perhaps more as well), and this may be a sign that, reasonable as love is in Austen's novels, it is not free of illusion.

In general, when Elinor's conduct is mistaken or she misjudges someone's character, it is not due to the "excess of sense" with which she is sometimes charged.[38] We can look at the example of Elinor's attitude toward the seriousness of Marianne's illness. Now, Elinor may not have acted improperly in this case at all, for only *her* statements indicate that she did, and this self-condemnation is partly due to her (perhaps excessive) fears for Marianne. When we hear that "Elinor *fancied* . . . that everything had been delayed too long" and so reproached herself for trifling with the illness (312, emphasis added), it is implied that everything perhaps was *not* improperly delayed. The long narrative about the progress of Marianne's illness in fact demonstrates Elinor's constant attention to her sister, even at times when she does not fear the worst (307), and the narrator points out the fact that Marianne's condition *had* improved—confirming Elinor "in every pleasant hope" (310)—just before the scene in which Elinor criticizes herself. In other words, misleading pleasant hopes—the opposite of excessive sense— would be to blame *if* any omissions of care on Elinor's part were what led to Marianne's relapse.

Austen argues that hope is inevitable, and the deepest root of it seems to be religious. Even Elinor's decency is grounded on an ultimate hope. She explains to Marianne how she can be composed without Edward, concluding:

> [a]fter all that is bewitching in the idea of a single and constant attachment, and all that can be said of one's happiness depending entirely on any particular person, it is not meant—it is not fit—it is not possible that it should be so (263).

Elinor's sudden broken speech, which follows sentences in which she determinedly implies that she has gotten over her love for Edward, reveals that she still loves him. Her statement is a sad hope—not hope that she will somehow have Edward, but hope that she can be happy without him. "It is not fit" and finally "it is not possible" that there is no support in the world for her happiness. Elinor's struggle seems to be a religious one: she does not appeal to reason, but after "constant and painful exertion" (264) has faith that there *must* be meaning and fitness in the world.

The narrator seems to approve of Elinor's efforts in this case to seriously struggle with, and finally accept, hope. For to say that happiness is based on hope is not to say that it is all simply the "imaginary happiness" in which Marianne sometimes indulges herself (91–92, see also 58). Such happiness need not be illusory if the hope is well-founded; and denying oneself happiness because one has refused to admit a *justified* hope would certainly be unfortunate. The occasional irony about Elinor's unwillingness to hope may suggest that she sometimes does deprive herself of happiness unnecessarily.

The same idea appears in *Persuasion*, in which it seems that Anne Elliot is somehow to blame for the lack of hope that has diminished her chances of happiness. Anne—"saved as we all are by some comfortable feeling of superiority from wishing for the possibility of exchange" (notice that self-satisfaction is not limited to any one class of people, just as we are told that all people, and not just Mr. Darcy, like to have their own way)—has no wish of exchanging "her own more elegant and cultivated mind" for all the "enjoyments" of the more shallow Musgrove girls (40–41). No reader could wish, any more than Anne does herself, that she exchange her superior mind for the pleasures of the Musgrove girls, but is Anne perhaps a little unwilling to admit the importance of being "happy and merry"? Anne says that she would have "suffered more" by keeping her engagement than by doing what she thought to be her duty, because she would have "suffered in her conscience" (246), and *Persuasion* does not attempt to refute the idea, implicit in all of Austen's novels, that virtue is necessary for happiness. It does, however, raise some questions about whether Anne's sense of duty was influenced by the lack of enough hope in Wentworth's success, and—perhaps even more—whether she was right to have become so hopeless without him.

Anne at the outset is faded and spiritless, and her recollections, when admiring autumn scenery, of sonnets about "images of youth and hope, and spring, all gone together" (85) carry personal weight. On an autumn walk she glimpses farmers with their ploughs at work, "meaning to have spring again" (85), a scene that, of course, foreshadows Anne's own "second spring of youth and beauty" (124). There is almost the suggestion that spring somehow will be due to the determined effort of these farmers, which raises a question that oddly haunts the first part of this novel—whether or how Anne is responsible for her continued loss of youth and beauty.

This question is also suggested by the novel's peculiar insistence on Anne's loss of "bloom."[39] Anne had been "very pretty," "extremely pretty" (6, 26), but "her bloom had vanished early" as the lasting effect of her lost love (6, 28). Anne has not simply grown too old—a woman is usually as handsome (or more so) at age 29 as at 19, we are told (6). But she is somehow lifeless, is always "necessarily" in the place of "least animation" (90, see 100, 123). Beauty here seems to be a grace that crowns all the things—such as happiness and hope—that Anne is without. The question is whether Anne is held accountable for this lack of hope. Captain Wentworth warmly advises Louisa that if she would be "beautiful and happy in her November of life, she will cherish all her present powers of mind" (88), and the conversation shows that he is thinking of Anne's overcautiousness. Certainly in Wentworth himself, who is as confident as ever, Anne sees that "the years which had destroyed her youth and bloom had only given him a more glowing, manly, open look" (61).

It is interesting that in Anne's reflections about her broken engagement, the closest she comes to blame is in lamenting her lack of hope, of "a cheerful confidence in futurity" (30), at the time. She now regrets "that over-anxious caution which seems to insult exertion and distrust Providence" (30). Anne fears she did not trust enough to her own strength or to the help of God. Lady Russell had urged her to break the engagement precisely because she could not bear to see Anne sunk "into a state of most wearing, anxious, youth-killing dependence" (27), a state without hope, the state Anne is now in. Setting aside the question of whether Anne should have had more hope at age 19, there is some question about whether she was right to give in to hopelessness once Wentworth was gone. She has had too little activity or change of scene, we are told (15, 28), and sure enough, when she does go to the sea, the wind and her pleasure restore "the bloom and freshness of youth" to her, as well as "animation" (104). This moment and the glance of admiration it produces from a passing stranger give Anne the pleasure of "*hoping* that she was to be blessed with a second spring of youth and beauty" (124, emphasis added). Her return of bloom and hope are necessary for her to attach anyone to herself, and the role of the stranger here gives a hint that Anne's new hopes for happiness do not depend entirely on Captain Wentworth. It seems that *Persuasion* endorses Elinor's hope that there is fitness in the world that makes happiness not depend on any one person. Anne cannot successfully "reason with herself" to feel less for Wentworth (60), but hope and faith may serve where reason could not.

Austen's emphasis on gratitude and hope in all her novels softens her rationalism. She is always highly aware of what is owing to others (even the right-minded Fanny owes much to the fallible Sir Thomas). And she tries to show that following reason is not a matter of harsh self-denial: a hope for pleasure is often justified. (Again, we see her focus on happiness: self-denial is not defended for its own sake, but because it leads to virtue and happiness.) To understand Austen's view of the world, it is useful to consider her interest in the sea, which is almost a character in *Persuasion*. Anne's father objects to the navy as being "the means of bringing persons of obscure birth into undue distinction" (19), a statement that reveals his pride of arrogance and conceit. Austen herself seems to *like* the fact that the sea offers an opportunity for distinction to those who have enough pride and hope to accomplish it. The sea, this place of beauty and unpredictability, is what restores Anne's hope. (In *Emma*, Emma and Mr. Knightley will begin their marriage with a trip to the sea.) The best pride is not the self-satisfaction of Sir

Walter Elliot (or a host of other characters), but rather the habit of all her heroes and heroines of requiring high things of themselves. Their pride is less conceited, we could say, in part because they are more grateful.

Notes

1. See Aristotle, *Ethics*, 1123a34–1125a16. Again, I would not insist that Austen used Aristotle as a model, or even had read him; only that her outlook is similar.

2. Ibid., 1125a6–8.

3. Ibid., 1125a8–9.

4. Ibid., 1124a20–21.

5. For a similar account see Aristotle, *Ethics* 1125a16–35. Even many small details echo Aristotle, as, for example, we see Mr. Collins "longing to publish his prosperous love" (123) in the manner of Aristotle's vain men, who "wish to have their good fortunes be made public and speak about them, thinking that through these they will be honored."

6. Samuel Kliger, in a defense of this thesis, says that "Darcy is the spokes-man for civilization" while Elizabeth represents "man-in-nature." (See Kliger, "Jane Austen's *Pride and Prejudice* in the Eighteenth-Century Mode" in *Twentieth Century Interpretations of Pride and Prejudice*, ed. E. Rubinstein [Englewood Cliffs, N. J.: Prentice-Hall, Inc., 1969], 53–54.) Tanner (*Jane Austen*, 136) similarly sees Elizabeth as the "freely rambling individual" and Darcy as the "rigidified upholder of the group" and their marriage as bringing together these principles. For similar ideas see also Litz, *Jane Austen*, 104–105; Nardin, *Those Elegant Decorums*, 60–61; Duckworth, *The Improvement*, 118; Mordecai Marcus, *Twentieth-Century Interpretations*, Rubinstein, 84; and Poovey, *The Proper Lady*, 189, 201.

7. See, for example, Morgan, who argues that Elizabeth's freedom is "a freedom to keep from becoming involved" and that she, like her father, refuses to commit her intelligence to seriousness and to a moral life (Morgan, *In the Meantime*, 83–92). See also Butler, who agrees with most critics that Elizabeth is fearless and independent and finds her similar to her father in her misanthropy (Butler, *Jane Austen and the War*, 199, 210). Elizabeth's tendencies to be vexed at people seem to me precisely to indicate her involvement with the world and to distinguish her from her father, who never gets upset and is hardly ever annoyed. The more foolish his acquaintances, the more he likes them (e.g., 68, 213, 364).

8. Mary Poovey, *The Proper Lady*, 194. See also Johnson who argues that in *Pride and Prejudice* "pursuing happiness is the business of life" and that Elizabeth has "a philosophy of pleasure" (C. Johnson, *Jane Austen*, 78, 80). The examples discussed above suggest that in Jane Austen's novels, pursuing happiness and hedonism are not the same.

9. See, for example, Nardin, who says that in *Pride and Prejudice*, if "a man or woman always displays good manners, it is perfectly safe for the reader to assume that his character is truly good" (Nardin, *Those Elegant Decorums*, 47).

10. Tanner, *Jane Austen*, 231. See also Auerbach, who says *Persuasion* shows "a revolution of values in Jane Austen's mind" ("O Brave New World," 117.)

11. I have argued elsewhere that Austen's account of love resembles Aristotle's discussion of friendship. But he is not primarily talking about friendship between a man and a woman, and does not present love as necessary for marriage. For a subtle application of Rousseau's psychology of love, or *amour-propre*, to *Pride and Prejudice*, see Allan Bloom, *Love and Friendship*, 191–208.

12. It is thus quite surprising that this novel, in particular, is often perceived as asexual, a view that seems to miss the forest for the trees. Tanner says that "passion, as such, is hardly differentiated from folly, in terms of the book" (Tanner, *Jane Austen*, 133). It is true that Lydia's passion is disparaged, but passion surely takes a more noble form in Mr. Darcy and Elizabeth. Butler sees Elizabeth's and Darcy's marriage "less as a sexual union between two individuals than as the stabilizing cornerstone of society" (Butler, *Jane Austen and the War*, introduction to 1987 ed., xliii). I would point out that it is not only Mr. Darcy who feels sexual desire for Elizabeth. To take one example, what else are we to think—but that she is strongly attracted to him—of the fact that after his proposal she is too weak to support herself and sobs for half an hour?

13. C. Johnson, *Jane Austen*, 81.

14. Thomas Hobbes, *Leviathan* (Harmondsworth, Middlesex, England: Penguin Books, 1968), 211.

15. Cf. Aristotle, *Ethics* (1124b5–6): "The high-minded man shows contempt justly (for his opinion is true) while ordinary men [imitating him] do so at random."

16. Austen, *Letters*, 309–10, 312 (24 May 1813).

17. Hobbes, *Leviathan*, Part I, Chapter 11, 161.

18. See again Aristotle's account of the high-minded man: "And he is the kind of man who does service to others but is ashamed to receive services from them" (*Ethics* 1124b9–10). See also 1168a10–12: "the service of the benefactor is not noble to the person who receives it but is, if anything, only expedient to him, and this is less pleasant to him and less worthy of being loved." This is precisely Elizabeth's reaction to Mr. Darcy's great service to her family. She would rather focus on its usefulness to herself than on its nobility in him because it is "painful, exceedingly painful" to know her family is "under obligations to a person who could never receive a return" (326).

19. Austen's whole treatment of gratitude—her suggestion that it is not simply a relation of debtors and creditors—is in line with Aristotle. Compare, for example, Mr. Knightley's claim that the good of his services to Emma was "all

to myself, by making you an object of the tenderest affection to me'' (E 462), with Aristotle, *Ethics*, 1167b31–33, ''those who have conferred services feel love and affection for those they have benefitted'' even if the latter are not useful to them.

20. C. Johnson, *Jane Austen* 73.

21. Poovey objects that a romance such as this ''makes women dream of being swept off their feet; [and] ends by reinforcing the helplessness that makes learning to stand on their own two feet unlikely'' (Poovey, *The Proper Lady*, 243). It is hard to imagine many people more able to stand on their own two feet than Elizabeth Bennet.

22. Kant, *Foundations*, 17.

23. This is also Aristotle's view. See *Ethics*, 1104b8–13 and 1110b30–33.

24. Ibid., 1106b32–33.

25. R. W. Harding quotes this passage and comments, '' 'Nothing worse'!— that phrase is typical. It is not mere sarcasm by any means. . . . 'Nothing worse' is a positive tribute to the decency, the superficial friendliness, the absence of the grosser forms of insolence and self-display at the dinner party. . . . And yet the effect of the comment, if her readers took it seriously, would be that of a disintegrating attack upon the sort of social intercourse they have established for themselves'' (Harding, ''Regulated Hatred: An Aspect of the Work of Jane Austen,'' *A Collection*, ed. Watt, 170). Harding is right to point out both the positive and negative force of the passage, but I would suggest that the tone of the novels as a whole makes the balance tilt toward the positive. It is possible to take this comment seriously, and see how the deficiencies of conversation are a sign of what is *truly* wanted in human intercourse. The phrase, in my view, points toward friendship rather than toward radical individualism.

Nor does Austen give up on the possibility that conversation can be good. We see examples (such as the witty exchanges between Elizabeth Bennet and Mr. Darcy and his friends Mr. Bingley and Colonel Fitzwilliam in *Pride and Prejudice*), and Anne Elliot's definition of good company—''the company of clever, well-informed people, who have a great deal of conversation''—is not suggested to be hopelessly fastidious, despite what Mr. Elliot might think (150). Such is the conversation that she is likely to find in the family and friends of Captain Wentworth (251). Austen's satire on conversation is close in spirit to Swift's Essay on Conversation, in which he says that the ''truest Way to understand Conversation, is to know the Faults and Errors to which it is subject, and from thence, every Man to form Maxims to himself whereby it may be regulated,'' for there are many men who might be more agreeable than they are. (Jonathan Swift, *A Tale of a Tub and other Satires* [London: J. M. Dent & Sons, 1975], 245–46.

26. Samuel Johnson, *A Dictionary of the English Language.* (London: Times Books, 1979), s.v.

27. S. Johnson, *Rambler* 185, *Works*, 209 emphasis added.

28. The many instances of luck that bring about Anne and Wentworth's re-

union are recounted by Paul N. Zietlow in "Luck and Fortuitous Circumstance in *Persuasion*: Two Interpretations," *ELH* 32 (June 1965): 179–95.

29. See also P 131, 224, 235, 237. Austen frequently uses expressions such as "upon my soul" or "poor soul," but, aside from these many references in *Persuasion*, the word is used with moral significance only two other times in all of her work (SS 92 and MP 269).

30. Archbishop Richard Whately writes, on reading *Mansfield Park*, that "Miss Austin has the merit (in our judgment most essential) of being evidently a Christian writer: a merit which is enhanced, both on the score of good taste, and of practical utility, by her religion being not at all obtrusive" (*Quarterly Review* xxiv [January 1821], reprinted in Southam, *The Critical Heritage*, 95).

31. Austen, *Letters*, 410 (18 November 1814).

32. Ibid., 256 (24 January 1809). Later, however, she tells her niece Anna that she does not suppose they differ "in our ideas of the Christian Religion. You have given an excellent description of it. We only affix a different meaning to the Word *Evangelical*" (Ibid., 420 [30 November 1814]).

33. Mary Augusta Austen-Leigh, *Personal Aspects of Jane Austen* (London: John Murray, 1920), 85.

34. Austen, *Letters*, 410 (18 November 1814).

35. See William and Richard Arthur Austen-Leigh, *Jane Austen: Her Life and Letters* (New York: Russell and Russell, 1965), 333.

36. Martin Price, *Forms of Life: Character and Moral Imagination in the Novel* (New Haven: Yale University Press, 1983), 86–87.

37. Mudrick, *Irony as Defense and Discovery*, 85.

38. See, for example, Kenneth Moler, *Jane Austen's Art of Allusion* (Lincoln, Neb.: University of Nebraska Press, 1968), 46, 70; Claudia Johnson, "A 'Sweet Face as White as Death': Jane Austen and the Politics of Female Sensibility," *Novel: a Forum on Fiction* 22:2 (Winter 1989), 172; Mudrick, *Irony as Defense and Discovery*, 84; Nardin, *Those Elegant Decorums*, 32.

39. Litz points out that there is something "idiosyncratic and almost obsessive" about the use of the word "bloom" in this novel ("*Persuasion*: Forms of Estrangement," in Halperin, *Jane Austen: Bicentenary Essays*, 223). I count at least nine appearances of the word (6 [2], 8, 28, 37, 61, 104, 153 [2]), not including the descriptions of Anne's returning color and looks (e.g., 114, 167, 243, 245).

Chapter 4

Men, Women, and Female Modesty

Nothing is more characteristic of Austen's heroines, or more separates them from their acquaintances, than their refusal to be in pursuit of a man or marriage. The author would seem to reject the reasons often stated as compelling women of her time to marry—both the practical reason that women had nothing else to do with their lives and the theoretical one that a woman needs a man. Nevertheless, all of the heroines *do* find their happiness in marriage. Furthermore, for all of Austen's interest in the nature and importance of friendship, including that between women, it is notable that she shows us no women (or men) who have with each other the truly open, equal, and fully satisfying friendship that we see between the hero and heroine when they marry. The question of whether and how women need marriage must be considered if we are to understand Austen's view of the way virtue relates to happiness.

To begin, it must be noted that Austen sees *both* sexes as naturally inclined toward marriage. The "universally acknowledged" truth that a single man of fortune must want a wife (PP 1) has its source in the public's wishes, and yet there may also be truth in it. For Austen shows us that men do desire wives and that they cannot marry without any money. Of course this does not mean that Mr. Bingley has taken his house with the object of finding a wife, any more than the Dashwood sisters' curiosity about the men in their neighborhood means that "*catching*" a man is "an employment to which they have been brought up" (SS 44). The simplest way to put Austen's attitude would be to say that humans are naturally inclined to form couples. Emma Woodhouse points out that everybody thought, for many reasons, that Mr. Weston would never marry again, but she "believed none of it" and was right (E 12). Mr. Knightley aptly says of Emma herself: "She always declares she will never marry, which, of course, means just nothing at all. But I have no idea that she has yet ever seen a man she cared for" (41). The same point is made in *Mansfield Park*, when we see how Henry Crawford quickly forgets his long-time resolve against marriage when he sees a woman he can love. The idea of opposing marriage *in principle* is always presented as a delusion.

Austen suggests that a general inclination toward marriage is not all that men and women share. Much of the discussion of the nature of men and women in Mary Wollstonecraft's *A Vindication of the Rights of Women*, the most important feminist writing of Austen's time, could find support in Austen's novels. In general, she and Wollstonecraft share a belief that "reason is absolutely necessary to perform any duty properly and sensibility is not reason."[1] In addition to believing women capable of reason and virtue, both also believe that these things are essential for friendship (or love). As Wollstonecraft says and Austen always shows, real friendship must be "founded on principle and cemented by time."[2] Margaret Kirkham plausibly argues that Austen shared "the essential convictions of rational feminism," and she further points out that this fact does not make her a political radical, because feminists such as Wollstonecraft emphasize the need for "reason and restraint in sexual matters."[3]

Nevertheless, there are important differences. The most obvious of these is that Austen does not urge political and social reforms. Unlike Wollstonecraft, she does not blame social attitudes and institutions for women's plight; indeed, it is not clear in her novels that women as a group have a plight. Anne Elliot's reflections on women's lack of activity and diversion are understanding, and certainly not bitter; there is a similar kind of compassionate reflection in Emma Woodhouse's "musings" about "the difference of woman's destiny" as she compares Jane Fairfax to Mrs. Churchill (384). Austen never presents the world as perfectly (or even very nearly) just—chance or "destiny" plays a significant role.

Paradoxically, perhaps, not only Austen's belief that good fortune will always be necessary for happiness, but also her greater belief in the importance of personal responsibility explain why she does not agitate for social change. Her heroines' capacity for reason and virtue is not dependent on opportunities outside of marriage, any more than it depends on the feminine conduct books that Wollstonecraft attacks. Nor does *essential* virtue even require a particular education, however beneficial a proper education is shown to be. Such women as Jane and Elizabeth Bennet have fended remarkably well for themselves, and even some with greater odds against them—Fanny Price's younger sister Susan or Lady Susan's neglected daughter—can do their duty and form real attachments.

Not only does Austen hold a woman (or man) personally responsible for her (or his) virtue, she also seems—more than Wollstonecraft[4]—to rely on the fact that real virtue will earn the respect of those whose respect is worth having. Mr. Bennet tells Elizabeth not to worry about her sister Lydia's improprieties, for "wherever you and Jane are known, you must be respected and valued" (PP 232). Now this is an exaggeration, for Austen knows well how much of respect is due to prejudice. Anne Elliot "was nobody" with her father and sister, and her fine piano playing is "little thought of" by her larger circle (P 47); nevertheless, we are assured that her mind and character "must have placed her high with any people of real understanding" (5). Fanny's Portsmouth neighbors see nothing to respect in her, which reflects badly on them, and the fact that Henry Crawford loves her is presented as a credit to his understanding. Certainly, Austen is aware (as the beginning of *Persuasion*, for example, shows) that a good husband is not the *inevitable* reward of virtue. Nevertheless, she suggests that the possibility that someone of good mind and character will find another such person to respect and love is not outlandish. Above all, she indicates—again a sign of her reliance on personal responsibility—that her heroines would be capable of happiness even if they did not marry.

In addition to differing from Wollstonecraft in her greater acceptance *not* of the rightness of the status quo but of the enduring possibility for humans (women as well as men) to live a virtuous life, Austen differs from her in her love of the graces and refinements of virtue that are especially exhibited in relations between the sexes. (Austen often makes fun of the affected forms of refinement, but this only points to her high regard for *real* graces.) Wollstonecraft's moralism is more austere:

> I who love simplicity would gladly give up politeness for a quarter of the virtue that has been sacrificed to an equivocal quality which at best should only be the polish of virtue.[5]

She makes this comment as a reply to Rousseau's dictum to women in *Emile*: they should require themselves to say "only what is pleasing to those to whom they speak" while yet making this rule subordinate to "the first law, which is never to lie."[6] Austen's sympathy with Rousseau on this point is indicated by the line in *Pride and Prejudice* that has

become classic because it seems so characteristic of her own method:
"Elizabeth tried to unite civility and truth in a few short sentences"
(PP 216). One of the themes of all the novels—it is what Marianne
Dashwood learns and Anne Elliot, among others, relies on—is to show
how truths can be conveyed while still respecting politeness.

The dispute about this point may be more fundamental than first appears, for Austen's interest in the *cultivation* of virtue, the part of virtue
that goes beyond what justice requires (truth is necessary, saying it
pleasantly is less so) concerns her fundamental belief that virtue is not
only strict duty toward others, but also is becoming to oneself. She
suggests that civility and propriety preserve a certain relation between
men and women that contributes to the pleasures of life. Now Austen,
as much as Wollstonecraft, wants to show that "elegance is inferior to
virtue"[7] and that delicate sensibility is not a woman's virtue; she seems
to share Elinor Dashwood's belief that Marianne places "too great importance" on "the delicacies of a strong sensibility" and the "graces
of a polished manner" (SS 201). (See also Austen's criticism not only
of the false elegance of Mrs. Elton but also the more genuine elegance
of Jane Fairfax or Mr. Bingley's sisters).[8] But she does not, like Wollstonecraft, "despise . . . elegancy of mind" as "weak."[9]

Even the novels' criticism of false forms of delicacy[10] point to the
possibility of a true "delicacy of mind,"[11] or "elegancy of mind" (P
5, cf. 28, 41, 153; MP 294) or "natural grace" (E 326, P 68). To be
sure, these qualities can belong to both sexes and are a mark of a general ability to discern what virtue calls for in a specific case. But there
is a sexual element to them as well, a sense in which cultivation has to
do with a (true, not affected) sensitivity to the proper relation between
men and women. Jane Fairfax's "delicacy of mind" relates to her sense
of propriety in her engagement (E 439, cf. MP 140), and Anne Elliot
has

> delicacy which must be pained by any lightness of conduct in a well-
> meaning young woman, and a heart to sympathize in any of the sufferings
> it occasioned (P 77).

Delicacy in these cases is connected to feminine modesty, a virtue that
Wollstonecraft would refuse to call sexual.[12]

Austen's greater interest in politeness goes along with an interest in
the relations of men and women as such that is greater than we find
in *A Vindication*, which is almost silent about love. Wollstonecraft's
Vindication is in large part an attack on Rousseau's *Emile*, a fundamen-

tal source of the Romantic movement of the eighteenth and nineteenth centuries. It would be surprising if Austen were not aware of this debate.[13] In *some* respects, Austen's portrayal of men and women has more in common with Rousseau's reasoned defense of the differences between the sexes than with Wollstonecraft. Of course, it can be seen, Austen disagrees with Rousseau in fundamental ways. For example, Rousseau derives the ideal relation between the sexes from bodily needs and desires,[14] whereas Austen's interest in the relations of the sexes seems to come from the perspective of the heights or refinements of human virtue: the possibility of conversation; and the attachment of friendship that seems to be a perfection of life. (It is tempting to say that Austen looks at the world in the way Aristotle does but from the perspective of a woman).[15] Men and women have different and complementary duties in life, she shows, which make them *generally* interested in marriage with each other. But this natural inclination does not imply for her—as for Rousseau in *Emile*—that a man or woman cannot be a complete moral person without marriage but must join together to be one "moral person" of which "the woman is the eye and the man is the arm" (377). It is a woman's capacity for virtue and the happiness that comes from it that allows her heroines to refuse marriage to men they do not love. (Perhaps Austen's greater insistence than Aristotle's on love in marriage reflects a greater belief in the potential independence of women as well.)

Despite all this, the different strengths of men and of women are shown to complement each other in marriage and thus to contribute to the attachment and dependence of each person on the other, and on this point Austen is more in accord with Rousseau than with Wollstonecraft. We can see her balance in the humorous portrait of the Crofts of *Persuasion*. As they are driving, Mrs. Croft cries out,

'My dear admiral, that post!—we shall certainly take that post.' But by coolly giving the reins a better direction herself, they happily passed the danger (92)

and Anne reflects that their style of driving is "no bad representation of the general guidance of their affairs." In this case, Mrs. Croft is both the eyes and the hands. This vigorous, intelligent woman, however, also depends on her husband. The winter spent on shore, apart from her husband, put her in "perpetual fright" (71), presumably in part for his safety, whereas she can brave life at sea because "while we were together, you know, there was nothing to be feared" (70). Austen's heroes and heroines are more evenly matched in intelligence, but we are always shown how they complement each other and feel their need for each other. The fact that they can survive without marriage does not mean that they are not inclined toward it and dependent on each other within it.

Differences Between the Sexes

Despite the fact that Austen always implies that women, like men, are "rational creatures," she nonetheless suggests that different virtues are dominant in each sex and that these differences are worth preserving. This idea is too pervasive in her works to admit of an accord on this point with Wollstonecraft, who wished to see "all distinction of sex confounded in society."[16] All of Austen's heroines, even the most spirited, have—in addition to intelligence—a combination of firmness of principle and the capacity to be persuaded on matters to which they are morally indifferent (what Austen often calls gentleness). Both qualities are related more to reason than to submissive obedience to a law or to a husband. Her heroes, in addition to intelligence, for the most part have a courage that is more spirited.

The misunderstandings of Anne and Captain Wentworth have something to do with the difference in their natures: he has "a great deal of intelligence, spirit and brilliancy," while she has "gentleness, modesty, taste and feeling" (26). Austen takes pains to defend these qualities. Spiritedness is Captain Wentworth's most prominent characteristic, and this is one of the virtues for which the navy, which has "done so much for us" (19), is praised. Admiral Croft says of Captain Benwick that "his reading has done him no harm, for he has fought as well as read" (219). Even Elinor Dashwood "presumed not to censure" Colonel Brandon—"a man and a soldier"—for fighting a duel (SS 211). As for women, what seems to be daring and spirit in Louisa Musgrove is suggested to be selfishness (94, 116), and her fall teaches Captain Wentworth to distinguish "between the steadiness of principle and the obstinacy of self-will" and to see in Anne "the loveliest medium of fortitude and gentleness" (241–42). This combination is typical of all Austen's heroines. Sir Thomas Bertram (presumably in line with nineteenth-century ideas of feminine perfection) meant to "recommend Fanny as a wife by shewing her persuadableness" (281), but he did not reckon upon the strength imposed by her sense of right.

Firmness of Mind in **Pride and Prejudice**

Firmness of principle is the solid foundation of even Austen's most timid and passive heroines. Fanny Price is one who is "firm as a rock in her own principles" and has a "gentleness of character so well adapted to recommend them" (MP 351). The mild and yielding Jane Bennet is "firm when she felt herself to be right" (59). She has a "*steady* mildness," a "mild and *steady* candor" (129, 138, emphasis added). But Austen's more spirited heroines also are characterized by firmness and gentleness. Elizabeth Bennet's manner, for example, combining "a sweetness and archness . . . which made it difficult for her to affront anybody" (PP 52), seems a case to prove Anne Elliot's argument against "the too common idea of spirit and gentleness being incompatible with each other" (P 172). These are the same qualities recommended by Rousseau for his Sophie.[17]

Elizabeth's extraordinary love and praise for her sister is one clue that her own character is not unfeminine.[18] Her softer side may be eclipsed by her older sister Jane, who is gentleness itself. Yet most of the praise of Jane's yielding disposition comes from Elizabeth (e.g., 15, 134, 186, 348), who, by pointing out that Jane's mildness is due to generosity rather than to lack of intelligence or lack of concern for others (as we see in Lady Bertram of *Mansfield Park*, for example), shows the reader what is lovable in it.

Elizabeth is not as fearless and self-assured as she says she is. She asserts to Jane that "one great difference between us" is that "compliments always take *you* by surprise, and *me* never" (14). This statement is soon followed by her shock at receiving Mr. Collins's proposal of marriage. And when Mr. Darcy proposes to her, the word "astonishment" is used at least eight times to describe her reaction (189, 251, 254, 255, 261, 263, 266, 334). The author also insists on Elizabeth's lack of *daring* in her relations with Mr. Darcy. It is true that she vows to be "impertinent" with him so as not to "grow afraid of him" (24), but she nonetheless—though "blaming herself for her own weakness"—cannot deliberately pain him (92). She "trembles" lest her mother expose herself before him (45). Later, knowing she loves him, she has no courage to speak (257, 336); she does not even "dare" lift her eyes to his face (251, 335, 336, 366). She has not "dared" expose Wickham's character (277). She has "not dared" tell her sister of Mr. Darcy's affection for her (227, 334). She tells Mr. Collins she is not "so daring" as to refuse a marriage offer she really wants (107)—but we see her dare to refuse an offer from as great a man as Mr. Darcy because he insults her and because she doubts his virtue. Still, she displays not the daring of self-assurance, but the steady defense of principle as well as the anger of offended pride. Her extreme physical weakness at this moment and at the other most intense moment in the novel (when she learns of Lydia's fate) show both her vulnerability and involvement.

Elizabeth's strength takes the form of a fidelity to true propriety and serious principles, particularly on the subject of marriage.[19] She is "exceedingly shocked" by the charges Darcy makes against Wickham (205), and she is as shocked as anyone in the novel at Lydia's running away with Wickham. She is sure that neither Lydia's "virtue nor her understanding would preserve her from falling a ready prey" (280), and after Lydia and Wickham have married she is "disgusted" at their easy assurance and blushes for her sister (315–16). Elizabeth's moral judgments are self-reflective (Lydia's coarse language at one point shocks her into a realization of her own coarse sentiments [220]) and they are compassionate (she has tears in her eyes as she admits how "shocking" it is that she should doubt her sister's "sense of decency and virtue," and she can only say that she is very young, unrestrained, and not "taught to think on serious subjects" [238]). Still, her judgments are as firm as any of Austen's heroines.

This is what distinguishes her from the similarly vivacious Mary Crawford, who, like Lydia, can "hardly be serious even on serious subjects" (MP 87). (Fanny worries, too, that Henry Crawford does not think properly "on serious subjects" [MP 350].) Elizabeth half regrets that Wickham and Lydia must marry (304), for she sees "how little of permanent happiness could belong to a couple who were only brought together because their passions were stronger than their virtue" (312). Here we see *both* the feeling and the principle that are lacking in Mary Crawford's plan to have her brother and Maria marry after their adultery (MP 457).

Elizabeth's opinion of Lydia is humorous but decided. When Lydia offers to find husbands for all her sisters, Elizabeth replies, "I thank you for my share of the favor, but I do not particularly like your way of getting husbands" (317). This is a revealing comment, for it puts Lydia in the camp of husband hunters when we might have been inclined to see her as marrying for love. Her imprudence does not do away with the fact that her marriage is more for the sake of situation than anyone's in the novel. And, to some extent, Lydia has sought marriage for the sake of situation. Austen stresses her eagerness to find a husband (221, 316–317). Wickham has not intended to marry her (323), but it is quite clear that *she* has assumed they will be married (292, 323). Lydia has "wanted only encouragement to attach herself to anybody" (280), and it is not surprising that her love for him is not deep and lasts only a little longer than his affection lasts for her (387). Lydia's first delights after marriage are, in fact, in her immodest displays of her situation— pulling down the coach window to wave her wedding ring at a passerby (316) and insisting on her new right to be seated ahead of her oldest sister (317).

In other words, Lydia's marriage is not the overly passionate opposite of the overly prudent marriage between Charlotte and Mr. Collins, but rather a much more careless and indecent version of the same phenomenon. When we hear Lydia say she is "sure they should be married some time or other" (323), there may be even an echo of Charlotte, who having accepted Mr. Collins for the sake of an establishment, "cared not how soon that establishment were gained" (122). Some critics have taken exception to what they consider to be Austen's sexual moralizing in the Lydia episode.[20] But it should be taken into account that Elizabeth is almost as shocked at Charlotte Lucas's marriage as at Lydia's elopement (125, 135–36).[21] Her strong objections to both indicate a purity of principle about marriage itself, not just about extramarital sex. Elizabeth is typical of Austen's heroines in her belief that marriage is not a necessity for women—a belief that she holds precisely because she is convinced that its duties are not to be undertaken lightly.

Constancy in *Persuasion*

One of the most important qualities more typical of women than of men, according to Austen, is constancy, which seems to be not only loyalty in love (its usual specific context) but a more general adherence to one's principles. Alisdair MacIntyre has pointed out that in Austen's novels constancy implies the "recognition of a particular kind of threat to the integrity of the personality in the peculiarly modern social world."[22] In other words, Austen's concern with being constant to one's principles—with "integrity," a word she sometimes uses—is an example of the way we see her classical outlook as responsive to the conditions of her own time. Yet the novels do not praise loyalty to *any* commitment; constancy assumes other virtues. For example, none of the heroines are or could be constant to a man who lacks virtue—this is the sentiment that Emma expresses when she cannot understand how Jane Fairfax could be loyal to Frank Churchill and that Marianne admits when Willoughby's character is revealed to her. Sir Thomas Bertram says the fact that Henry Crawford has chosen so well gives "his constancy a respectable stamp,'' even though it still may not in itself be a merit (MP 330).

Anne Elliot analyzes the reasons why women are more apt to be constant in love:

> We do not forget you, so soon as you forget us. It is, perhaps, our fate rather than our merit. . . . We live at home, quiet, confined, and our feelings prey upon us. You are forced on exertion. You have always a profession, pursuits, business of some sort or other, to take you back into the world immediately, and continual occupation and change soon weaken impressions (232).

Constancy, as she portrays it, is not a virtue so much as a strength of feeling—more to be sympathetically pitied than praised. Anne seems to admit, as we have seen the novel generally to suggest, that it was not a merit in herself to be so hopeless after Wentworth was gone. At the same time we are led to wonder if the change that weakens impressions is not to be lamented. ''Men of the world,'' Henry Crawford says, have a memory of the past that is ''under . . . easy dominion'' (MP 98), but for Jane Austen's less worldly characters time and change cannot conquer everything. Constancy is a sign of the sensibility that is possessed by Austen's best characters.

Women's feelings especially can tend toward excess, Anne's speeches suggest, and this is not a virtue. (So we see a reference to ''the first ardour of *female alarm*'' in this novel [9, emphasis added]). Anne admits that ''true attachment and constancy'' are also felt by men (235)—but only while the woman a man loves is alive and devoted to him. The novel supports this view, for while Captain Wentworth has not married since leaving Anne, his ''more glowing, open, manly look'' attests to the fact that he has suffered less than she has. Women have the *unenviable* privilege of ''loving longest, when existence or when hope is gone,'' loving, that is, without reason. Austen's general conviction that disappointment in love can and should be overcome[23] is not absent from *Persuasion*, sympathetic as she is to Anne's retentive feelings.

Austen's insistence on the point that women's suffering is not in itself a virtue gives us reason to doubt that feeling, in *Persuasion*, has become the source of moral authority.[24] Here, as elsewhere in Austen's work, not feeling but duty is the proper guide to behavior. A small example of the primacy of duty for Anne appears in the painful moment at the music concert when she turns away from Wentworth just as they are at the brink of an understanding, in order to answer his rival's pressing inquiries: "never had she sacrificed to politeness with a more suffering spirit" (190). Anne's capacity for deep feeling, as we saw with Fanny Price, goes along with her habits of principle.

The difference in men's and women's feelings reflects (but does not prescribe) their different functions in life. Anne defends her brother-in-law for not offering to stay home with his sick child, for "nursing does not belong to a man, it is not his province." A sick child is "always" the mother's property, she says, and "her own feelings generally make it so" (56). She seems to see a division of labor as right, apart from feelings, but also believes that a man's or woman's feelings "generally" support such a division. Now Anne, of course, is the most domestic of Austen's heroines: marriage is a state for which she is "peculiarly fitted by her warm affections and domestic habits" (29). She loves and is good with children (e.g., 43–45), and we often see her caring for the ill or injured (her nephew, Louisa Musgrove, Mrs. Smith) counselling and comforting others (her sister Mary, Captain Benwick, Henrietta Musgrove, Captain Harville), and in general falling into "all her wonted ways of attention and assistance" (221). It should be noted that these actions are not passive: Anne is capable of giving orders and counsel to men. (She, the most domestic heroine, also makes the most direct feminist statement: she will "not allow books to prove anything" because men have always "had every advantage of us in telling their own story" [P 234].)

All the heroines have Anne's habits of caring for others to a significant degree. Emma Woodhouse devotes herself to her father, Elinor Dashwood nurses her sister,[25] Fanny is invaluable at Mansfield Park at a time of illness and upheaval.[26] These are not cases of heroic self-sacrifice. Austen has not abandoned the view that made her defend, in *Northanger Abbey,* Catherine's preference for cricket over "the more heroic enjoyments of infancy," such as "nursing a dormouse," that make this "heroine" seem "unpropitious for heroism" (NA 13). Nevertheless all the heroines can appreciate, as Anne does, "the satisfaction of knowing herself extremely useful" (P 121).

There is always an ambiguity in the novels about whether it is women's *nature* that makes their feelings prey upon them. Certainly it is partly due to the more passive habits that result from their limited opportunities. Yet Anne goes on to suggest that the nature of women's attachments might make it too difficult for them to have a more active life. She tells Captain Harville that men's feelings might be "strongest" but that women's are most "tender":

> Man is more robust than woman, but he is not longer-lived; which exactly
> explains my view of the nature of their attachments. Nay it would be too
> hard upon you, if it were otherwise . . . you are always labouring and
> toiling . . . your home, country, friends all quitted . . . it would be too hard
> indeed (with a faltering voice) if woman's feelings were to be added to all
> this (233).

I believe that this passage does not support the interpretation that Anne
blames society for making women victims of their feelings.[27] Now perhaps Anne may simply be turning Captain Harville's biological explanation against him and may not herself believe in a strictly physical
account of male/female differences. But the important point is that
Anne says that if, in addition to laboring away from family and friends,
men had "woman's feelings" as well, it would be too hard to bear: the
combination of such toil and such feelings would be too painful. In
other words, if it is not possible to do away with such feelings, the labor
of working away from family and friends might not liberate her but
only add to her burden. Now perhaps eventually "continual change"
would "weaken impressions," as Anne says, and we are left with the
further question of whether Austen thinks this desirable for women.

Women's Attachment to Convention

Women's greater constancy is shown to be related to their greater
attachment to duty, even in matters of convention. And this respect for
propriety is a necessary part of the relation between the sexes, and of
social intercourse in general, in the novels. The cases of Jane Fairfax in
Emma and of Anne Elliot in *Persuasion*, especially, show how women
suffer more than men do for violating duty. Frank and Jane fight under
the stress of their engagement, for she cannot understand his playful
attitude and he cannot sympathize with her distress at violating duty:

> the consciousness of having done amiss, had exposed her to a thousand
> inquietudes, and made her captious and irritable to a degree . . . that had
> been hard for him to bear (419).

The laudable women in these novels seem to feel a greater instinctual
attachment to propriety than men do, even though the laudable men do
their duty. Frank Churchill says that Jane has felt "every scruple of
mine with multiplied strength and refinement" (440). Her suffering
does not show a romantic nature as much as a respect for convention
and propriety.

Jane's suffering is not from social condemnation, but from her own sense of having acted improperly. *Emma* seems to support the view that a strong sense of duty is, as Anne Elliot says, "no *bad* part" of the lot that falls to a woman (P 246). Frank Churchill is blamed by others and by himself for not respecting Jane's scruples (E 441, 446, 477), and the solid marriages in these novels are grounded in part upon a man's respect for a woman's uprightness. Emma herself is no exception to this rule. Mr. Knightley's deference to Emma's firm sense of what she owes her father is a key reason why this marriage—and no other—can work for her. Frank's lack of true gallantry and real feeling is shown by his "persisting to act in direct opposition to Jane Fairfax's sense of right" (446). Significantly, Jane's difficult circumstances are not the *cause* of her respect for propriety but rather the reason she does not follow it more strictly.[28] Emma says that Jane's putting up with Frank's behavior—including his flirting with other women—shows "a degree of placidity, which I can neither comprehend nor respect" (397), but Jane's circumstances may explain it (122, 384).

The respect of men for what is due to women is a chief principle underlying Austen's whole system of manners. Austen defends this principle in a surprisingly *un*patriarchal fashion. Many of her heroes have to learn that what is due to women is not a condescending respect for their softness or weakness, but rather the more difficult respect for the sense of duty that is a sign of their strength of mind. Captain Wentworth, for example, at first displays a gallantry that is similar to the disingenuous flattery of Mr. Elton and Frank Churchill in *Emma*.[29] Captain Wentworth claims to be gallant in disliking to give passage to women on ships because he rates "the claims of women to every personal comfort *high*" (69). His sister charges that this gallantry—which obviously restricts the movements of women—is of "a superfine, extraordinary sort" for it presumes that "women are all fine ladies, instead of rational creatures" (69). The debate is not resolved, but there is other evidence that Captain Wentworth's gallantry is misplaced. We are told that Captain Wentworth was "not very gallant by [Anne]" when he first saw her again (60), and this is generally true of his reaction to her breaking of their engagement. For true gallantry in all of Jane Austen's novels is not so much shown by restraining women (i.e., refusing them passage on ships) as by respecting their sense of restraint (i.e., trying to understand Anne's deference to her godmother and to prudence). The latter kind is more difficult, of course, because it means less show and more sacrifice. Wentworth must come to understand the nature of Anne's tenderness and her *real* claims to protection.

Good manners and rules of propriety in this novel have much to do with respect for women. Mr. Bennet's improprieties, for example, are chiefly displayed in his disrespect for his daughters and especially his wife. It is the fact that he exposes his wife to the contempt of her own children that Elizabeth sees as "reprehensible," a "continual breach of conjugal obligation and decorum" (236). Nor does he believe his daughters need the protection of his respect. They are "all silly and ignorant, like other girls" (5), a dismissal that makes him not bother to ever guide or restrain Lydia, makes him able to embarrass his daughter Mary in public (101), and lets him "disconcert" his daughter Kitty (29) and even "most cruelly mortify" his favorite Elizabeth by teasing her about Darcy (364). What seems to be a general contempt for women is what makes him ill-mannered. Not surprisingly, Mr. Bennet detests dancing (13). Austen also delights in stripping bare the false deference to women that is not real respect. When Mr. Collins asks Elizabeth to "pardon me for neglecting to profit by your advice, which on every other subject shall be my constant guide" (97), we see the mock respect for her which is confirmed by his smug assurance about "the usual practice of elegant females" in his proposal (108).

Now, the idea that it is a woman's strong sense of duty that deserves respect or protection from men does not mean that Austen disdains other genuine acts of service. In *Persuasion*, the renewal of Captain Wentworth's attachment to Anne is shown by all the protective services he does for her, from plucking a troublesome child from her back, to placing her in a carriage when he sees she is tired, to offering her an umbrella. William Dean Howells, commenting on the first of these incidents, points out that "this is not the sort of rescue to bring about a reconciliation between lovers in a *true* novel. There it must be something more formidable than a naughty little boy that the heroine is saved from."[30] Austen's typically anti-heroic point is that women are not weak creatures who need to be saved by gallant men. The type of services that genuinely lead to attachment and mutual involvement are more modest, but reveal the man's real attentiveness to the woman's needs. (Again, we see Austen's version of a "sensitive" man, one not inclined to indulge his own feelings but rather to be of use to others.) It is typical of Austen's heroines to accept such acts of concern gratefully, seeing them as the result of affection rather than power.

Still, Captain Wentworth's greatest challenge is to see Anne's sense of duty as worthy of respect. It might be noted that Anne's willingness to take her godmother's advice about marriage is not the only way in which she respects what she sees as duty. The advice itself reflects an insight into the importance of convention that seems to belong more to women than to men. Anne may think, in retrospect, that Lady Russell's advice was wrong in her case, and yet all the novels support the idea that lies behind her advice: that love often cannot withstand a long engagement, but rather needs the support of the convention of marriage. It is implied that Anne and Captain Wentworth could not have immediately married, for her father said he would do nothing for her, and Wentworth had ''nothing but himself to recommend him'' (27). Lady Russell worries that Anne will be—not ''snatched off'' by him, for they wouldn't yet marry—but ''sunk'' by him ''into a state of most wearing, anxious, youth-killing dependence'' (27).

We see how such worries, and the mere passage of time, cause trouble for the love between Edward Ferrars and Lucy Steele in *Sense and Sensibility* and Frank and Jane in *Emma*. So, when the sensible Mrs. Croft says that an ''uncertain engagement; an engagement which may be long'' is what she considers ''very unsafe and unwise'' (231), Anne, applying it to herself, feels a ''nervous thrill'' and watches Captain Wentworth's reaction. Austen expresses a similar sentiment herself in a letter to a niece having doubts about an engagement:

> I should dread the continuance of this sort of tacit agreement. . . . Years may pass, before he is Independent. You like him [in my opinion] well enough to marry, but not well enough to wait.[31]

Implied in all these statements is the idea that love needs the support of convention. Austen's niece loves this man enough to marry him and thus to undertake the duties that will further attach the two to each other, but it is not a strong enough love to survive without this conventional support. Marriage does not require an exceptionally high sort of love, Austen indicates, however desirable such a love might be. Now Austen is always interested in the exceptions to general rules, and it is possible that Anne's and Captain Wentworth's love could have withstood any difficulties. (In retrospect, Anne thinks so.) The point, however, is that Lady Russell's and Anne's greater respect for convention is not simply selfish or unreasonable. And Captain Wentworth's refusal to see this is the chief sign of his lack of gallantry. He ''shut [his] eyes'' and ''would not understand [her],'' and refused to return a year later when her scruples would have been removed (247).

Part of the worth of marriage as Jane Austen portrays it is that it can impart constancy to men and courage to women. Anne protests the ''too-common idea of spirit and gentleness being incompatible with each other'' (172). Indeed, it is when Wentworth turns and speaks to her ''with a glow, and yet a gentleness, which seemed almost restoring the past'' that Anne first ''colour[s] deeply'' (114). It is the combination of *gentleness* with his spirited glow that makes Anne remember the past. As Wentworth has become more gentle, so Anne in the course of the novel is reanimated and her bloom and beauty are restored (see 104, 114, 145, 167, 178).

Vanity and Seriousness in Emma

Emma Woodhouse seems at first glance not to display the feminine qualities of the other heroines, chiefly because she is more apt to think too well of herself and to indulge her vanity. In Emma, however (as opposed to someone such as Mary Crawford in *Mansfield Park*), this vanity seems to be a (generally) harmless and even charming matter of style, because it is joined with what Austen so often calls ''seriousness on serious subjects'' (e.g., MP 87). Austen is reported to have said that Emma was a heroine ''whom no one but myself will much like,''[32] whereas she found Anne Elliot ''almost too good for me.''[33]

Austen is never terribly hard on feminine vanity, despite the confessions the heroines inevitably make in the end. She says in her own narrative voice in the unfinished *Sanditon*, ''I make no apologies for my Heroine's vanity.—If there are young Ladies in the World at her time of Life, more dull of Fancy & more careless of pleasing, I know them not and never wish to know them'' (MW 395). Vanity shows a desire of pleasing that Austen is not willing to criticize harshly, even though she is clear about the fact that it is not virtue and can get in the way of love (e.g., SS 331, MP 467). It contributes to the pleasures and agreeableness of life. Even though Austen makes her readers fully aware of the deficiencies of such people as the Crawfords and Willoughby, she is able to portray their charm. And even the most upright heroines are not free from vanity. In *Mansfield Park*, the narrator says (again in the author's voice) that while she supposes there *are* ''such unconquerable ladies of eighteen''—or ''one should not read about them''—who would never be persuaded into love against their judgment by talent, manner, and flattery, she does not believe Fanny to be one of them [MP 231]. Austen explicitly distinguishes herself from harsher moralists who would not allow that vanity can be combined with seriousness of principle.

At the same time, the reason Emma can be liked is that her ''vain spirit'' is intertwined with a ''serious spirit'' (330). There is something especially feminine about the nature of Emma's seriousness, as well as about the nature of her vanity. Emma shares with *all* the heroines the habit of always analyzing the rightness of her own conduct. She is as often engaged in self-doubt or criticism as in being carried away by her vanity (e.g., 133–39, 231, 315, 330, 377–78, 402–23), for,

> She did not always feel so absolutely satisfied with herself, so entirely convinced that her opinions were right and her adversary's wrong, as Mr. Knightley (67).

Now usually Mr. Knightley's opinions *are* right, but that is not the main point here, which is that Emma's thinking is not as straightforward and sure of itself as is his. It is typical in Austen's novels that women are more engaged in struggles with themselves over the rightness of their actions. (*All* the heroines debate with themselves in this way [e.g., MP 135].)

Emma's self-doubts and reflections about the past and future may be connected with her preoccupation with matchmaking and marriage. To some extent, Emma's pursuit of the feminine activity of matchmaking—the "greatest amusement in the world" (12, 69)—could be explained by Anne Elliot's comment about the lack of occupation for women. Emma, not especially interested in the accomplishments of piano or drawing or the more serious employment of steady reading (37, 44, 69, 231), usually does not have much to do. She quickly and willingly puts her matchmaking projects aside when she has preparations to make for the arrival of her sister's family (91). The men in *Emma* are, in contrast, industrious by necessity—even the gentlemen keep accounts and attend to parish concerns (e.g. 28, 100, 257, 383, 456–58). But there is more to it than this, more even than a wish on Emma's part to control others.

Matchmaking aims at reducing the role of chance in human affairs. Emma somewhat bitterly reflects on the inconsistency of the world when she fears that Mr. Knightley will marry Harriet:

> Was it new for [a man], perhaps too busy to seek, to be the prize of the girl who would seek him?—Was it new for anything in this world to be unequal, inconsistent, incongruous—or for chance and circumstance (as second causes) to direct the human fate? (413).

Emma is not surprised that a busy man might accept the woman who comes his way, but she despairs at such a giving in to circumstance.

(Emma's caveat, ''as second causes,'' implies that there is a higher power who ultimately directs and orders the world.) It is typical of many men in the novels to put themselves at the mercy of chance in marriage by marrying for fortune or for beauty. (Women who seek for husbands meet the same fate.) Austen's suggestion that marriage must be for love is not necessarily at odds with the idea of arranged matches, for she sees the deepest love to require a concern with character and suitability. Captain Wentworth is joking when he says he has come to Uppercross ''quite ready to make a foolish match'' (62), but then he does in fact court two foolish girls at once. If he had in fact had to marry Louisa, he would not be the only man in the novels so deceived. The idea of making matches presumes the need to choose a spouse carefully; it allows for the influence of reason upon feeling.

Emma's matchmaking indicates a difference between her and Mr. Knightley's way of thinking that is indicated to be characteristic of their sexes. When Mr. Knightley refuses to credit Emma for the match of the happy Westons, she plausibly defends her efforts as ''a something between the do-nothing and the do-all,'' pointing out that if she had not ''given many little encouragements'' and ''smoothed many little matters,'' it would not have come off. The reader, knowing the ultra-conservative habits at Hartfield, can agree (13). Emma does not insist on having things as clear-cut as Mr. Knightley does.

Her rationality is less single-minded than Mr. Knightley's. She claims to differ from her sex in ''set[ting] up . . . for Understanding,'' (427), and she teasingly tells Mr. Knightley that *his* sex thinks beauty and mild temper are ''the highest claims a woman could possess.'' The ensuing exchange is revealing:

'Upon my word, Emma, to hear you abusing the reason you have, is almost enough to make me think so too. Better be without sense, than misapply it as you do.'
      'To be sure,' cried she playfully. 'I know *that* is the feeling of you all . . . such a girl as Harriet is just what every man delights in' (64).

On the one hand, it is clear that both Emma and Mr. Knightley believe women possess reason and sense, while on the other, Emma's method of arguing shows how she can somewhat irrationally get him to say exactly what she wants. Her method is like that of Mary Crawford in *Mansfield Park*, who speaks with ''feminine lawlessness'' (94), so that Edmund reasoned with her, but in vain. She would not calculate, she would not compare. She would only smile and assert. The greatest degree of rational consistency could not have been more engaging (MP 96).

The charm of this does not rest on the idea that the woman is inferior: on the contrary, Emma and Mary are able to tease a man for his unbending reasonableness. Even Mr. Knightley can find rational inconsistency engaging, as when we hear on one occasion that " 'Nonsensical girl!' was his reply [to Emma], but not at all in anger" (214). The fact that she teases him to the end of the novel (e.g., 474) shows that she, thankfully, never does fully submit "to a subjection of the fancy to the understanding" (37). The difference between the sexes is not an impassable gulf in this novel. Mr. Knightley tells Emma that "nature gave you understanding" (462), and so nature has given him an imagination: he is the only person in the novel to observe signs of love between Jane and Frank Churchill (343).

Emma is by no means the only woman in the novels who, while possessing sense and firmly adhering to good principles, is not as convinced of her own *opinions* as are men. In *Mansfield Park*, Austen says in her own narrative voice, moderating Fanny's criticisms of Mary Crawford, that "impartiality would not have denied to Miss Crawford's nature that participation of the general nature of women, which would lead her to adopt the opinions of the man she loved and respected, as her own" (367). This does not mean that women are slavish. Austen can laugh at the eagerness of the naive Catherine Morland of *Northanger Abbey*, or the falsely sophisticated Mrs. Elton of *Emma*, for an exaggerated version of the very tendency she describes here; her more mature and intelligent heroines are not so worshipful. Nor do the heroes overtly instruct their wives (even Mr. Knightley implies that his reprimand at Box Hill will be the last instance of his tutoring). There is always the idea that marriage is a relation of equality: Anne, walking with Admiral Croft, reflects that "as she was not really Mrs. Croft she must let him have his own way" (P 170), and Mr. Knightley says that the only woman who will ever "invite what guests she pleases" to Donwell is Mrs. Knightley, when she is in existence (E 354). Nevertheless, Austen seems to think it is natural that women's opinions are adaptable and indicates that this is one hope for the happiness of marriage. Elizabeth's liberties with Mr. Darcy will soften his mind, and her own mind, Elizabeth feels, would receive "benefit of greater importance" from "his judgment, information, and knowledge of the world" (312).

The context of Austen's comment about the adaptability of women's opinions is, notably, in defense of marriage between the morally questionable Mary Crawford and Edmund Bertram. Someone more set on defending "patriarchal" relations than is Austen would more deplore the idea that an upright clergyman such as Edmund could be attracted to, and even justified in marrying, one so disrespectful of his position as Mary. Austen is willing to let such things take their course. If Mary really did accept Edmund—the attraction would have to be love and respect, given his lack (in her eyes) of worldly inducements—it can be expected that she will come around to his view. (The same is suggested of Lucy Steele if she were to marry the fortuneless Edward Ferrars in *Sense and Sensibility*.)

Women's Friendship

Anthony Trollope said of *Emma* that it shows "wonderful knowledge of female character, and is severe on the little foibles of women with a severity which no man would dare to use."[34] Austen herself likewise noted that a female acquaintance of hers "objected to my exposing the sex in the character of the heroine [of *Emma*]."[35] To see what these female failings are, we might turn to Emma herself. According to her, "the worst of all her womanly follies" was her failure to choose a proper friend (463). If she had sought to find a friend in Jane Fairfax— marked by "birth, abilities and education" to be her associate (421)— instead of developing a "wilfull intimacy" with Harriet Smith (463) she might have been "spared from every pain" regarding Mr. Knightley (421). While it might be argued that the novel somehow points to the potential of friendship between Emma and Jane Fairfax, we must wonder why it is a "*womanly*" folly to reject such an equal friendship. Austen deliberately suggests that this error is not unique to Emma. The novel's very emphasis on the reasons why Emma and Jane should have been friends (104, 166, 170–71, 203, 421), and the fact that they are not, seems meant to raise a question about the possibility of it.

Emma blames her mistake on vanity of an especially feminine sort. She was drawn to Harriet because Harriet wanted someone to look up to and to guide her (27); Emma is flattered, of course, but she also enjoys being of use. It would seem that she did not feel she could do anything for Jane. Of course, jealousy is part of what makes Emma dislike Jane—she has both "envious feelings" for Jane's accomplishments (421, see also 203) and perhaps some (unacknowledged) jealousy of Mr. Knightley's high regard of Jane. But the fact that her chief feeling is that Jane does not need her is substantiated by the fact that Emma only becomes friendly with Jane as she begins to pity her (168, 171, 363, 379–80, 391) and to see what she could do for her: she wants to show "regard or sympathy" and "wanted to be of use to her" (389).

The kind of friendship Austen portrays between women is not so much the deep friendship of two individuals as a kind of solidarity due to similar situation. Mrs. Weston thinks that "no man can be a good judge" of "the comfort a woman feels in the society of one of her own sex" (E 36). Austen always indicates that talk between women alone is less reserved than talk in mixed company [e.g., P 230]. The comfort of a woman's conversation that she defends here presumes the convention of feminine modesty with men. Interestingly, those heroines who are least modest are also least apt to be good friends to other women. Despite the professions of friendship between Lady Susan and Alicia Johnson, both are willing to set the practice of the friendship aside when it would require any sacrifice (MW 296, 307); see also the contrast between Isabella Thorpe's professions of friendship to Catherine and her actions (e.g., NA 98, 146). Fanny has reason to doubt the depth of Mary Crawford's friendship to herself, which Mary has made so much of (MP 433).

Fanny sounds more like a feminist than does Mary when she reflects that she *would* have thought "that every woman must have felt the possibility of a man's not being approved . . . by some one of her own sex" for it ought not "be set down as certain, that a man must be acceptable to every woman he may happen to like himself" (MP 353). The point of solidarity between women is to defend each other's feelings and choices, lest they be taken advantage of by men. Emma fears she has transgressed the duty of woman by woman in betraying her suspicions of Jane Fairfax's feelings to Frank Churchill (231, compare Isabella Thorpe's conduct with Catherine, e.g., NA 98, 146), and we are led to doubt her confidence that she "had done nothing which woman's friendship and woman's feelings would not justify" in regard to Harriet (67). By assuming that Harriet could not love Robert Martin (and so persuading her), she shows the same lack of feeling that Elizabeth Bennet showed in criticizing her friend Charlotte for her choice (PP 124–25).

There are many friendships between women in the novels, but none of them is the equal of married love, and many have a fundamental problem. Lady Russell, for example, is one of the most impressive friends. She is "capable of strong attachments" and proves this in the end when, because she "loved Anne better than her own abilities," she can make a friend of the man she has so long worked against (11, 249). This is a remarkable quality, for Jane Austen is fully aware of the tendency to hate those we have ill-treated: Mrs. Norris "disliked Fanny because she had neglected her" (MP 332). But, of course, all confidence on the most important points to Anne has ceased between them since Lady Russell's unfortunate advice. There is great affection between Emma and Mrs. Weston but again no turning to each other in matters of real importance. To repeat, Austen does not belittle such friendships. Even after Elizabeth has been disappointed in her friend Charlotte, she continues to correspond with her "for the sake of what had been, rather than what was" (PP 146). The novels never disparage this kind of delicacy, or the genuine affection that exists between many friends.[36]

The deepest friendships in the novels are not those between women as such but between siblings. The narrator of *Mansfield Park* says it is "*unnatural*" for children "of the same family, the same blood, with the same first associations and habits" to be estranged (235), although she admits "too often, alas! it is so" (235). (Lady Bertram and her sister Mrs. Price are one example of how such ties can become "little more than nothing" [428].) The friendship between Fanny and William Price is the most open and deep one Austen portrays, outside of marriage. Jane and Elizabeth Bennet, and Marianne and Elinor Dashwood are also examples of deep sibling affection: *Sense and Sensibility* ends by pointing out that one of their chief sources of happiness is that "though sisters, and living almost within sight of each other" they live without disagreement (380). There is a natural basis for these friendships, although even they require virtue to make them lasting.[37]

Emma's situation seems to be summed up by the line that is, in her words, "the cream" of the charade Mr. Elton has written for her: "And woman, lovely woman, reigns alone" (73). The solution to this charade is the word "courtship." Emma's delight in this particular gallantry (of course, she thinks it is meant for Harriet) reflects its aptness for herself. Emma feels herself to be in some sense self-sufficient; she does not have a strong need for an equal friend of her own sex. (Consider also Elinor Dashwood, who despite her great love for her sister does not confide in her because she is "stronger alone" [SS 141].) This womanly feeling may be a folly—Emma deprives herself of a good thing— but Austen seems to understand it. In the solution to the charade, "courtship," Austen perhaps alludes to something she never stresses, that the relation between a man and a woman—however much she may show it to be, at heart, friendship—contains an element that is different, one that is consistent with women reigning alone, one, that is, of ruling. One irony of this passage is that the charade does not make Emma reflect on her belief that "love is not my way, or my nature" (84).

Feminine Power and Feminine Modesty

Mr. Elton's charade is the passing pleasantry of a minor and unimpressive character, but the issue raised by it is a serious one for Austen's work as a whole. The question is what the differences between women and men—which she plainly admits—mean for the relations between them. This issue is the one at stake between Rousseau and Mary Wollstonecraft. Rousseau's *Emile* suggests that women are able to manipulate or rule men, precisely because of their different nature: "The more women want to resemble [men], the less women will govern men, and then men will truly be the masters."[38] Wollstonecraft, citing this passage, says, "This is the very point I aim at. I do not wish them to have power over men but over themselves."[39]

On the matter of power, perhaps more than anything, we see how Austen distances herself from both these thinkers. Unlike Rousseau, she does not believe that power over men is the only option for women, whom she always portrays as rational creatures. The point Wollstonecraft makes here rings more true to the novels and it is important to see that Austen is much more like Wollstonecraft than like the modern feminists who have tried to read her novels as a matter of power relations.[40] Nevertheless, there is a certain way in which both Wollstonecraft and Rousseau are part of a liberal tradition that focuses not only on an individual's duties (which are not dictated by human nature but by one's consent) but especially on his or her rights, a subject that Austen conspicuously avoids. She writes no more to vindicate the rights of man than the rights of woman.

The sort of loyalty to other women that Austen describes is distinguished from the pursuit of women's rights. Emma's reason for preventing Harriet from marrying a suitable man who would have her happy is that she considered Harriet's refusal to be a point of "female right and refinement" (65). Emma explains her action to Mr. Knightley by appealing again to the claims of women in general: "a man always imagines a woman to be ready for anybody who asks her" (60). With such comments Emma can resemble the insufferable Mrs. Elton, who declares,

I always take the part of my own sex. I do indeed. I give you notice—You
will find me a formidable antagonist. . . . I always stand up for women
(306).

Mrs. Elton, who snubs Emma and Harriet and whose services for Jane
Fairfax are a sort of parody of Emma's for Harriet, shows how such
advocacy in the abstract does not translate into real respect for other
particular women. Anne Elliot's fretful sister Mary is another whose
speeches for the rights of women—"if anything disagreeable is going
on, men are sure to get out of it," for example (56)—indicate a lack of
self-knowledge. The point is not that Austen thought women had fewer
rights than men, but rather that she thought that an insistence on one's
rights is not only in poor taste but also does not contribute to the best
kind of happiness.

Austen's reticence about rectifying the wrongs toward women ac-
cords with her general tendency, as I have argued, to be silent about the
side of justice that makes claims upon others. Wollstonecraft worries
that "the being, who patiently endures injustice, and silently bears insults, will soon become unjust, or unable to discern right from
wrong."[41] She implies that justice is a mean between committing injustice and suffering from it.[42] Nothing in Austen's novels denies this fact,
and yet it is important that she does not seem to worry much about
suffering unjustly. It is implied, of course, that her heroines would not
put up with such insults as Mrs. Palmer receives from her husband in
Sense and Sensibility, not to mention more serious mistreatment. Elizabeth Bennet's calm, pointed, and controlled retorts to Lady Catherine's
abuse of her (PP 356–58) are a model of how to stick by one's principles even in the face of injustice. (Fanny Price's ability to withstand her
uncle's unjust charges and keep her resolve against Henry Crawford is
another such example.) As we have seen in other matters as well, Austen
is more interested in the gracefulness that does not insist on one's due.
We see, for example, how Anne and Elizabeth Elliot are both "very,
very happy" as they enter a particular concert. For Elizabeth this is due
to the dignity of arriving with her noble cousins—in "looking on the
broad back of the dowager Viscountess Dalrymphle" she had "nothing
to wish for which did not seem within her reach" (P 185). Austen argues that it is an "insult" to the nature of Anne's happiness—that of
"generous attachment"—to compare it to this "selfish vanity" that is
happy to receive its due.

The Possibility of Feminine Power

Austen was, of course, a modern writer. This is why her defense of
the possibility that happiness can come from virtue, and of the true

pleasures (including romantic ones) of controlling one's desires, takes the form of a criticism of the prevailing counterview that would focus not on happiness but on power. Mary Crawford, urging Fanny to marry Henry, says she will have "the glory of fixing one who has been shot at by so many," and of having it "in one's power to pay off the debts of one's sex! Oh, I am sure it is not in woman's nature to refuse such a triumph" (MP 363). (Mary's view, like Emma's appreciation of the charade, shows that there is something in woman's nature that does seek power.) Austen sets out to show that it is also in woman's (better) nature to refuse such power and glory. Fanny *can* refuse the triumph Mary describes, not because she is too unassuming but because she has too high a regard for her own happiness. Maria Bertram, unlike Fanny, finds the only pleasure in her engagement to be "showing her power over Mr. Rushworth" (MP 70), and her desire to show her independence from Henry Crawford makes her go ahead with her marriage (202). Her pursuit of power and independence (the words "cool" and "cold" are constantly applied to her [e.g., 200, 202, 423, 466]) is *not* the pursuit of happiness: she can in fact only "throw a mist" over her future (107).

Austen's most thoroughgoing critique of feminine power is in the portrayal of the heroine of her early *Lady Susan*.[43] She seems to consider such a coquettish woman only fit for a quite funny parody,[44] and then she rejects female power as a central subject for her mature novels. In this early work, we can especially see the grounds for difference between her and Rousseau. Lady Susan is a master of art (contrast how the artlessness of the later heroines is always stressed): "artlessness will never do in love matters" (MW 274). But her highest art is an imitation of nature. Lady Susan can be seen as a satire on Rousseau's thesis that "to be a woman means to be coquettish, but her coquetry changes its form and its object according to her views."[45] Lady Susan's grand designs are on the virtuous (if somewhat shallow) Reginald de Courcy, and for him she cannot be giddy and frivolous. As she says, "I have never behaved less like a Coquette in the whole course of my life, tho' perhaps my desire of dominion was never more decided. I have subdued him entirely by sentiment and serious conversation" (MW 258). She loses her man, however, because she ultimately cannot conceal the evidence of her vice. ("Facts are such horrid things!" [303]). Of course Rousseau would require the woman to be truly, and not just seemingly, virtuous; nevertheless, Austen makes fun of the way in which a coquette obscures the difference. There is an echo of Lady Susan in Mary Crawford's attempt to win over Edmund. Mary remembers with exquisite happiness seeing ''his sturdy spirit to bend as it did! Oh! it was sweet beyond expression'' (MP 358). The aftermath of *Lady Susan*, in which Mrs. Vernon waits on her and almost ''turns from her with horror'' when she sees ''no consciousness of guilt'' or ''look of embarrassment'' (MW 311) is replayed too in Edmund Bertram's final parting from Mary Crawford. Austen (unlike Rousseau) always seems to associate a woman's conscious use of power with selfishness and separateness.

Nor is Austen's criticism of power limited to these instances of its misuse. We have seen how Elizabeth Bennet, despite Charlotte's belief that she would love Mr. Darcy once she knew him to be in her power, actually loves him when she sees her power declining and thus realizes how much she needs him, and how Emma Woodhouse similarly recognizes her love at the moment she feels a *loss* of independence. Real attachment means becoming part of another person, and feminine modesty facilitates this attachment. Wollstonecraft objects that when modesty is made a sexual virtue, women's virtue has ''no other foundation than utility'' (51). Austen does not disdain the utility of virtue so much as Wollstonecraft does. At the same time, Austen indicates that modesty is not primarily calculating but has a more natural or reasonable foundation.

Reasons for Feminine Modesty

Female modesty is generally portrayed as a *positive* quality in Austen's novels; it is not a duty imposed by an unfeeling society. Although one of her critics defines modesty as ''the extent to which women do *not* feel, express, and pursue their own desires,''[46] Austen's novels argue the reverse: it is the women who *most* feel their own desires (such as Elinor Dashwood, Fanny Price, and Anne Elliot) who are most modest. Modesty is a way to avoid being controlled by one's feelings; it is not expected to deny those feelings' existence. Austen makes fun, in *Northanger Abbey*, of the idea that because a woman should not profess her love first, she therefore can't *feel* love for a man before he does for her. Austen's most modest and timid heroine, Fanny Price, does this very thing.

Austen usually, in fact, indicates that modest reserve is a *sign* of particularly deep feeling. ''Bad indeed must the nature of Marianne's affliction be, when her mother could talk of fortitude'' (SS 213), Elinor thinks. And in *Emma*, Emma Woodhouse worries that Harriet's second disappointment in love will be more severe than her first, for she is "judging by [the second love's] apparently stronger effect on Harriet's mind, producing reserve and self-command" (E 403). Self-command seems to be a natural response to deep feeling: as usual, Austen indicates that ease of conversation does not reveal great moral and emotional depth. Elinor responds to feeling with increasing self-command (her "exertion of spirits . . . increased with her increase of emotions" [130]), Anne Elliot only freely gives reign to her fears at the moment they become much less foreboding—when she is sure that the man she loves does love her (P 190–91). In contrast to Anne, the Musgrove girls openly encourage Captain Wentworth. They are more in love with him than he is with them, Anne thinks, yet even with them, "it was not love. It was a little fever of admiration; but it might, probably must, end in love with some" (82). Their immodest ease is what tells Anne they do not really love. Interestingly, while Austen suggests that such encouragement shows precisely a *lack* of love, she does acknowledge that these attentions might lead to love (as we see with Marianne Dashwood). In other words, we see again how love—even of the shallow kind felt by women like the Musgroves—is the result of what one gives to the other person even more than what one receives.

Of course there is some truth to Marianne's belief that "they who suffer little may be as proud and independent as they like" (189), for reserve does not *always* indicate deep feeling—in Lady Middleton it is due to the shallowness of her passions (see 215). And a show of emotion can be a relief, as when Elinor discovers her sister's pain at Willoughby's desertion and then herself gives way to "a burst of tears, which at first was scarcely less violent than Marianne's" (182). Elinor's tears are real but this is not the moment of her *greatest* emotion in the book (cf. 135, 264). And her tears are only "at first" as violent as Marianne's: even they are a means to composure.

Modesty is not simply a sexual quality, but even there, Austen indicates it is natural. This is especially apparent in the scene in *Sense and Sensibility* in which Marianne meets Willoughby. Austen stresses the naturalness of this scene. Marianne and her sister "caught in their faces" the "animating gales" of a high wind and "pursued their way against the wind, resisting it with laughing delight" (41); they seem to feel a kinship with nature.[47] Marianne is caught by rain, trips and falls, and is carried away by a handsome stranger—and yet this is all done matter-of-factly:

> The gentleman offered his services, and perceiving that her modesty declined what her situation rendered necessary, took her up in his arms without further delay, and carried her down the hill (42).

Marianne and Willoughby's chance encounter is not improbable, for she is usually outdoors and he is usually hunting and her accident is a natural one. It is only Marianne's romantic imagination that makes this an instance of a knight saving a damsel in distress. Willoughby simply performs a natural and protective service. And, most interestingly— while Marianne's romantic imagination is partly responsible for her later lack of modesty with Willoughby—at this moment she is instinctively modest. We must wonder if modesty is as unnatural as she later insists.

Modesty is natural, Austen suggests, because it is reasonable; it is not *simply* a social convention. It is not in the spirit of *Sense and Sensibility* to say that "if one submits to society, every dream will come true."[48] The point is not that love is the inevitable reward of following convention, but that female modesty and propriety—far from being an affront to love—can contribute to attachment between two people. Marianne sees propriety to aim at "the restraint of sentiments which [are] not in themselves illaudable" (53), but the novel as a whole does not present it this way. Propriety does not simply require self-restraint, but rather the "delicacy" that discerns what is right.

To put this another way, in talking about love Austen does not stress the *feeling* of affection so much as the attachment itself, the involvement of two people in each other's concerns. This sort of attachment usually takes time but always requires the assurance of the other person's goodness. Marianne says she could not love Willoughby, nor could Elizabeth love Wickham or Fanny love Henry Crawford, once they believe these men lack virtue. Marianne, like the other heroines, "has not a heart, to be made happy with such a man" (SS 350). The problem is that her immodesty made it harder to determine his worth.

It has been argued that Austen's novels "burden their heroines with acquired notions about propriety" that do not protect them, for "it makes no difference whether one holds back with Elinor's modest caution or hurries forward with Marianne's dauntless ardour" as both are led to unwarranted hopes.[49] But the point is that a woman's modesty and virtue help her to be sure of a man's love—for Elinor's confidence in Edward's love for her is fully warranted. Elinor and Edward have each discerned the other's love despite all their regard for propriety (21–22, 139, 336). Elinor's chief consolation, the greatest "softener of the heart," is that Edward "certainly loved her" (140), a consolation that is not at all available to Marianne. In addition, Elinor has the consolation of knowing that it is a respect for *duty* that keeps Edward from marrying her and that she has nothing for which to blame herself (140–

41). None of these consolations is available to Marianne, who is tormented not only by the knowledge that someone she loved was so wicked, but also by how she appears to herself, given the possible consequences of her "most shamefully unguarded affection" (345). Elinor and Marianne both suffer deeply, but one has behaved in such a way as to let her overcome her misfortune, while the other's actions cause her almost to die from it. A woman's modesty may not protect her from all contingencies, any more than it protects her from loving, but her virtue allows her happiness not to rest *solely* on good fortune.

Furthermore, a woman's modesty is shown to influence a man's behavior toward herself. Marianne encouraged Willoughby's attentions by flattering attentions to him (see 46–48), ignoring propriety to the extent of writing letters to him because, as she tells her sister, she felt "as solemnly engaged to him, as if the strictest legal covenant had bound us" (188). Elinor points out that "unfortunately he did not feel the same" (188). And Willoughby later confesses that Marianne's attentions did not win his heart (it was left "insensible") but his vanity only was elevated (320). Marianne's sexual and romantic interest in Willoughby has aroused in her a sense of loyalty to him, but his similar interest in her was not enough to enforce a sense of duty. (This may be another sign of a woman's greater conventionality.) To the good-hearted Mrs. Jennings, it is "the oddest thing" that "a man should use such a pretty girl so ill" (194), but it is implied that this statement is as naive as the one preceding it, in which she expresses surprise that her dried cherries have not cured Marianne's romantic disappointment. Austen does not rely on charm, even the charm of virtue, to secure loyalty.

Just as there is no equivalence in the situations of Marianne and Elinor, so we should not let a certain outward similarity between Edward and Willoughby—both arouse expectations of marriage that they do not intend to fulfill—blind us to the fact that they are in important ways opposite in their behavior. Many of Austen's critics have been disturbed by the fact that the novel implicitly suggests that Edward was right to uphold his engagement to a woman he no longer loved.[50] But it should be kept in mind that Edward behaves no differently than the more charming Captain Wentworth of *Persuasion*, who says he would have been bound to marry Louisa Musgrove, despite his love for Anne Elliot, if Louisa had wished it—even though in this case there was no formal engagement (P 242). And even Marianne, who so often scorns conventional propriety, never suggests that Edward should break his engagement to Lucy; on the contrary, she as much as Elinor appreciates the "true merit" in his behavior (270). Edward *is* blamable for allowing himself to become attached to Elinor (140), but—to her—this is a forgivable mistake. What she could not forgive would be him breaking his word to another woman, even if that woman is so little worthy of it as is Lucy (see 141, 179, 260, 270, for the role of Elinor's esteem for Edward's virtue in her love for him). Edward is caught unawares by love and resists it out of duty, while Willoughby indulges his vanity and then manages to overcome love by attention to self-interest.

Marianne's immodesty makes her fail to look within Willoughby for the concern for virtue that Austen always shows to be needed if love is to last. Elinor points out (and Marianne admits) that if Willoughby had married Marianne, their poverty would have forced Marianne to "abridge his enjoyments" and "is it not to be feared that . . . you would have lessened your own influence on his heart?" (351). If she only influences him insofar as she contributes to his pleasure, there is no security that their love will last. As Rousseau puts it of Sophie, she would disdain a man who "did not love her for her virtues as much as, and more than, for her charms, and which did not prefer [his] own duty to her and hers to everything else . . . she did not want a lover who knew no law other than hers."[51] This is why Elinor would not want to marry Edward if he forsook his duty to Lucy.

Austen makes fun of the idea of a woman being the only law to a man in the Box Hill scene in *Emma*, where Frank Churchill's gallantry is shown at its worst. He (in jest, of course) tells Emma that hers is the only command he knows and goes on to demand that everyone pay homage to her charms (369–73). His conduct is brutal to Jane, embarrassing to Emma, and offensive to almost everyone else; Austen clearly mocks this type of lover and suggests that he ought to be under "self-command" (369).

In *Northanger Abbey*, the author offers an explicit discussion of the way in which a woman's virtue influences a man's behavior. Catherine says she cannot like Henry Tilney's brother Frederick, for what if by flirting with Isabella he had made her in love with him? Henry replies that this assumes Isabella "had a heart to lose," in which case she would "have been a very different creature . . . and would have met with very different treatment" (NA 219). Isabella's "vain coquett[ery]," her obvious flirtation with Frederick, made Frederick think she has no heart. Henry suggests that true feeling and virtue would have earned more respect. Marianne condemns herself for having behaved in a way typical of women like Isabella, and it is true that her manners made her the sport of a man's vanity. Nevertheless, Austen never indicates that "heart" is all a matter of outward manner. Marianne is not Isabella, and she *almost* meets with different treatment. Although Willoughby, like Frederick, at first tries to please Marianne only for his own amusement, he does recognize her merits and real feeling, begins to love her, and—for at least a short while—determines to "justify the attentions" he had paid her (SS 321).

Modesty and the Pursuit of Marriage

Of course, a modest manner is not always a guarantee of a woman's virtue, any more than Austen suggests that good manners are an assurance of any virtue. In *Mansfield Park*, Edmund and Mary criticize the way in which many girls' "coming out" produce a change from complete reserve to too much "confidence" of manner (MP 49). Edmund objects that this shows the girls' vanity, and that they have no more "real modesty" before appearing in public than afterwards. Mary nonetheless defends the convention, arguing that it is much worse "to have girls *not out*, give the same airs and take the same liberties as if they were," which she finds "disgusting" (MP 50). The hint of something questionable in this is confirmed by Tom Bertram's rapid endorsement of her view, citing the "scrapes" he has gotten into by not knowing whether a girl was "out." The point of the convention of coming "out" is to let a man know that a woman is eligible for marriage. Mary's and Tom's defense of it shows an attitude toward marriage that the novels do not particularly endorse: Mary does not want girls "not out" competing for men with the girls who are "out," and Tom only wants to be able to flirt without making anyone angry.

Immodesty always goes along with a lack of seriousness about marriage in the novels. That is to say, Austen reflects upon the irony that those who do not take marriage seriously are most in pursuit of it—most dependent on men. Neither Mary Crawford nor Charlotte Lucas takes seriously the possibility that marriage can be a meaningful attachment. Mary believes that 99 out of 100 people are "taken in when they marry" (MP 46) and Charlotte that "happiness in marriage is entirely a matter of chance" (PP 23). And yet both of them are in pursuit of marriage, seemingly eager to take their chances. For Charlotte, "without thinking highly either of men or of matrimony, marriage had always been her object" (PP 122), and for Mary "matrimony was her object, provided she could marry well" (MP 42). (The thoughtless Lydia Bennet also belongs in this camp, as we have seen.) Both the aggressiveness and the resignation shown by these opinions seem to be signs of the lack of heart that Elizabeth complains about in her friend. Charlotte and Mary, in fact, both doubt that there is much "heart" in the world (PP 22, MP 359), and it is the possibility of this sort of attachment that Austen defends. Mary says that at Mansfield Park there is "more *heart* among you, than one finds in the world at large" (MP 359).

Modesty is shown to be the result of a heart that feels deeply and properly; nevertheless, Austen does not disdain its useful purpose in helping a woman determine the nature of a *man*'s heart. Charlotte Lucas's advice, early in *Pride and Prejudice*—that a woman should show even more affection than she feels, because few [men] have "heart enough to be really in love without encouragement"—might seem vindicated by the fact that Mr. Bingley has *not* been able to tell that the modest and reserved Jane loved him. But the novel seems ultimately to support Elizabeth's view, that if a woman "is partial to a man, and does not endeavor to conceal it, he must find it out" (22). Mr. Bingley *did*, he admits, suspect that Jane liked him, and the fact that he allowed his friends to persuade him otherwise—the fact, perhaps, that he needed more overt encouragement from her—only shows that he does not have the highest kind of "heart." (So we might have suspected from the fact that he has often been in love before [PP 197].) Jane does not blame Mr. Bingley's friends as much as Elizabeth does, for she rightly points out that if he really were attached to her, they could not succeed in keeping him away (137).

It might be pointed out that Rousseau's Sophie in *Emile* feels the same distaste in searching for a husband as do all of Austen's heroines. Rousseau attributes it to pride:

> For the haughty Sophie carried in the depth of her heart a noble pride in knowing how to triumph over herself; and whatever need she had of a husband, she would rather die a maiden than resolve to look for one.[52]

Austen is fully aware of the praiseworthy sort of pride that takes pleasure in overcoming desires. But she is much less inclined than Rousseau to insist on a woman's desire or need for marriage. We cannot imagine *any* of the heroines becoming, like Sophie, despondent, distracted, and in ill-health because she so much felt her need for a husband and also felt the impossibility of choosing.[53] Even Anne Elliot is not reduced to this state. Nor could Austen allow a romance such as *The Adventures of Telemachus*—or any book—to play such a fundamental role in the direction of the heroine's desires. To indulge one's feelings in this fashion is always presented as immoral in the novels. Just as Austen herself did not pine away without a husband, so she always suggests that her heroines—much as they will find happiness with the man they truly love—have minds that are capable of happiness without marriage.

Austen's lack of interest in adultery as a theme—a fact that distinguishes her from the Romantic tradition that followed Rousseau— reflects this belief. For her, marriage is not the source of all duty and attachments. As Elinor Dashwood puts it, explaining why she kept her secret about Edward's engagement, "I did not love only him" (263). The reason for Sophie's distress is that she must choose both a "lover" and a "husband," and Rousseau believes these qualities are difficult to combine.[54] Many reasons could be suggested for why Austen does not see this as an impossible problem, but one of them is that her best characters do not feel that it is absolutely necessary to have either a lover or a husband. Their "firmness of mind" means that they do not require a happy marriage to survive, as certain lesser characters do (consider Harriet Smith's "safety" in a happy marriage [E 482]).

Austen explicitly suggests that one with a "firm mind" might not need a happy marriage (this is not to say it wouldn't be desirable) in the story of the two Elizas inserted in *Sense and Sensibility*. This story is one of the few places where Austen does discuss adultery. Colonel Brandon puts particular emphasis on the fact that the young Eliza's disgrace mirrored that of her mother and namesake. Perhaps Austen means to call our attention to the "strikingly great" resemblance between Marianne and her mother, who, despite her age, shares Marianne's "happy ardour of youth" and "romantic delicacy" (85, 159). Colonel Brandon compares Marianne to the younger Eliza and predicts that she will not have Eliza's fate because her "natural sweet disposition" will be "guarded by a firmer mind or a happier marriage" (208). As Eliza's fate followed her mother's, so Marianne will be protected, as her mother was, by a happier marriage rather than a firmer mind (for Mrs. Dashwood's marital happiness, see p. 18). Marianne's sweetness will be protected by Colonel Brandon's true love, and she will find "her own happiness in forming his" (379).

Eliza's case is a cautionary tale about the importance of being sure of a man's love and virtue, not only because of the risk of rape instead of marriage, but also because of the temptation to infidelity after marriage if one has misjudged.[55] A happy marriage will guard against the temptations of desire. Austen, however, allows for the possibility that *some* women with "firmer minds" do not need a happy marriage to keep them from being in control of their desires. Some men also need this protection. Mrs. Norris may speak in the "blindness of her anger" in blaming Fanny for the fate of Henry and Maria, but while her blame is inappropriate, her suggestion that a marriage between Fanny and Henry might have prevented this outcome may be true (MP 448). As Mary Crawford puts it, Fanny "would have fixed him" (MP 455–6). Of course Fanny, no more than the other heroines, would not wish to be married to someone whose *own* firmness of mind could not be relied on.

To Austen, the fact that a woman does not *need* a man is not an aggressive statement of independence, but rather an expression of the feminine delicacy that her best characters possess. Elizabeth's belief in the potential happiness of marriage makes her unwilling to accept just any husband, and unwilling to go out in search of a husband. Her delicacy on this point seems to be a sign of her femininity. In a scene in Austen's unfinished novel, *The Watsons*, Penelope Watson's pursuit of a husband and situation is said to show "too masculine and bold a temper" (MW 318). Mary Crawford is not "perfectly feminine" when she speaks lightly of marriage, and a significant detail about the fearless and bold Lydia (8, 315) is her delight in dressing up a male servant in women's clothes (231). Charlotte's aggressive beliefs about conduct in courtship seem to Elizabeth to be "not a proper way of thinking" (22, 135). Charlotte's choice is condemned on the grounds of being improper or distasteful, even if she has not, like Lydia, violated "virtue and decency."

Elizabeth's pure principles let her criticize *both* the marriage of Charlotte (whose prudent marriage is quite proper by conventional standards) and that of Lydia (whose marriage is necessitated by propriety). What Edmund Bertram might call her "feminine loathings" make her disapprove not only of extramarital sex but also of conventionally acceptable marriage that is not justified by real love. The novel does not judge only by the opinion of the world: the criticisms of both marriages come from the point of view of love and integrity, not worldly respectability.[56]

Just as a woman's virtue is shown to earn a man's respect, Austen often suggests that a woman finds a man's respect for his duty to be lovable. This is the charm of Mr. Knightley, and even Mary Crawford surprises herself by being charmed by the "sincerity, steadiness and integrity" of Edmund Bertram (MP 65). In *Persuasion*, we see a scene in which Captain Wentworth, unseen and unheard of "for two whole days," returns to Uppercross to justify himself. He explains that he was kept away because he discovered an old friend in poor health after a battle wound, and had to stay with him. When the women hear his story, "his acquittal was complete, his friendship warmly honoured, a lively interest was excited for his friend" (94). His humane act more than justifies his lack of gallant attentiveness to them.[57] This story is almost an exact retelling of the scene in *Emile* in which Emile is delayed in coming to Sophie because he stops to help a crippled peasant and his needy family. After hearing Emile's explanation—"do not make me forget the rights of humanity. They are more sacred to me than yours"—Sophie accepts him as a husband.[58] Now, Austen's portrayal of compassion and humanity is different in fundamental ways from Rousseau's.[59] Nevertheless, like him, she shows how a sense of duty toward others makes a woman trust the promises of love.

Modesty and a Woman's Choice

One point of the presumption that men will keep their promises is to allow women, despite the requirement that they be modest, a real choice in marriage. A woman's choice of a husband may be only the power of refusal—"man has the advantage of choice, woman only the power of refusal (NA 77)," says Henry Tilney, comparing an agreement to dance to one to marry—but Austen assumes in all her novels that this choice, to decline or break an engagement, belongs to women alone. Edward Ferrars's honor is not just a matter of form. He has continued his engagement because, until Lucy's last letter, "he had always believed her to be a well-disposed, good-hearted girl, and thoroughly attached to himself" (367), and there is ample evidence in the novel of Lucy's ability to misrepresent herself so. The implication—here again is Austen's lack of extremism or legalism—is that some considerations *would* allow Edward to break his engagement. These would be evidence of her own lack of love for him; not his lack of love for her.

Austen is not defending a code of honor but a willingness to fulfill one's reasonable obligations to another. It is implied in *Northanger Abbey* that James Morland broke off his engagement with Isabella after seeing evidence that she loved someone else. He does not "enter into particulars" of the breaking-up (202), but Isabella's later disingenuous comment—she is afraid "he took something in my conduct amiss" (217)—implies that her actions, not her words, led to the end of the engagement. What to do in a given case always depends on the circumstances, for Austen, and here we see that a man is not bound to marry a woman who obviously does not care for him and flirts with others, even if, "to the very last, she declared herself as much attached to [him] as ever" (202). (A "yes" does not always mean "yes.") This does not deny the fact that a man must keep a promise to a woman who has kept hers. As Captain Wentworth puts it about Louisa, he is "hers in honor *if she wished it*" (P 242, my emphasis).

Women's right to refuse or annul an engagement is not a condescending courtesy but rather a way to equalize relations between men and women. The requirements of modesty do not let a woman choose a man, but her right to refuse allows her to be the judge of his virtue. Henry Tilney's analogy of dance to marriage is deliberately overdrawn, but it is true that in both the man lets the woman judge his merits. We see the first proof of Mr. Darcy's attraction for Elizabeth in the scene in which he asks her, one evening, to dance a reel. Elizabeth claims that he does not really want to dance but rather to despise her taste, and thus she will say she does *not* want to dance. She adds "and now despise me if you dare," and he replies, simply, "Indeed I do not dare" (52). His response shows that he does not take her regard for granted: he desires her good opinion. (Rousseau argues that the fact that no man wants to be despised by a woman is what makes women the natural judges of men.)[60] The problem with Mr. Darcy's proposal of marriage is that it (unlike the request for a dance) *is* contemptuous—he only *speaks* of "apprehension and anxiety" (189). Elizabeth cannot accept him until he takes seriously her responsibility to accept or reject him. He must explain his character to her.

Austen always stresses the element of choice in virtue. A man's duty is what he can always *choose* to do (E 146); humans are responsible for their actions. This is why the woman's choice to accept or refuse an engagement is so important. Edmund says that there is "no sacrifice" in Maria's engagement to Mr. Rushworth, for "it is entirely her own doing" (108). Austen does not seem to *insist* that it is immoral to marry someone one doesn't love, if the man and woman both respect duty. (Perhaps it is better to say that the type of love need not be very romantic or deep. Charlotte's marriage to Mr. Collins is not inspiring but it may work, as have the marriages of such couples as the senior Bertrams and Bennets.) Nevertheless, it clearly *is* immoral to marry one person while loving someone else, for the simple reason that this love would threaten the duties of marriage. This is why it is essential that the woman be able to refuse a match. It is also why Austen is against long engagements as a rule, for she does not rely on love alone to keep two people together. (There is too much risk that one of them, not being bound by marriage, will allow him or herself to love someone else.)

Modesty and Women's Education

That some modesty is affected does not allow the conclusion that a modest manner is not the natural result of real "heart." Austen's careful distinctions in the scene about "ins" and "outs" are typical of the way she holds conventions to the light of reason. Her defense of modesty is not one of the artificial restraint of young girls. Elizabeth Bennet defends to Lady Catherine the fact that all of her sisters are "out," arguing that it would not be fair for the youngest sisters to miss the pleasures of society because "the elder may not have the means or inclination to marry early." And "to be kept back on such a motive" [of getting the older ones married off]—"I think it would not be very likely to promote sisterly affection or delicacy of mind" (165). This convention, instead of promoting true modesty, promotes the *lack* of delicacy in its treatment of marriage as a market and a necessity. In *Mansfield Park*, "coming out" is explicitly called a "trade": "Miss Price had not been brought up to the trade of *coming out*" (267).

This language—that Fanny has not been "brought up to the trade" of displaying herself in public—is reminiscent of Edmund saying about the theater that he does not want to look at the efforts of those "who have not been bred to the trade" of acting (124). *Mansfield Park* only makes explicit the sense in all of the novels that the author wishes to defend women as belonging to a private sphere. The word "trade" is degrading in both of the above contexts, suggesting that this sort of public display is like selling oneself. The objections to this private theater, all carefully outlined (125), have to do with the particular circumstances of this family, and especially to Maria's "delicate" situation (the stress on the delicacy of it alludes to the unstated truth that she is engaged to a man she doesn't love). The immodesty of the women's parts in the play that is chosen adds deeper objections, including the idea of the women displaying themselves before strangers (125, 148–49, 154). Fanny feels the women's parts are

> so totally improper for home representation—the situation of one, and the language of the other, so unfit to be expressed by any woman of modesty (137),

and even Maria instinctively blushes when Edmund, shocked at the choice of play, asks what they will do for women (139). Of course none of the women who wish to take part are "acting" at all; the play is a vehicle for the expression of their not-so-hidden passions. Austen chiefly objects to this play, at this time, but there is also a more general critique of the immodesty of women displaying themselves and their emotions. Maria's and Julia's lack of principle is directly blamed on their (encouraged) habit of seeking public distinction: their "authorized object" has been to be "distinguished for elegance and accomplishments" (463).

Austen criticizes womanly "accomplishments" not only from the point of view of reason but also from the point of view of modesty. There is an ascetic tone to the criticism in all Austen's novels of the concern with frivolities and affected "elegance" that she often associates with increasingly popular schools for women. The sense of change that is often discovered in *Persuasion* is present from the start of Austen's work and has to do with women's education. We hear in one well-known passage how "the Musgroves, like their houses, were in a state of alteration, perhaps of improvement" (P 40), for while the parents are "friendly and hospitable, not much educated, and not at all elegant," their children have "more modern minds and manners," having brought from a school at Exeter "all the usual stock of accomplishments" (40). This is almost identical to the account in Jane Austen's earlier novel, *Sense and Sensibility*, of the difference between Mrs. Palmer and her daughters. The uneducated, but friendly and hospitable, Mrs. Palmer was the wife of a tradesman in a less elegant part of town (153), and since his death she moves with her daughters in altered, *perhaps* improved, circles. Austen describes the Palmers' modern improvements with the same ironic distance used with the Musgroves: the wall displays "a landscape in coloured silks" done by her daughter Charlotte, "in proof of her having spent seven years at a great school in town to some effect" (160).

Austen laughs at these frivolities, and Wollstonecraft resents them, because while both believe in a woman's rationality, Austen has more confidence in her ability to exercise it whatever her circumstances. Women such as she writes about can discern well enough what is really worthwhile. One could say this is the very proof of their rationality (for rationality in Austen always means practical reason that is directed ultimately at happiness.[61]) Elizabeth Bennet's formal education was no more than the encouragement to read (165); the narrator of *Mansfield Park* says "a fondness for reading, if properly directed, must be an education in itself" (22). (Perhaps Elizabeth's father, like Edmund Bertram to Fanny, made reading "useful" by talking to her of what she read and "heightened its attraction" by judicious praise [MP 22].) Austen would never, with Wollstonecraft, recommend public schools in which the top students of both sexes would study the dead and living languages, the elements of science, and continue the study of history and politics, on a more extensive scale, which would not exclude polite literature.[62]

Austen often makes fun of lists like this (Emma has such plans, as does Marianne Dashwood after her illness, and Mr. Darcy in his prescription for a desirable woman), most humorously in *Mansfield Park*, when one of the Bertram girls brags that she has known for years all the kings of England, "Roman emperors as low as Severus; besides a great deal of the Heathen Mythology, and all the Metals, Semi-Metals, Planets and distinguished philosophers" (19). Her mother scolds her to remember there is much more to learn, and she replies "Yes, I know there is, until I am 17." The truth is that Austen does not think much of scholars. (We also see this caricatured in Mary Bennet and in Lady Catherine's suspect belief that "nothing is to be done in education without steady and regular instruction" [PP 165].)

Austen opposes a great concern with "accomplishments" in large part because the purpose is usually public display. Austen's heroines, having good taste, do not disdain the talent of, say, a musician such as Jane Fairfax. Yet, Mr. Darcy smiles at Elizabeth's criticism of her own piano-playing, saying

> You have employed your time much better. No one admitted to the privilege of hearing you, can think anything wanting. We neither of us perform to strangers (PP 176).

Mr. Darcy's smile indicates his perception that Elizabeth is really complimenting herself, and he includes himself in the praise. But along with the ironies is as always a certain surface truth: no one who sees Elizabeth can wish more accomplishments, and her genuine capacity to please has to do with the fact that she does not "perform," does not seek praise. In this context, it is worth remembering the comment Austen makes about Mr. Darcy prizing any picture of Elizabeth too much "to like it should be exposed to the public eye," a feeling he has out of "love, pride and delicacy."[63]

Now it could be argued fairly that Austen seeks a private life for *both* sexes. There is an explicit criticism of male ambition in *Sense and Sensibility* and *Mansfield Park*, whose heroes must defend themselves against those who want them to choose a more powerful or lucrative career. Even *Persuasion*, which features a more ambitious hero, has his highest hopes rest upon domestic happiness, and his profession is

"more distinguished in its domestic virtues than in its national importance" (252). The point of education for both sexes is the ability to act
in a way that shows discernment and, especially, to converse. Austen's
high value for conversation tempers the moralism of her view of education. Neither Fanny nor the author morally object, as has been suggested, to Henry Crawford's elegance and refinement.[64] In fact it is
the upright Fanny in whom "taste was too strong" to ignore Henry
Crawford's excellent reading of Shakespeare, or his good acting, despite her doubts about his character (337). In this same spirit, Austen
herself was pleased that her brother "admires Henry Crawford: I mean
properly, as a clever, pleasant man."[65]

The point on which education between the sexes is not identical,
however, concerns public exposure. It is true that Mr. Darcy, no more
than Elizabeth, "performs" for strangers. Men who do so (ranging
from the foppish Mr. Yates and Mr. Rushworth, to the smoother Mr.
Churchill, to the more dangerously insinuating Mr. Willoughby and Mr.
Wickham) are criticized. Austen, like Wollstonecraft, wants personal
reserve in both sexes, but she always implies that it is more important
for women. The idea that women should not be "exposed" does not
mean that they must be physically restrained. In fact, the outward restraint imposed on Maria by her father is one cause of her wish to
proceed with her engagement (202), and Julia's fear of greater severity
and restraint makes her elope after Maria's adultery (466). What the
Bertram girls lack, of course, is the ability for self-restraint (463); Lydia
Bennet, too, is marked by her "assurance and disdain of all restraint"
(231). In all these cases we see Austen's typical insistence that vanity
be tempered (but not destroyed) by seriousness. Lydia has "been given
up to amusement and vanity" (283), just as this was the authorized
object of Julia and Maria's youth.

Austen accepts the idea that women must not only be good, but must
appear to be good. (This is the basic principle of Rousseau's education
of women.)[66] Sir Thomas makes this distinction when he talks of
"snatching [Maria] from farther vice, though all was lost on the side of
character" (MP 451). A woman's "character" or reputation, then, is
not her only virtue. In *Lady Susan*, one sign of the heroine's lack of
real worthiness is that she so often speaks of what she owes to her
"own character," used in the sense of worldly reputation (MW 294,
300). And Austen uses Mary Bennet's moralizing to mock the idea that

'loss of virtue in a female is irretrievable—that one false step involves her
in endless ruin—that her reputation is no less brittle than it is beautiful . . .'

Elizabeth lifted up her eyes in amazement, but was too oppressed to make any reply (PP 289).

Aside from revealing her lack of real feeling on the occasion, Mary equates virtue and reputation in a way Austen does not. Lydia's reputation, furthermore, *is* retrievable. She will have "whatever of honour and credit could now be purchased for her" (308, cf. 387), says the narrator in language that is more humorous than cynical. Maria's reputation is hopeless because her behavior reveals vice and not just folly. (Adultery is worse than living with a man before marriage.) The narrator, reflecting on the fact that Maria will be punished so much more severely than Henry, reflects that "the penalty is less equal than could be wished," but, interestingly, seems to imply that *both* should be so punished. The "public punishment of disgrace" for men is not one of the protections "which society gives to virtue" (468). Like the convention of marriage, the purpose of this convention is to aid virtue.

Austen's superior characters are not tormented by adultery because a heart that can really love deeply has a kind of virtue, Austen always suggests, that makes it inconceivable to love someone who is married to someone else. Their respect for this conventional propriety does not indicate a lack of feeling, but rather a simple unwillingness to do something base or hurtful. Even those people in the novels with the "superior sort" of nature in which feelings are "acute and retentive" (such as Fanny Price and Anne Elliot) do not love eternally if there is no possibility of return. Their lasting, unrequited love would find another object, we are told, if the men they love were to marry someone else. And their love would not be so worth having, Austen suggests, if they could act otherwise.

Notes

1. Mary Wollstonecraft, *A Vindication of the Rights of Women*, 2d ed. Carol H. Poston (New York: W. W. Norton & Co., Norton Critical Edition, 1988), 64.
2. Ibid., 73.
3. Kirkham, "Feminist Irony," 234–35. The convictions of what Kirkham calls "rational feminism" were, as she points out, tame by modern feminist standards: that women have the same moral status and accountability as men and should be educated in line with this view, and that marriage is a partnership based on friendship and esteem.
4. Wollstonecraft is less reliant on virtue getting respect. Like Austen, she points out how reputation and outward manner can differ from real character,

and says that although a *man*'s real character will "work its way to light," for a woman, "morality is very insidiously undermined" by the fact that reputation is more important than virtue (Wollstonecraft, *A Vindication*, 135).

5. Ibid., 86.

6. Jean-Jacques Rousseau, *Emile*, trans. Allan Bloom (New York: Basic Books, 1979), 376.

7. Wollstonecraft, *A Vindication*, 9.

8. I discuss this theme in chapter 2 of the text.

9. Wollstonecraft, *A Vindication*, 9.

10. Austen makes fun of "romantic delicacy" (SS 85) or false "delicacy of feeling" (MW 249) or Mr. Collins's sense of "the true delicacy of the feminine character" (PP 108).

11. For some of the non-ironic uses of "delicacy of mind" and phrases like it, see SS 127, 140, 283; PP 128, 165; MP 81, 140, 231, 293, 321, 326, 397, 407, 431, 456; E 51, 149, 179, 439, 448; P 77, 230.

12. Wollstonecraft, *A Vindication*, 51.

13. There is no direct evidence that Austen knew the works of either Wollstonecraft or Rousseau, and yet it would be remarkable if she did not. Kirkham points out that she would have had access to Wollstonecraft's writing (*A Vindication* was published in 1792, five years before Austen's first novel) in her years in Bath (Kirkham, "Feminist Irony," 236). Equally accessible and well known would have been Rousseau's *Emile* (published in 1762 in Paris, with several English editions available at the end of the century) and especially his *Nouvelle Heloise*. (See James H. Warner, "Eighteenth-Century English Reactions to the *Nouvelle Heloise*, *PMLA* 52 [1937], 803–819; see also Edward Duffy, *Rousseau in England* [Berkeley: University of California Press, 1979].)

14. Feminists, including Wollstonecraft, do not often acknowledge the fact that Rousseau's most outrageous-sounding pronouncements about women in *Emile* are presented as the psychological component of biological needs. "Woman is made specially to please man," for example, is explained to be the consequence of the fact that sexual intercourse requires the arousal of the male but not the female. And women need men not because of their passive timidity but because they desire sex so much and because the consequence of it is pregnancy (Rousseau, *Emile*, 358.) I point this out not to make Rousseau's argument more palatable, but to indicate how the sexual qualities he goes on to describe are presented as *reasoned* responses to human desires and needs. Austen, as I have suggested, does not begin from Rousseau's low ground—nor does she argue, on any ground, that women *need* men in order to be moral—but they do share an interest in showing what is reasonable about the passion of love.

15. I do not intend to give an account of Aristotle's teaching about women in part because I do not argue for his *influence* on Austen. Austen shares his view that humans do not come together only because of sexual needs and desires (see for example, *Ethics*, 1162a20–22), and, in general, that human satisfaction comes through virtue and conversation (see, for example, Aristotle, *Eth-*

ics, 1098a16–17 and book 1 as a whole; cf. Aristotle, *Politics,* 1253a7–18). I have pointed out before that he allows for the possibility of a friendship of virtue between husband and wife (*Ethics,* 1162a24–26).

16. Wollstonecraft, *A Vindication,* 57.

17. Understandably put off by the way in which Rousseau directs Sophie's education toward a man, feminists often overlook the tough-minded strengths she is to have. Kirkham rightly points out that Rousseau was the "*bete noir* of English Enlightenment feminism" because he was seen to make "Man rational and Woman emotional" (Kirkham, *Jane Austen: Feminism and Fiction* [Sussex, England: The Harvester Press, 1983], xii); but this is too simplistic a view of his project. Fanny Price's "feebleness" (and "timidity" and "self-abasement") are not a mark of "anti-Rousseauist, feminist irony" upon her (Kirkham, "Feminist Irony," 231, 239) or—since there is no evidence external to the novels of what Austen thought of Rousseau—we should say that such qualities do not accurately mock him. Elizabeth Bennet, with the wit and cleverness that make her more truly able to please, is closer to his ideal than is Fanny (see Rousseau, *Emile,* 371, 375–76). He recommends that girls *not* be too soft but that they should "play, jump, run, shout" (366); they should dress simply, be "vigilant and industrious" (368–69), adhere to virtue (the rule of politeness is subservient to the rule never to lie [376]). Finally, Rousseau famously divides the world into two classes—"people who think" and "people who don't think"—and says that a man from one class should not marry a woman from the other (408). The purpose of women's education is that they be able to rule men: "the gentleness of a woman brings [a man] around and triumphs over him sooner or later" (370). If Austen caricatures this, it is not in the withdrawn Fanny Price but in that masterful coquette, Lady Susan.

18. As Judith Lowder Newton aptly puts it, "it is as if Austen could not be indirect or qualified enough in presenting this self-assertive heroine." She points out that it is Austen's qualifications of Elizabeth's power that account for most of the irony in the first two-thirds of the novel. See Newton, *Women, Power and Subversion,* 80. This is not the usual view of feminist critics. Nancy Armstrong claims that Elizabeth's "particular assets are the traditionally masculine qualities of rational intelligence, honesty, self-possession, and especially a command of the language" (*Desire and Domestic Fiction: A Political History of the Novel* [New York: Oxford University Press, 1987], 50). As I will argue, Austen does not present any of these characteristics as masculine. The masculine qualities she portrays have to do with courage—spirit and daring—and not with intelligence and honesty (which can belong to both sexes).

19. For a discussion of Elizabeth's social propriety, see chapter 4 of the text.

20. Mudrick argues that it is only on the subject of extra-marital sex that Austen allows herself no irony. "She must truncate, flatten, falsify, disapprove . . . and the process in *Pride and Prejudice* is so out of key with its surroundings as to be immediately jarring" (*Irony as Defense and Discovery,* 111). See also Ten Harmsel (*Fictional Conventions,* 67, 81). Some critics, perhaps troubled by

such sternness of judgment, simply ignore the evidence. Claudia Johnson (*Jane Austen*, 81) wrongly asserts that Austen leaves censure of Lydia only to the spiteful old ladies in Meryton.

21. Elizabeth's criticisms of Charlotte's marriage may not, however, be as sound as her criticisms of her sister. For a discussion of Charlotte's decision, see chapter 3 of the text.

22. MacIntyre, *After Virtue*, 225.

23. See the discussion of hope in Chapter 4 above. See also Austen's advice to her niece Fanny, who is hesitating about marriage, in which Austen minimizes the risk of turning down a man and then discovering she loves him: "it is no creed of mine, as you must be well aware, that such sort of Disappointments kill anybody" (*Letters*, 411 [18 November 1814]).

24. For this claim see especially the analyses by Howard S. Babb, *Jane Austen's Novels: The Fabric of Dialogue*, (Ohio State University Press, 1962), 238 and Mary Poovey, *The Proper Lady*, 226–28, both of whose arguments are in other ways valuable. Poovey, arguing that Austen "redeems romance by purging it of all traces of egoism" (200, cf. 214, 220) admits that there comes to be a problem (she is speaking of *Persuasion*) in knowing "whose desires to trust" (235). I would argue that the problem is that Austen does not believe that desire as such *is* trustworthy. In general, Poovey wants morality to be more pure than Austen allows it to be. It is not a "compromise of ethical and moral absolutes" that finally "imperils" the teaching of *Pride and Prejudice* (207) because Austen does not portray morality to be a set of absolute rules, or to be free of self-concern. What to do depends upon circumstances, and Austen always suggests that there is nothing shameful about the thought that there is a reward for virtue.

25. Elinor's method of nursing her sister is sometimes criticized, but see my defense of it toward the end of chapter 4 of the text.

26. For a good discussion of the importance of nursing the ill in the novels, see John Wiltshire, *Jane Austen and the Body: The Picture of Health* (Cambridge: Cambridge University Press, 1992).

27. See Lloyd W. Brown, "Jane Austen and the Feminist Tradition," *Nineteenth-Century Fiction* 28 (1973): 326; or Nina Auerbach, "O Brave New World: Evolution and Revolution in *Persuasion*" *ELH* 39 (1972): 125–26.

28. If Jane does not marry Frank she will become a governess, which she says may be more miserable than slavery (300–301). Arnold Kettle in "Emma," in Watt, *Critical Essays*, 117–18, argues that the willingness of someone so good as Jane to marry a man who is inferior shows Jane Austen's awareness of the vulnerable position of poor women in her society.

29. Austen always presents this sort of gallantry as French. Tocqueville's criticism of French gallantry is relevant to her point here: Americans, he says, "seldom lavish upon women the eager attentions which are often paid to them in Europe, but their conduct always shows that they assume them to be virtuous and refined" (Tocqueville, *Democracy in America*, 602).

30. William Dean Howells, *Heroines of Fiction*, vol. 1 (New York: Harper and Brothers, 1901), 54–55.

31. Austen, *Letters*, (30 November 1814) 418.

32. James Edward Austen-Leigh, *Memoir of Jane Austen* (New York: Macmillan, 1906), 148.

33. Austen, *Letters*, (23 March 1817) 487.

34. From comments written by Trollope in his copy of *Emma* in 1865, reprinted in Lodge, *Jane Austen: A Casebook*, 51.

35. "Opinions of *Emma*: Collected and Transcribed by Jane Austen," December 1815, reprinted in *The Critical Heritage*, ed. Southam.

36. Janet Todd's claim that the novels disparage female friendship because of its "strangely threatening potential" (246) seems at odds with the warmth with which Austen presents these relations (Todd, *Women's Friendship*, 246–301.)

37. See chapter 3 of the text for a more extensive discussion of the requirements of friendship, especially as relates to Elinor and Marianne.

38. Rousseau, *Emile*, 363.

39. Wollstonecraft, *A Vindication*, 62.

40. Almost all recent criticism of Austen, especially from a feminist perspective, has shared this belief, despite differences on other grounds. I would argue that the belief that Austen wrote chiefly about power is assumed from our own views about sexual relations rather than derived from the text. As Rachel M. Brownstein argues, "*Pride and Prejudice* is about women's lives in relation to sexual roles and to marriage; therefore—that the connection is inevitable is Jane Austen's point—it is about power, and independence, and authority." See "Jane Austen: Irony and Authority," *Women's Studies* 15 (1988), 64. There is something to this, as some of the similarities between Austen and Rousseau attest. But I would argue that Austen's point is precisely that power is *not* what love and marriage are ultimately about. The fact that Charlotte Lucas believes marriage is a matter of power, or that Elizabeth believes Mr. Darcy loves power—some of the evidence Brownstein cites—is not sufficient to show that "courtship as power play" is her chief subject, for these claims are discredited in the novels. Newton gives a more subtle account of power in *Pride and Prejudice*, but we must wonder, when she concludes that it is an "astoundingly modest power fantasy" and that Elizabeth's real "power is her ability to turn her critical vision upon herself" whether Mr. Darcy really is her "oppressor," that is, whether power is the right way to analyze it at all. See Newton, *Women, Power and Subversion*, 80–81. See also Julie Shaffer, "Not Subordinate: Empowering Women," *Criticism* 34 (Winter 1992): 51–73; and Cy Frost, "Autocracy and the Matrix of Power: Issues of Propriety and Economics in the Work of Mary Wollstonecraft, Jane Austen, and Harriet Martineau," *Tulsa Studies in Women's Literature* 10 (Fall 1991), 253–71; Leroy W. Smith, "*Mansfield Park*: The Revolt of the 'Feminine Woman,' " in *Jane Austen in a Social Context*, ed. David Monaghan (New York: Macmillan, 1981), 143–57.

Nor is the perspective of power limited to women. Claudia Johnson argues, rather implausibly I think, that "the male spectators of *Sense and Sensibility* do not sympathize with the distress of women. Rather, they look at that distress as a reflection of their own power (as in Willoughby's case) or powerlessness (as in Brandon's). (See C. Johnson, " 'A Sweet Face as White as Death,' " 171.) See especially the speeches themselves (SS 205–206, 319–33), where the dominant concern is hardly power.

41. Wollstonecraft, *A Vindication*, 83.

42. Compare Aristotle: "a just action is a mean between acting unjustly and being treated unjustly" (*Ethics*, 1133b30–31).

43. Lloyd W. Brown makes this point well in "Jane Austen and the Feminist Tradition," *NCF* 28 (1973): 334–35.

44. It has been argued that the parody is not so obvious. Mary Poovey suggests that the novel's epistolary form grants "no moral authority because there is no narrative authority," and that while Austen's family might have had the "moral consensus" to be amused at Lady Susan's expense, we cannot assume such a consensus elsewhere (See Poovey, *The Proper Lady*, 178). Surely Austen thought a larger audience than her family would share the morals that the satire presumes: that it is wrong, for example, to take advantage of a friend's hospitality to try to win the love of her husband *and* the suitor of her daughter; to send one's child to a school without any intention of paying the bill; to prevent one's brother from buying the family estate because its possession by a younger brother would be undignified; to wish for the death of a former friend and of the husband of another friend.

45. Rousseau, *Emile*, 365.

46. C. Johnson, *Jane Austen*, 14.

47. R. W. Chapman points out that "the famous description of Charmouth [in *Persuasion*] is not a bit more 'romantic' than the description of the high wind on a Devonshire hill, and the girls' delight in it, in *Sense and Sensibility*" ("A Reply to Mr. Duffy on 'Persuasion,' " *Nineteenth-Century Fiction* 9 [1954–55]: 154). It is the love of nature that is romantic here; this is a highly *naturalized* scene.

48. Mary Poovey, *The Proper Lady*, 193.

49. C. Johnson, *Jane Austen*, 59–60.

50. Henrietta Ten Harmsel (*Jane Austen: Fictional Conventions*, 54) says the reader should not forgive Edward or the author for his "scrupulous loyalty to his meaningless engagement" (54) See also Mudrick in *Jane Austen: Irony as Defense and Discovery*, 87, and Nardin, *Those Elegant Decorums*, who says Elinor unreasonably wants Edward to obey "the letter of a law of honor" (35).

51. Rousseau, *Emile*, 439.

52. Ibid., 402.

53. Ibid., 403–405.

54. Ibid., 404. Rousseau develops this theme especially in the *Nouvelle Heloise*, which concerns Julie's struggle between her respect for her husband, Wolmar, and her love for St.-Preux. (One can imagine what Austen would have thought of the fact that these three have such an understanding of each other

that St.-Preux comes to live with the Wolmars and tutors their children. Butler seems correct to say that Julie is an "unthinkable heroine for a Briton [Butler, *Jane Austen and the War*, 44]). Both of the marriages envisioned by Rousseau are shown to be failures because of the impossibility of combining a lover and a husband in the same man. In *Emile et Sophie,* the fragmentary sequel to *Emile,* the couple divorces. Julie, on the other hand, is happy to come to an early death. For an excellent discussion of these novels as well as Rousseau's sexual teachings in general, see Joel Schwartz, *The Sexual Politics of Jean-Jacques Rousseau* (Chicago: University of Chicago Press, 1984).

55. One of the points of Eliza's story, then, is that modesty has the practical purpose of protecting one from rape. When Johnson describes the eighteenth-century countryside as "full of Jacobin riffraff out to ruin English families by seducing women away from fond fathers and rightful husbands" (C. Johnson, *Jane Austen,* 14), her sarcasm implies that rules against sex outside of marriage are simply self-serving patriarchal conventions. Johnson makes her sarcasm about adultery more explicit when she says that "far from being a cautionary tale about the duty of fidelity, Eliza's story . . . indicts the license to coercion, corruption, and avarice available to grasping patriarchs and their oldest sons" (Ibid., 56). *Sense and Sensibility* surely attacks parents and legal inheritors as much as it attacks excessive romance, but this is hardly Colonel Brandon's point or the point of his story's insertion in the novel. Austen never cares so much about reforming the countryside as about showing how, as Henry Tilney explains, one's character and behavior affect how one is treated (see NA 219). In the other instance of adultery in the novels—Maria Bertram and Henry Crawford—the point again is not that Maria is the victim of the grasping son of a patriarch, but rather that she is a victim of her own loveless grasping in marriage. While the narrator laments the fact that Henry Crawford is not punished in the same measure as Maria, her guilt is never disputed; "Maria had destroyed her own character" (MP 465, 468).

56. It seems quite unfair to say, as Martin Amis has, that Austen loses sight of her characters "at exactly the same point that 'respectability'—or stock response—loses sight of them." See "Miss Jane's Prime," *The Atlantic* 265, no. 2 (February 1990): 102.

57. Consider also Emma's comment when she arranges for Harriet to meet Mr. Elton on their visit to some sick neighbors: "to meet in a charitable scheme; this will bring a real increase of love on each side" (E 87). Such is Henry Crawford's strategy when he hopes to win Fanny's favor by telling her of his efforts to help a poor and industrious family in his neighborhood. "To be the friend of the poor and oppressed! Nothing could be more grateful to her" (MP 404).

58. Rousseau, *Emile,* 441.

59. As I have pointed out elsewhere, Austen suggests that compassion, like any feeling, is in need of guidance from virtue; she does not encourage pity and sensibility in the way Rousseau does in *Emile.* It would be possible to use

evidence from her novels to dispute his three maxims about compassion (Ibid., 223–25). To give one example, Austen often suggests that pity is for *unde-served* suffering, that we pity only those who suffer unjustly, whereas for Rousseau the justice of the sufferer is not relevant. (The "disappointments of selfish passion can excite little pity," we are told of Maria and Mr. Rushworth; "Maria had destroyed her own character" [MP 464–65]. Elinor can pity Lucy for the poor abilities that are due to her lack of education but not for her lack of rectitude and integrity, for which she is responsible [SS 127].) Austen's view is in line with Aristotle (see *Rhetoric*, 2.8.2)

In general, Austen suggests that reason can be brought to bear on pity without destroying it. We see this in *Pride and Prejudice* when Mr. Collins' harsh advice regarding Lydia is contrasted to more superior characters who have a "more gentle, less dignified, forgiveness" (SS 330). In fact, Jane and Elizabeth feel more compassion for Lydia than she does for herself (PP 315); their sympathy comes not from the fact that they see her suffering (for she seems not to) but from what they see, objectively, as her misfortune (contrast Rousseau's third maxim, that the pity one has "is measured not by the quantity of that misfortune but by the sentiment which one attributes to those who suffer it" [Rousseau, *Emile*, 225]). Austen's precise reasonableness applies to compassion as much as to anything: Lydia's actions cannot be forgotten or defended (305); she must be sent away, but not cruelly, and she will have her sisters' sympathy and monetary support.

60. Rousseau, *Emile*, 390.

61. Reason is grounded by what she calls "understanding." All the novels show the problems that result to those who "shu[t] their eyes while they look, or their understandings while they reason" (MP 107).

62. Wollstonecraft, *A Vindication*, 168.

63. Austen, *Letters*, 309–10, 312 (24 May 1813). See also my discussion of this quote in chapter 4 of the text.

64. The suggestion about Fanny is most provocatively made by Moler (*Jane Austen's Art of Allusion*, 148–54). Duckworth also seems to exaggerate the extent to which Henry Crawford's taste for refinement is in itself disapproved of. When Edmund says he "must be satisfied with rather less ornament and beauty" and give "the air of a gentleman's residence without any very heavy expense, and that must suffice me" (242), he implies that he might do more if he had more money. It is the fact that Fanny has "so much taste" that makes it likely she could have married Henry, had Edmund been out of the picture (231).

65. Austen, *Letters*, 377–88 (2 March 1814).

66. Rousseau, *Emile*, Book V, (e.g., 361, 364–65).

Conclusion: The Romantic Rewards of Moderation

Jane Austen's novels make a case for moderation that is seldom seen in modern writers. It is a case not for the lowering of expectations, but for pursuing what she presents as the deepest kind of happiness and love. If passion does not seem to dominate her work, it may be precisely because she is so confident that desires and feelings will always be around. Feelings are not so fleeting and fragile that they will vanish if regulated by virtue and judged by reason. In fact, Austen argues the reverse. She has Elizabeth Bennet say that poetry, far from being the food of love, "will starve it entirely away" (PP 44–45). Poetry, like anything, will nourish what is already a "fine, stout, healthy" love, but in the case of a more "thin sort of inclination" dwelling on the feeling will drive it away. Austen shows how, in contrast to the indulgence of feeling, confidence in the rightness and reasonableness of one's feelings *strengthens* those feelings of attachment.

Austen, then, attacks romanticism on the ground of love. The love that emerges from real suitability, a knowledge of one another's goodness, and time to get to know one another and to exchange favors, is not praised only because it is more sensible or proper, but even more because it is deeper and more lasting than the kind of love that comes from desire alone. Love is in some real sense the reward of virtue. This is not because a modest woman is always guaranteed a good husband— for Austen is highly aware of the role of good fortune—but rather because the most lasting and meaningful love is simply not possible without virtue and intelligence. To put this another way, Austen never denies that certain external goods that are a matter of good fortune (including a husband or wife) are needed for, or at least contribute to, the best happiness. But she also denies that "happiness in marriage is entirely a matter of chance" (PP 23). She would agree with Aristotle that "activities in accordance with virtue play the dominant role in happiness,"[1] and she shows how those who act virtuously can form the kind of attachment that will make marriage not a "take in" (MP 46).

Austen forecasts happiness for the unions she creates because they display more genuine *love* than is typical. She suggests that the deepest attachment to another comes when one can "rationally as well as passionately" love (MP 469). Love is domesticated or civilized in Austen's novels. Except to attack on occasion, she does not concern herself with grand ambitions for power and glory. She writes about a "very quiet set of people . . . more disposed to stay at home than engage in schemes of pleasure" (E 274). But it would go too far to say that she has flattened the human soul. Her novels defend the nobility and dignity of "the quiet of the private life" (SS 16). Private life is superior, Austen suggests, because it offers a more substantial (not just more attainable) happiness, the core of which is love.

Austen's perspective could not be described as submissive to society, nor as subversive of it. Her novels describe an unmodern middle ground in which humans do not have to choose complete selfishness (radical individuality) or complete sociability to avoid being split between the two.[2] She appeals to a standard beyond both society and individual desire, that of virtue and the happiness that comes from it. Austen defends convention, but not on conventional grounds. Her choice of marriage as a subject is central to her thought as a whole. Marriage follows naturally, we might say, from the sort of love she describes, a love that is salutary for society as well as for the individuals because it is grounded on the virtue aimed at by both.

Jane Austen's heroes and heroines stand apart—and are able to choose each other—because they have the better taste that comes from a better accord between their desires and their virtue. It is this "better taste" that Mary Crawford acquires at Mansfield Park, and which makes her so long in finding a husband among the "idle heir apparents" she sees in London (MP 469). Living a measured life requires the kind of taste that takes pleasure in noble things. Austen's novels are themselves an education in this sort of "moral taste" (MP 235). Mary and Henry Crawford grew up in "a bad school for matrimony" (46), says Mary's sister, but she adds "stay with us and we will cure you" (47). In the end, however, they are not cured, for ultimately Austen does not reduce morality to taste. Virtue is acquired by habit: Mary's carelessness and ambition overcome her better taste because "habit, habit carried it" (MP 458, cf. 467; PP 207, 231; SS 331).

Jane Austen's novels are striking for their unusual combination of warmth of heart with clearness of judgment. As Mary Crawford puts it, in a statement that could apply to all Austen's heroines, "you all have so much more *heart* among you, than one finds in the world at large" (MP 359). Both qualities are present in almost every aspect of the novels. Austen writes with a clear-sighted irony from which no character is spared, and yet also with a warmth that makes her characters win over her readers. She can make us hear the "large fat sighings" of a Mrs. Musgrove and yet also indicate that the superiority of Captain Wentworth is the "natural grace" that lets him respect what is "real and unabsurd" in Mrs. Musgrove's feelings (P 68). Austen shows, at the end of each novel, how *moving* is the joy that comes from the sense of the rightness of love. She portrays those who reject the importance of such virtues as prudence, moderation, and modesty, not as possessing sensibility so much as selfishness. Austen's wit and her moralism are ultimately not at odds, any more than sense and sensibility are, for the novels suggest that real unselfishness relies more on judgment than on feeling.

Notes

1. Aristotle, *Ethics*, 1100b9–10.
2. Her novels can be seen to share Rousseau's criticism of the "bourgeois"—the person who, "always in contradiction with himself, always floating between his inclinations and his duties . . . will be good neither for himself nor for others" (Rousseau, *Emile*, 40.) (Consider Willoughby of *Sense and Sensibility*, Mr. Knightley's criticisms of Frank Churchill in *Emma*, or any of the characters who are unfavorably portrayed.) But Austen does not, with Rousseau, conclude that any way of life that is internally consistent is good. She appeals, through her better characters, to an objective end or nature for humans that is constituted by virtue.

Bibliography

Amis, Kingsley. "What Became of Jane Austen." In *Jane Austen: A Collection of Critical Essays*, ed. Ian Watt, 141–44. Englewood, N. J.: Prentice-Hall, Inc. 1963.

Amis, Martin. "Miss Jane's Prime." *The Atlantic*, 265, no. 2 (February 1990): 100–102.

Aristotle. *Nicomachean Ethics*. Edited by Hippocrates G. Apostle. Grinnell, Iowa: Peripatetic Press, 1984.

———. *Politics*. Translated by Carnes Lord. Chicago: University of Chicago Press, 1984.

———. *Rhetoric*. Loeb Classical Library. Cambridge, Mass.: Harvard University Press, 1948.

Armstrong, Nancy. *Desire and Domestic Fiction: A Political History of the Novel*. New York: Oxford University Press, 1987.

Auerbach, Nina. "O Brave New World: Evolution and Revolution in *Persuasion*." *ELH* 39 (1972): 112–28.

Austen, Jane. *Jane Austen's Letters to Her Sister Cassandra and Others*. Edited by R. W. Chapman. 2d. ed. Oxford: Oxford University Press, 1952.

———. *The Novels of Jane Austen*. Edited by R. W. Chapman. 5 vols., 3rd. edition. Oxford: Oxford University Press, 1933.

———. *Minor Works*. Edited by R. W. Chapman. Vol. 6 of *The Works of Jane Austen*. Oxford: Oxford University Press, 1954.

———. "Opinions of Emma: Collected and Transcribed by Jane Austen." December 1815. Reprinted in *Jane Austen: The Critical Heritage*, ed. B. C. Southam, 55–57. London: Routledge & Kegan Paul, 1968.

Austen-Leigh, James Edward. *Memoir of Jane Austen*. New York: Macmillan, 1906.

Austen-Leigh, Mary Augusta. *Personal Aspects of Jane Austen*. London: John Murray, 1920.

Austen-Leigh, William and Richard Arthur. *Jane Austen: Her Life and Letters*. New York: Russell and Russell, 1965.

Babb, Howard S. *Jane Austen's Novels: The Fabric of Dialogue*. Athens, Ohio: Ohio State University Press, 1962.

Banerjee, A. "Dr. Johnson's Daughter: Jane Austen and *Northanger Abbey*," *English Studies* 2 (1990): 113–24.

Bayley, John. "The Irresponsibility of Jane Austen." In *Critical Essays on Jane Austen*, ed. B. C. Southam, 1–20. London: Routledge & Kegan Paul, 1968.

Bloom, Allan. *Love and Friendship*. New York: Simon & Schuster, 1993.

Bloom, Harold, ed. *Modern Critical Views: Jane Austen*. New York: Chelsea House Publishers, 1986.

Booth, Wayne C. "Control of Distance in Jane Austen's *Emma*." In *Jane Austen, Emma: A Casebook*, ed. David Lodge, 195–216. London, Macmillan, 1968.

———. "Emma, *Emma*, and the Question of Feminism." *Persuasions*, 5 (1983): 29–40.

Bradbury, Malcolm. In *Jane Austen, Emma: A Casebook*, ed. David Lodge, 217–31. London: Macmillan, 1968.

Brissenden, R. F. "*Mansfield Park*: Freedom and the Family." In *Jane Austen: Bicentenary Essays*, ed. John Halperin, 156–71. Cambridge, Cambridge University Press, 1975.

Brown, Lloyd W. "Jane Austen and the Feminist Tradition." *NCF* 28 (1973): 321–38.

Brownstein, Rachel M. "Jane Austen: Irony and Authority," *Women's Studies* 15 (1988): 57–70.

Burke, Edmund. *Reflections on the Revolution in France*. Edited by William B. Todd. New York: Reinhart, 1959.

Butler, Marilyn. "Introduction." In Jane Austen, *Emma*, v–xxxii. Everyman's Library, 1991.

———. *Jane Austen and the War of Ideas*. Oxford: Clarendon Press (1975), 1987 edition.

Cecil, Lord David. *Jane Austen*. The Leslie Stephen Lecture. Cambridge: Cambridge University Press, 1935.

Chapman, R. W. "A Reply to Mr. Duffy on 'Persuasion.'" *NCF* 9 (1954–1955): 154.

Churchill, Winston S. *The Second World War*, vol. 5. Boston: Houghton Mifflin Co., 1951.

Conrad, Joseph. *Heart of Darkness*. London: Pan Classics edition, 1976.

DeForest, Mary. "Jane Austen and the Anti-Heroic Tradition," *Persuasions* 10 (1988), 11–21.

De Rose, Peter L. *Jane Austen and Samuel Johnson*. Washington, D. C.: University Press of America, 1980.

Duckworth, Alistair. *The Improvement of the Estate*. Baltimore: Johns Hopkins University Press, 1971.

———. "Jane Austen and the Conflict of Interpretations." In *Jane Austen: New Perspectives*, Women & Literature New Series, vol. 3, ed. Janet Todd, 39–51. New York: Holmes & Meier, 1983.

Duffy, Edward. *Rousseau in England*. Berkeley: University of California Press, 1979.

Duffy, Joseph M. "Moral Integrity and Moral Anarchy in *Mansfield Park*," *ELH* 23 (March 1956): 71–91.

Fleishman, Avrom. *A Reading of Mansfield Park*. Minneapolis: University of Minnesota Press, 1967.

Frost, Cy. "Autocracy and the Matrix of Power: Issues of Propriety and Economics in the Work of Mary Wollstonecraft, Jane Austen and Harriet Martineau," *Tulsa Studies in Women's Literature* (Fall 1991): 253–71.

Gilbert, Sandra and Gubar, Susan. *The Madwoman in the Attic*. New Haven: Yale University Press, 1979.

Grove, Robin. "Austen's Ambiguous Conclusions." In *Modern Critical Views: Jane Austen*, ed. Harold Bloom, 179–90. New York: Chelsea House Publishers, 1986.

Halperin, John, ed. *Jane Austen: Bicentenary Essays*. Cambridge: Cambridge University Press, 1975.

Harding, D. W. "Regulated Hatred: An Aspect of the Work of Jane Austen." *Scrutiny* 8 (1940): 346–62. Reprinted in *Jane Austen: A Collection of Critical Essays*, ed. Ian Watt, 166–79. Englewood Cliffs, N. J.: Prentice-Hall, Inc., 1963.

Hardy, Barbara. *A Reading of Jane Austen*. New York: New York University Press, 1976.

Hobbes, Thomas. *Leviathan*. Harmondsworth, Middlesex, England: Penguin Books, 1968.

Howells, William Dean. *Heroines of Fiction*. New York: Harper & Brothers, 1901.

Johnson, Claudia L. *Jane Austen: Women, Politics and the Novel*. Chicago: University of Chicago Press, 1988.

———. "A 'Sweet Face as White as Death,': Jane Austen and the Politics of Female Sensibility," *Novel: Forum on Fiction* 22 (Winter 1989): 159–74.

Johnson, Samuel. *The Yale Edition of the Works of Samuel Johnson*. Vols. 1 and 3. New Haven: Yale University Press, 1969.

———. *A Dictionary of the English Language*. London: Times Books, 1979.

Kant, Immanuel. *The Critique of Judgement*. Translated by James Creed Meredith. Oxford: Clarendon Press, 1952.

―――. *Foundations of the Metaphysics of Morals*. Edited by Robert Paul Wolff. Indianapolis: Bobbs-Merrill, 1969.

―――. *Lectures on Ethics*. Translated by Louis Inflield. New York: Harper & Row, 1963.

Kaufmann, David. "Law and Propriety, *Sense and Sensibility*: Austen on the Cusp of Modernity," *ELH* 59 (1992): 385–408.

Kettle, Arnold. "Emma." In *Jane Austen: A Collection of Critical Essays*, ed. Ian Watt, 112–123. Englewood Cliffs, N. J.: Prentice-Hall, Inc., 1963.

Kirkham, Margaret. *Jane Austen: Feminism and Fiction*. Sussex, England: The Harvester Press, 1983.

―――. "Feminist Irony and the Priceless Heroine of *Mansfield Park*." In *Jane Austen: New Perspectives*, Women & Literature New Series, vol. 3, ed. Janet Todd, 231–47. New York: Holmes & Meier, 1983.

Kliger, Samuel. "Jane Austen's *Pride and Prejudice* in the Eighteenth-Century Mode." In *Twentieth Century Interpretations of Pride and Prejudice*, ed. E. Rubenstein, 46–58. Englewood Cliffs, N. J.: Prentice-Hall, Inc. 1969.

Knuth, Deborah J. "Friendship in Jane Austen's *Juvenilia* and Lady Susan." In *Jane Austen's Beginnings*, ed. J. David Grey, 95–106. Ann Arbor, Mich.: UMI Research Press, 1989.

Litz, A. Walton. *Jane Austen: A Study of her Artistic Development*. New York: Oxford University Press, 1965.

―――. "*Persuasion*: Forms of Estrangement." In *Jane Austen: Bicentenary Essays*, ed. John Halperin, 221–34. Cambridge: Cambridge University Press, 1975.

Lodge, David. *Language of Fiction*. London: Routledge & Kegan Paul, 1966.

Lodge, David, ed. *Jane Austen, Emma: A Casebook*. London: Macmillan, 1968.

MacIntyre, Alisdair. *After Virtue: A Study in Moral Theory*. Notre Dame, Ind.: University of Notre Dame, 1981.

Marcus, Mordecai. "A Major Thematic Pattern in *Pride and Prejudice*." In *Twentieth Century Interpretations of Pride and Prejudice*, ed. Rubinstein, 83–87. Englewood Cliffs, N. J.: Prentice-Hall, Inc., 1969.

Melzer, Arthur M. *The Natural Goodness of Man: On the System of Rousseau's Thought*. Chicago: University of Chicago Press, 1990.

Moler, Kenneth L. *Jane Austen's Art of Allusion*. Lincoln, Neb.: University of Nebraska Press, 1968.

Montesquieu, *The Spirit of the Laws*. Translated by Anne M. Cohler, Basia Carolyn Miller and Harold Samuel Shue. Cambridge: Cambridge University Press, 1989.

Monaghan, David, ed. *Jane Austen in a Social Context.* New York: Macmillan, 1981.

Morgan, Susan. *In the Meantime.* Chicago: University of Chicago Press, 1980.

Mudrick, Marvin. *Jane Austen: Irony as Defense and Discovery.* Princeton, N.J.: Princeton University Press, 1952.

Nardin, Jane. *Those Elegant Decorums: The Concept of Propriety in Jane Austen's Novels.* Albany: State University of New York Press (SUNY), 1973.

Neill, Edward. "The Politics of Jane Austen," *English* 40: 168 (Fall 1991): 205–13.

Newton, Judith Lowder. *Women, Power and Subversion: Social Strategies in British Fiction 1778–1860.* Athens, Ga.: University of Georgia Press, 1981.

Orwin, Clifford. "Compassion," *American Scholar* (Summer 1980): 309–33.

Pangle, Thomas L. *Montesquieu's Philosophy of Liberalism.* Chicago: University of Chicago Press, 1973.

Pickrel, Paul. "Lionel Trilling and *Emma*: A Reconsideration," *NCF* 40 (December 1985): 298–303.

Poovey, Mary. *The Proper Lady and the Woman Writer.* Chicago: University of Chicago Press, 1984.

Price, Martin. *Forms of Life: Character and Moral Imagination in the Novel.* New Haven: Yale University Press, 1983.

Rousseau, Jean-Jacques. *Emile.* Translated by Allan Bloom. New York: Basic Books, 1979.

Rubinstein, E., ed. *Twentieth-Century Interpretations of Pride and Prejudice.* Englewood Cliffs, N. J.: Prentice- Hall, Inc., 1969.

Ryle, Gilbert. "Jane Austen and the Moralists." In *Critical Essays on Jane Austen*, ed. B. C. Southam, 106–122. London: Routledge & Kegan Paul, 1968.

Said, Edward. *Culture and Interpretation.* New York: Alfred A. Knopf, 1993.

Schorer, Mark. "Fiction and the 'Matrix of Analogy,' " *The Kenyon Review* 11 (Autumn 1949): 539–60.

Schwartz, Joel. *The Sexual Politics of Jean-Jacques Rousseau.* Chicago: University of Chicago Press, 1984.

Scott, Sir Walter. Unsigned review of *Emma. Quarterly Review* xiv (March 1816): 188–201. In *Jane Austen: The Critical Heritage*, B. C. Southam, 58–69. London: Routledge & Kegan Paul, 1968.

Shaffer, Julie. "Not Subordinate: Empowering Women in the Marriage-Plot," *Criticism* 34 (Winter 1992): 51–73.

Simpson, Richard. "Memoir," *North British Review* lii (April 1870): 129–52. Reprinted in *Jane Austen: The Critical Heritage*, ed. B. C. Southam, 241–65. London: Routledge & Kegan Paul, 1968.

Sinclair, Upton. *Mammonart*. Pasadena, Calif.: published by author, 1924.

Smith, J. M. " 'My Only Sister Now': Incest in *Mansfield Park*," *Studies in the Novel* 19 (Spring 1987), 1–15.

Smith, Leroy W. "*Mansfield Park*: The Revolt of the 'Feminine' Woman." In *Jane Austen in a Social Context*, ed. David Monaghan, 143–58. New York: Macmillan, 1981.

Southam, B. C., ed. *Critical Essays on Jane Austen*. London: Routledge & Kegan Paul, 1968.

———, ed. *Jane Austen: The Critical Heritage*. London: Routledge and Kegan Paul, 1968.

———. *Jane Austen*. *Writers and their Work*, no. 241. Edited by Ian Scott-Kilvert. Longman Group, Ltd. for the British Council, 1975.

Sulloway, Alison G. *Jane Austen and the Province of Womanhood*. Philadelphia: University of Pennsylvania Press, 1989.

Swift, Jonathan. *A Tale of a Tub and Other Satires*. London: J. M. Dent & Sons, 1975.

Tanner, Tony. *Jane Austen*. Cambridge, Mass.: Harvard University Press, 1986.

Tave, Stuart. *Some Words of Jane Austen*. Chicago: University of Chicago Press, 1973.

Ten Harmsel, Henrietta. *Jane Austen: A Study in Fictional Conventions*. The Hague: Mouton & Co., 1964.

Tocqueville, Alexis de. *Democracy in America*. Edited by J. P. Mayer. Garden City, New York: Anchor Books, 1969.

Todd, Janet, ed. *Jane Austen: New Perspectives*. Women & Literature New Series, vol. 3. New York: Holmes & Meier Pub., 1983.

———. *Women's Friendship in Literature*. New York: Columbia University Press, 1980.

Trilling, Lionel. "Mansfield Park." *Jane Austen: A Collection of Critical Essays*, ed. Ian Watt, 124–40. Englewood Cliffs, N. J.: Prentice-Hall, Inc., 1963.

———. *The Opposing Self*. New York: Harcourt Brace Jovanovich, 1950.

Warner, James H. "Eighteenth-Century English Reactions to the *Nouvelle Heloise*," *PMLA* 52 (1937), 803–19.

Watt, Ian, ed. *A Collection of Critical Essays*. Englewood Cliffs, N.J.: Prentice-Hall, Inc., 1963.

Wilson, Edmund. "A Long Talk About Jane Austen." *Classics and Commercials: A Literary Chronicle of the Forties*. New York: Farrar, Straus & Cudahy, 1950.

Wiltshire, John. *Jane Austen and the Body: the Picture of Health*. Cambridge: Cambridge University Press, 1992.

Wollstonecraft, Mary. *A Vindication of the Rights of Woman.* 2nd edition. New York: W. W. Norton & Co., Norton Critical Edition, 1988.

Woolf, Virginia. *The Common Reader.* New York: Harcourt, Brace & Co., 1925.

Yeazell, Ruth Bernard. *Fictions of Modesty: Women and Courtship in the English Novel.* Chicago: University of Chicago Press, 1991.

Zietlow, Paul N. ''Luck and Fortuitous Circumstance in *Persuasion*: Two Interpretations.'' *ELH* 32 (June 1965): 179–95.

Index

About the Author

Anne Crippen Ruderman lives in Dallas, Texas. She received her Ph.D. in 1990 from the University of Chicago, where she was a Mellon Fellow in the Humanities. She has taught political theory and literature at Colgate University and Cornell University.

DATE DUE